Sustainable Beekeeping:

Surviving in an Age of CCD

Creating New Paradigms for Today's New Challenges

Grant F. C. Gillard

Sustainable Beekeeping: Surviving in an Age of CCD

Creating New Paradigms for Today's New Challenges

By Grant F.C. Gillard

copyright 2014 Grant F.C. Gillard

ALL RIGHTS RESERVED
No part of this publication may be reproduced, stored in a retrieval system, or transmitted, in any form or by any means--electronic, mechanical, photocopying, recording, or otherwise--without prior written permission.

For more information:

Grant F.C. Gillard
3721 North High Street
Jackson, MO 63755
gillard5@charter.net

Grant F.C. Gillard is a Presbyterian Pastor and Beekeeper. He has been keeping bees since 1981. He speaks at bee conferences and conventions across the nation. Contact him at **gillard5@charter.net** to check his availability for your next event.

You can find more information about the author at the conclusion of this book, or www.grantgillard.weebly.com

Dedication:

This manuscript is dedicated to the
"Forehanded Farmer."

From the 1927 edition of
The Old Farmer's Almanac:

The successful farmer is always forehanded.

*He pushes his work instead of allowing
his work to push him.*

*He plans his necessary work well ahead
and gets much of it done before
the rush of the season.*

*This policy gives opportunity for more thorough,
intelligent and productive work.*

It is my hope and prayer, in these challenging and
difficult times, to survive in this age of CCD,
we would discern the power of sustainable practices
and adopt the best ideals and noble intentions of a
"Forehanded Beekeeper."

Acknowledgements

Jack Canfield, author of numerous inspirational books, quoted one of his professors who said, *"If you can't find the book you're looking for, it must be you're supposed to write it."*

What you hold in your hands is the book I was looking for on sustainable beekeeping, more specifically, how I might learn the subtle tricks which keep me keeping bees in this challenging age in the shadow of Colony Collapse Disorder. In reality, I wrote this manuscript for me.

This manuscript is a prayerful answer to my struggles, hardships, challenges and obstacles, not to mention my frustration and embarrassment as I have attempted to keep honey bees over the past 30-plus years.

I appreciate those many talented apiarists who have traveled with me on this thought-provoking journey hoping someday we might find the solutions to lighten the load of those who come behind us.

It also contains my joy and celebration, for those momentary slices of lucidity and clarity thinking I finally figured something out.

Not one of my manuscripts can be complete without an acknowledgement of my nuclear family as they lived with and endured my consuming passion with which I keep bees. They have been a great help, supportive in many different ways, patient in most ways, particularly parking their cars outside on the driveway while my expansive beekeeping hobby occupied the garage.

My special thanks to my long-suffering wife of twenty-seven years, Nancy, along with my grown children, Barbara Gillard Morton and her husband, Jeremy Morton, and my other two children, Austin Gillard and Claire Gillard.

I am indebted to my church family at First Presbyterian Church in Jackson, Missouri. They have graciously allowed my introspective dalliances in the bee yards and commercial endeavors at the local farmer's markets.

Boatloads of thanks go, as well, to my apicultural family, specifically those beekeepers I have met through several local associations and the Missouri State Beekeepers Associations. In particular, I am thankful to MSBA President John Timmons, and his wife, Jane, for their gracious friendship and capable leadership. It's been a blast serving alongside of both of you.

As a beekeeper, you meet some of the most interesting people. It is a great joy to be able to speak a language others understand and appreciate, as well as the many things we hold in common and have learned from each other.

I am also grateful for the Wednesday Night Writing Class and my coach, Linda Culbreth and the serendipitous manner in which God brought us together.

A good coach gets you in the game, but they can't play the game for you. This book, along with my other published works, would not be possible without Linda's invaluable help and her faithful obedience to Jesus Christ which keeps me in the game.

Prior to meeting Linda, I was but an aspiring writer. Under her guidance and accountability, today, I am a published author. You can find more information about Linda at her web site found at www.bookdesignbylinda.com

I can't help but express my gratitude to our Creator for these little pollinators which delightfully capture our attention and imagination, without which we might lack a veritable cornucopia of delights as "the land yields up its bountiful increase." (Psalm 67:6, paraphrased).

And lastly, my gratitude to the late Richard Trump, a retired high school biology teacher and Presbyterian elder at the Collegiate Presbyterian Church in Ames, Iowa. We worshipped on Sunday mornings listening to the sermons of Rev. Harry Strong, another person who had a profound affect on my life and faith.

"Dr. Trump," as we called him, was a marvelous instructor teaching Entomology 222 at Iowa State University. His teaching style baited my interest and his gentle manner set the hook. I give him much of the credit for inadvertently launching my fledgling beekeeping career in the Spring Quarter of 1979.

As an aside, he only gave two grades for this course; an "A" or an "F." As we entered the University bee yard to inspect the hives, if we got stung, proving that we were working the hives, we received an "A." If we didn't get stung, we received an "F," presuming we were not "close up and personal" with the bees.

Needless to say, we all got "A's." With a sheepish smile he added, "And I don't give out any "B's" (the pun fully intended).

Mr. Trump passed away at the age of 98 on November 1, 2010.

I am grateful for many opportunities to speak and share my passion for beekeeping. Many doors have opened before me, merely because I continue in this time-honored craft. I owe a great deal of thanks to my bees.

Table of Contents:

Introduction: Where are we at, and what do we know?   page 13

Chapter 1: Sustainable Perceptions and Observations   page 53

Chapter 2: What constitutes, "Sustainable?"   page 75

Chapter 3: More practical thoughts on sustainable beekeeping   page 123

Chapter 4: Are you, yourself, sustainable?   page 137

Chapter 5: The Queen - The Heart of Sustainability   page 191

Chapter 6: Frames and Foundation - The Womb of Sustainability   page 226

Chapter 7: Knowledge   page 245

Chapter 8: Swarm Prevention, Control
and Management   page 263

Chapter 9: Mite Suppression   page 295

Chapter 10: Nucs   page 329

Chapter 11: Wisdom and Education   page 343

Chapter 12: Diversity of Forage   page 357

Chapter 13: Time Management
and Self Management   page 370

Chapter 14: OMG! Do I Have CCD?   page 389

Chapter 15: Has Beekeeping
Become a Game of Attrition?   page 401

Chapter 16: Is Treatment-Free Beekeeping
the Gateway to Sustainability?   page 411

Other Popular Beekeeping Resources by Grant F. C. Gillard

Beekeeping with Twenty-five Hives:
From Passion to Profits
www.createspace.com/4152725

A Ton of Honey:
Managing Your Hives for
Maximum Production
www.createspace.com/4111886

Free Bees!
The Joy and the Insanity of Removing and Retrieving Honey Bee Swarms
www.createspace.com/4107714

Keeping Honey Bees and Swarm Trapping:
A Better Way to Collect "Free" Bees
www.createspace.com/4106626

Why I Keep Honeybees
(and why you should, too!):
Keys to Your Success

www.createspace.com/4043781

Beekeeping 101:
Where Can I Keep My Bees?

www.createspace.com/4044187

Honey! It Turned to Sugar!
Dealing with Issues of Granulated Honey

www.createspace.com/4044721

Simplified Queen Rearing:
A Non-Grafting Approach Using
The "Nicot" Queen Rearing Kit

www.createspace.com/ 4542113

Introduction:

Where are we at, and what do we know?

"The secret to change is to focus all your energy, not on fighting the old, but on building the new." --Socrates

Beekeeping is in crisis as I put this manuscript together. In reality, this is nothing new. We've been facing a mysterious catastrophe with broad implications for several years now and there is no relief in sight.

The three most commonly assumed, probable culprits of this crisis, if you want to "round up the usual suspects," are Colony Collapse Disorder or CCD, systemic pesticides (the neonicotinoids), and genetically modified organisms (GMO crops).

These alleged problems do not fully define the complete predicament we're facing, but they are easy to blame, play well with the non-beekeeping community, and make alarming headlines which intentionally pique the curiosity and sympathies of the general public.

As a beekeeper, I have grave concerns where our craft is headed, or where it will end up. The general public, even those previously oblivious to our need for pollination in roughly one-third of our food source, have taken notice.

While the news of CCD has fallen off the front page of our informational media, the potential implications, both real and imagined, continue to haunt the periphery of our consciousness.

And there is good cause to be troubled, after all, everyone agrees, "We need the bees," and unless you've been living under a rock for the past decade, everyone knows our bees are dying. The next logical leap arrives at the conclusion: our food sources are now in jeopardy, thus, we are in trouble. We need the bees; we need to save the bees; we need to save humanity...but we're not exactly sure what we're facing or how to fix this nebulous dilemma.

From my perspective, I choose not to jump on the bandwagon of public opinion, affixing blame on these three, easily, and ignorantly presumed culprits, nor am I searching for some nefarious governmental conspiracy, i.e. "chemtrails." ("Google" it.)

And don't get me started on cell phones. There is no connection...literally or figuratively. Can you hear me, now?

Some days I wonder if it's even possible to know what we're really facing other than an uncertain future. There's a lot of things we don't know, and a host of things where we don't know what we don't know. Ignorance can be bliss. But things are changing, rapidly, and we cannot continue on with an ignorant, business-as-usual, the Emperor-is-not-naked frame of mind.

Much is at stake, not just the future of the bees, not just the future of beekeeping, not just the future of humanity. We are in trouble, deep trouble, but the depth of this bottomless pit has not yet been realized. We are presently making the best decisions based on what we do know, hoping to right the ship, in order to set the most appropriate course of action to securing a better future, a future with hope.

Symptoms and Root Causes

Personally, I'm not sure we know what the real problem is, that is, identifying the root cause of these unexplained bee deaths. Dead bees are more likely a symptom of a greater environmental problem, which likely includes those three "usual suspects," but I fear deeper implications of other factors, factors we may not readily agree to surrender if the cost to our lifestyle, our supply of cheap food or our consumer-driven economy proves too great.

There are powerful corporate interests at stake, as well. We're playing with the big boys. As a beekeeper, I fear the old aphorism used by poker players reminding me, *"If you've been in a poker game for a while, and you still don't know who the patsy is, you're the patsy."*

The mysterious bee deaths have been compared to the old analogy of the "canary in the coal mine." And let's face it, dead canaries are not the problem, but rather a symptom of a more sinister conundrum lurking in the coal mine. The dilemma becomes finding out why the canary died and finding a workable solution to making the coal mine safe.

Until we discover those solutions, canaries will continue to perish in coal mines. Once we get tired of dead canaries piling up in the bottom of coal mines, perhaps we'll look at different ways to harvest coal other than digging long, dark tunnels into the depths of the earth. Or we may need to find additional fuel sources other than coal, but that means we need to invent different technology to adapt to alternative fuel sources. We call such change, a "paradigm shift."

Such changes may challenge, even compromise our comfortable lifestyle, or they may open the door to cleaner, more efficient energy consumption. Fear of change and what it portends will always be an intangible obstacle. We'll always hearken back to the good old days when...

These kinds of changes necessitate a paradigm shift, not just how we do things, but how we *think* about doing things.

The Power of a Paradigm

We may not find ourselves concerned about piles of dead canaries at the bottom of mine shafts, but we've reached the point where dead bees piling up on bottom boards or vacating hives, en masse, flying off to who knows where and disappearing has grabbed our attention.

As beekeepers, we ask ourselves, "If CCD, pesticides, and GMOs are the legitimate problems, obviously beyond the scope of our individual control, what I can do, personally, in my back yard apiary, to address these challenges, how they impact my bees, and how do I change my management to preserve my beekeeping operation?"

Instead of reacting to these presumed problems directly, not that I can do anything about them anyway, how do I form a proactive response based on what is within my power to change?

To borrow a worn-out cliché, "we need a new paradigm." A paradigm is nothing more than a model, a framework containing some common assumptions that inform our ways of getting things done, or how we *think* about getting things done.

The word, "paradigm," used to be kind of trendy until we wore it out, but like my plaid golf pants, things have a way of coming back into style. Consider me ahead of the trend. "Paradigm," resonates with me.

Likewise, another phrase that was beat like a dead race horse was, "paradigm shift." It's likened to, "thinking outside the box," which too, has been retired to the vocabulary nursing home.

Despite being over-used, they are nice illustrations of our need to change our thinking in how we approach today's challenges of keeping bees, and changing that which continues to frustrate our attempts at keeping bees alive.

Forces That Shift Our Paradigms

The beekeeping community built a nice paradigm prior to the arrival of varroa. It was a framework of how we kept bees, basically throwing bees in a box and getting the heck out of their way. We really didn't have to think how we kept bees; they kept us. We dosed our hives with powdered sugar and what was then an effective antibiotic to control our only real problem, American Foul Brood.

But with the arrival of varroa, we had to switch gears, think differently and create a new model to deal with varroa mites. So our management included a chemical response, hence, a new paradigm.

And if you've been keeping bees as long as I have, you know the story of chemical miticides and their declining effectiveness, kind of like our human illnesses that once responded quite well to penicillin. Times have changed, as they always do, forcing our hand to develop a new model, another shift in our paradigm. Was anyone really surprised by the rapid resistance those pesky varroa developed?

In hindsight, we followed the best management practices we could devise, given the mitigating circumstances and the available information, at that time. We just didn't think long enough, or far enough out into the future. Everything has future implications. But then, how could anyone imagine the present problems facing us today? And it's only been a few decades ago when they crested the horizon.

Every new challenge forces a modification to the existing model and how we operate and respond, given what we know. Knowledge is vital, otherwise we're shooting in the dark or merely rolling the dice, gambling away our future.

But our problems seem to always be about two miles, or two years ahead of our knowledge. Every challenge today seems to evolve with a greater acceleration than the previous one. Those on the front lines of developing more effective pharmaceuticals run the tortuous gauntlet of governmental approval and registration, not to mention the vast amounts of money to develop these products even before the first package is sold.

Leaving the Past Behind, Moving Forward

A paradigm shift does not throw the baby out with the bathwater (another trite cliché, sorry). We save what still works, yet we discard those old assumptions invalidated by the new challenge, then work to find, even create the next best management practice.

Then we pray the new practice works.

What works today is almost destined to disappoint us tomorrow. It is the nature of our present industry. We seem to be building and rebuilding new paradigms, hoping we've finally mastered our problems.

When I was a little boy growing up in Minnesota, a horrendous, late-summer thunderstorm ripped through our community. In my grandparent's yard, on the family farm where my grandfather was born, stood several old, gnarled apple trees, raised from seeds planted by my grandfather. Grandpa didn't really care what kind of apples the seeds produced. I think he had more fun taking seeds from good tasting apples and seeing if he could get a tree to produce.

My grandfather, instead of giving the trees names from the variety of the apple they produced, gave them regular names reflecting a personality as if they were pets or people. I vaguely remember some of the names were, "Pearl," "Sylvia," and "Myrtle." They were always women's names, for some reason. Maybe his old, childhood sweethearts.

My father was a young teen when many of these trees were planted. He likened the trees as if they were part of the family, lovingly offering gifts of fruit in exchange for my grandfather's doting care.

After the storm blew through and the skies cleared, we arrived at the farm, as did many of my aunts and uncles. With my grandparents, we assessed the damage and the prospects of cleaning and clearing debris.

We focused on one of those cherished apple trees, top-heavy with an abundant crop, ruby jewels on a crown of broadly spreading branches. It proved no match to withstand the ravaging winds. The trunk was strong and did not snap, but the roots gave way from the sodden soil and the tree lay on its side as if asleep. We stood around the tree in silence, as if fearing we might wake it.

My grandfather, a stoic Norwegian and not unfamiliar to many of life's tragedies, spoke plainly, breaking the silence. "We'll harvest the fruit and cut up the rest for firewood."

With the help of my cousins, we picked every apple and hauled them by wheel barrow to the "summer kitchen" where my grandmother canned the garden produce. My aunts bustled around each other in the cramped kitchen, peeling and slicing apples, washing jars, sweating through their long aprons from their close proximity to one another and the boiling pots on the stove.

Wheel barrows of apples were traded for buckets of apple peelings. I lost count how many buckets we dumped into the hog trough.

The sound of a chainsaw ripped through the late afternoon as all the cousins were conscriped to carry firewood using the same wheel barrow. My grandfather's pocket bulged with two, choice apples he selected, planning to recover the seeds for a new generation of apple trees.

One of the genetic defects in our family, passed from one generation to the next, is an uncommon, somewhat impractical frugality that wastes nothing, saves everything and hangs on to it until it finds a suitable use or another home. It's something I inherited and it drives my wife crazy and she prays the gene finds a terminal end before our children choose their respective spouse.

The demise of this old apple tree, whose name escapes my memory after all these years, is an example of a paradigm shift. The thunderstorm presented an unexpected situation, a new challenge forcing my grandfather's hand. His path forward moved him to 1) salvage the fruit, 2) cut up the tree for firewood for the coming winter, and 3) retain a couple of apples for seeds to plant new trees. He didn't abandon the good, but discarded that which wasn't going to work for him anymore.

Then he resolved to move forward. A proper paradigm shifts moves us into a new future, a future with hope.

His paradigm shift opened the door to a new future with new apple trees. Instead of moping around the fallen tree, reminiscing over the past about what might have been or cursing the injustice of the situation, a paradigm shift moved us into action, clearing the way for a proactive response. A paradigm shift is nothing more than a new model of how we get things done.

As beekeepers, we've experienced a lingering, pervasive, "disturbance in the force," which we've generically lumped under the ubiquitous term,

"CCD." The sudden deaths and mysterious disappearances of the honey bee and the decline of their productivity has forced our hand requiring changes in how we keep bees, even how we *think* about keeping bees.

The million dollar question becomes, "What needs to change as we seek a path forward, or what model gives us the best opportunity to successfully manage our bees in the wake of this storm?"

In a sense, we need not abandon the good, but we must discard those practices and management regimes that don't work anymore. We'll never be able to keep bees like our grandparents and there's little value in reminiscing over the past, except to remember what doesn't, and won't, work any more.

I can't personally change the reality of CCD, pesticides, and GMOs, no more than my grandfather could change the reality of a devastating thunderstorm and how it forced his hand.

So my paradigm shift, as it pertains to my beekeeping operation, is to find new ways in which I keep my bees such that I can overcome these challenges and work around them.

The new questions become, "How do I change the way I keep bees to survive in these difficult times? What can I do to keep me keeping bees? How do I reframe the situation and develop a new paradigm for an uncertain future, and make it a future with hope?"

Shrewd people know how to play a good hand from the cards they are dealt. Often times they are forced to do so, pondering when it's best to hold them, or if they should, in fact, fold them. Bluffing is hardly recommended unless a person is prepared to lose.

Beekeepers are no exception. We've been dealt some difficult cards and we're sitting around the table with some rather unsavory characters like the small hive beetles. It makes me wonder what they have up their six sleeves.

However, our resolve is to move forward to the best of our abilities with the present information we have at our disposal. Despite the odds against us, many of us resolve to keep on keeping bees.

We will also likely continue to lose bees, but our mission to pollinate crops and the steely determination to produce honey encourages us despite every negative thing we read or hear in the news media about the mysterious problems and the massive losses of colonies of bees.

But the questions of "how?" persist, nibbling annoyingly at our illogical optimism. We seem to be finding more ways that don't work than the ways that do.

Public Perception and Support

Once people find out I keep honey bees, I'm immediately asked if "they" have found a cure for that "thing that's killing the bees." I respond rather vaguely, "No, but we've got our best researchers working on it."

And I sincerely believe we do.

I interpret their reference to this "thing that's killing the bees" to be CCD, and no, we have not found a cure. Colony Collapse Disorder is an unexplained collection of several different problems which seem to interact inconsistently in malevolent and mysterious ways.

Researchers meticulously track down one problem and conclude, "This (*fill in the blank*) is the problem that's responsible for killing the bees." Then another team of researchers finds ten healthy hives, all prospering despite the presence of the same detected problem. It makes no sense other than to deduce there are many interacting factors and we've yet to figure out what combination is responsible.

It's complicated, and we're still searching for definitive answers.

If we could narrow the problem down to one culprit, then we could apply the most effective, single pharmaceutical remedy to address that lone problem.

But there is more than one issue, and hence, we are looking at multiple applications to remedy the predicament in order to find the best way forward.

At best, it's like herding feral cats that scatter once we open the barn door. It's a challenging and complicated time to try and keep honey bees, and not for the faint of heart, let alone the inexperienced beginner who optimistically hopes to be the strategic catalyst to "save the honey bee."

I love their idealism, but I have my doubts. However, we're at a point where we could definitely use a little more optimistic hope, no matter how improbable. Just give me something encouraging to hang my veil on.

Basically, we have to live with bees dying in this age of CCD. And this is where I'm coming from with this manuscript. Bees are dying and we have to find ways AROUND this problem because it seems there is no way THROUGH this problem.

This is just another way of saying we have to work smarter, not harder. And note how I use the plural form of "ways." There is no one problem and there is no one way to get around it. It is a multifaceted problem that will take a multifaceted approach...and a bit of creative ingenuity, not to mention some old fashioned perseverance.

And stubborn resolve.

Don't leave out that illogical and idiotic sense of obstinately hanging in there despite all the suggestions to the contrary. Maybe some of the lucky ones will be those beekeepers who are just too stubborn to quit and too foolish to leave the profession.

As a beekeeper, facing this seemingly insurmountable, rather undefined issue of dead and dying bees, I have to ask myself,

- ✓ How can I keep on keeping bees?

- ✓ What can I do that is within my power and my resources to overcome the difficulties this industry shares?

- ✓ What things can I control and what things are outside the realm of my influence?

- ✓ How do I marshal the fortitude, and the financial resources to give it another shot next year?

- ✓ How can I rise above the expected losses and counteract the anticipated deaths of my bees?

- ✓ How do I convince my spouse I haven't completely lost my mind?

And please don't share that old axiom of, "What doesn't kill us will only make us stronger." These problems ARE killing us.

But it's not just about me and my little pity-party. I lay awake at night wondering what the future holds for all of us beekeepers.

- ✓ We look around at our association meetings and wonder, who will be with us next year? Who won't?

- ✓ My phone rings each spring with people looking for nucs, packages and queens to fill the hives that died over the winter. Where do these nucs and packages come from? Prices keep going up. Who is going to afford a nuc in five years?

- ✓ How does my generation make the adjustments to our management such that those who come after us will enjoy the same opportunities to keep bees? Are we taking our privileges for granted? How much longer will this profession last?

- ✓ How does my generation pass on the knowledge and philosophies we've built, many of them still reminiscing on the simplicity of the pre-varroa years, and empower the next generation of beekeepers?

- ✓ How does my generation insure there will still be bees around to keep?
- ✓ Will there be a next generation of beekeepers?

At the farmer's markets where I sell honey, people continually ask me if the bees are still dying. My answer is, "Yes, they are still dying, but bees and beekeepers are resilient and we're bouncing back the best we know how."

Such an optimistic answer seems to assuage their ignorant fears, many of them believing the urban legend that if the honey bee should perish we'll all starve within four years.

This quote is totally false, mistakenly and fictitiously attributed to some guy with a last name of "Einstein," but not the real one called, "Albert." When my customers recite this quote (as if I've never heard it before), I usually smile and gently remind these wonderfully astute inquirers that our diet is based largely on corn, wheat, rice and potatoes, all of which are not dependent upon bees for pollination.

We will not starve and we'll be able to feed our livestock. We'll still enjoy bacon and eggs. I don't have time to get into all the vegetables, like tomatoes, which do not require honey bees as pollinators yet manage to produce nicely with other kinds of bees or wind. We will still savor our BLTs. If the bees all die, we will survive, but our diet will miss a lot of good things like melons, berries and fruit...and honey.

Sometimes I'm asked if *my bees* are dying, or if I've seen "this CCD thing," to which I guess these customers at the farmer's markets are thinking of the national headlines in the mass media and their local access to honey.

I answer simply, "No, my bees are doing relatively well." With that answer, they smile as if I have fixed all their problems.

For the most part, my bees are doing relatively well, or at least, better than the national average. Maybe I'm one of the lucky ones, but I have yet to see the narrowly-defined symptoms of CCD in my hives. Much of my problems focus around the varroa mite and my somewhat natural, non-chemical approaches to keeping honey bees that are not 100% effective.

There is some truth to my simplistic replies, however, as bees all around the country are still dying and my bees are still dying, but we are still keeping bees, or at least, trying our hardest to keep on keeping bees. We are resilient and we know how to raise queens and make splits. We have not given up, at any rate, not yet.

The Collateral Damage of CCD

Yet an attendant tragedy to the loss of the bees is the fact that old beekeepers are also dying, and if not dying, they are retiring or simply getting out of the business of keeping bees. We're struggling to stay ahead of the wave, but the tide is pulling some beekeepers under, unable to fight the current or continue to tread water.

As one of my buddies forlornly said, "It's like spending your life banging your head against the wall. You don't really want to quit, but it just feels so much better when you finally do."

One fairly large Missouri beekeeper, now retired for about five years though he still hangs out at the annual state conventions, told me, "Retirement is great. I no longer get up in the morning wondering and worrying about how many hives died since the last time I visited that bee yard."

We beekeepers are an aging population and most of us who keep bees are age-challenged, Caucasian males (read: old, grey-haired, white guys).

Yes, we have an incredible upsurge of beginners and a renaissance of backyard beekeepers, but the collective knowledge of 5,000 beginners, each with two hives, cannot replace the expertise and experience of one retiring, commercial beekeeper with 10,000 hives. Nor can those 5,000 new beekeepers marshal the resources to pollinate the vast acreage of crops covered by that single beekeeper.

Still, there is a place for the backyard beekeeper whose bees will find the neighbor's fruit trees and gardens, but backyard beekeeping is not the answer to our problem of hundreds of thousands of acres of pollinator-dependent crops and the society that has grown quite fond of affordable food produced on this kind of scale, with the highest quality at the lowest cost.

Part of the problem is when these old beekeepers die or retire, there is no one to fill their shoes. Many experienced beekeepers, the mid-sized sideliners who would naturally be ready to move up to the commercial ranks, are getting out of the business, as well. Many of them are calling it quits for a variety of reasons, but no one is ready, willing or able, vocationally, physically or financially, to pick up where they left off, either.

We are experiencing a top-level vacuum of commercial-level beekeepers. While nature abhors a vacuum, no one is scaling the ranks to fill the void.

And if an experienced, commercial beekeeper can't figure things out, what makes an inexperienced beginner optimistically think he, or she holds the secret key?

Desperate Hope; Blind Hope

Quite a number of beginners and "wannabees" approach me at various conventions and conferences, thinking they have magically stumbled upon the apicultural Holy Grail to successful beekeeping. They tell me they've been "researching" on the Internet, as if no one else knows of this source.

They pull me aside, eagerly sharing this new-found, secret knowledge, often spoken in hushed tones as they take me into their confidence, "The future of the honey bee lies in natural beekeeping."

Sometimes they use the word, "ecological" or "biodynamic beekeeping." "Organic" is a word thrown in here and there. I've heard the word, "permaculture," and one that really caught my ear was, "dynamic, adaptive transactional change."

I usually nod contemplatively and smile as they share this perceived secret, but in truth, it is not as secret as they think. At least I'm glad they're thinking about the future.

As one critic posted on a popular Internet forum, with respect to these enthusiastic newcomers to apiculture, "*It is not enough that they aspire to learn to keep bees, they approach the task convinced before reading the first book on the subject that they can "save" the bees from the stupidity of all current beekeepers by abandoning some large swath of the practices and/or equipment that has seemed to be useful for the past 200 or so years, replacing it with something that is a minor variant of a concept unjustly rejected by beekeepers several times over the past decades."*

I tend to agree with this position, and recall many years ago when family farms were failing and hordes of young, inexperienced, urban agrarians roamed the hinterlands hoping to, "buy land, farm organically, and pay off the bank loan from the profits."

You got to love their idealism, but the paper projections worked out on the kitchen table rapidly disintegrate when planted in the dirt. Still, they had vision. I respect them for their sense of vision.

Like the Internet poster previously quoted, I have experienced similar encounters, but God bless them, anyway. We're in a funk and we need some new ideas, even old ideas repackaged in shiny paper that seems fresh. We're ready to believe just about anything, even if it means trading the family cow for a handful of magic beans...especially if we're told the bean blossoms make really good honey.

It's like a fast-talking salesman who came to our small town in southern Minnesota about forty years ago. He spoke to a standing-room-only crowd shoehorned into the American Legion. The overflow huddled against the winter chill outside the front entry hoping to hear his salvific solutions.

I had to admire this salesman. He smoothly articulated a vision offering a limited-time, ground-floor opportunity regarding a new, highly-profitable miracle crop that was going to save the family farm. It was going to solve the energy crisis. It would bring us prosperity.

If the price for this seed was a first-born son, I might not be here to put this memory in writing. Several in attendance frantically searched their pockets for pens to sign the contracts.

I could tell many of those beleaguered farmers in attendance had their doubts, but their desperate hope, listening to this stranger offering a shiny ray of good news dispelling their gloom, would not allow them the luxury of disbelief.

My father's stoic response, reinforced by uncommon frugality, was unenthusiastic and skeptical. "If this miracle crop is so special, why aren't more farmers growing it right now? Why haven't we heard about it before this time?"

One of Dad's mantras in life was, "Anything that sounds too good to be true usually is." Ironically, in his later years he lamented his stubborn skepticism often kept him a day late and a dollar short. But he also said he never lost money on a speculative project he never started.

As it turned out, the potential market for this miracle crop never developed. Those who bought into the program ended up plowing the crop under. We didn't even come close to solving the energy crisis. If any good came out of the experience, it provided ample fodder fueling the conversation at the local coffee shop. A few lawyers tried to assemble a class-action lawsuit, but most of our neighbors were too ashamed to admit their gullibility. They opted for healing rather than picking off the scab in what would have been a lengthy, likely futile, legal battle.

So the bees are dying, but so are the beekeepers. The perceived consensus of the average consumer is, "We need the honey bees! We need to save the honey bees!" But we're not quite sure how to go about accomplishing our desires.

A lot of interest is brewing in the public, itching to help save the bees. If I were to take a guess, I'd say nine out of every ten conversations I've heard in the last two or three years begins with, "I've heard of keeping bees in a new kind of hive. It's called a top bar hive. It's all-natural and it's the cure to this CCD thing that's killing all the bees. It's so natural you don't even need to use smoke."

I just don't know how to best counsel these enthusiastic, hopeful beekeepers. There was a time I felt justified in correcting them, critically, though gently, steering them in the "right" direction of conventional Langstroth hives, but with my own losses, I may be lining up, myself, to drink the same Koolaid®.

Losses Continue

Every season brings bad news and the past winter of 2012 and 2013 recorded devastating losses across the nation. Personally, in southeast Missouri, it was my worst winter as I logged in losses around 25% of my hives, which, again, I will reiterate was not from CCD.

When I conversed with my colleagues over the Internet, they commonly exclaimed, "Wow! Only 25%? You're one of the lucky ones." They shared losses that ranged from 30% to 50%, with a few as high as 75% to 80% of their hives.

As spring rolled around, they found themselves scrambling and competing with other beekeepers to find package bees and nucs to replace those losses. Some complained they didn't have the money to buy replacement bees. It's tough out there; tougher than you may think; tougher than we want to admit.

Nationally, the average losses of this past year floated around 30 to 35% depending on the source of the data. My losses are attributed to the long drought of the 2012 growing season. The bees went into the winter with low reserves of stored honey, or as the beekeepers like to say, "The hives were light."

Actually, beekeepers DO NOT like to say, "The hives were light." It means we need to feed and get that feed to the bees before winter weather closes the door on that opportunity.

With hives light and short on reserves, coupled with the long, extended winter and subsequent late spring of 2013, my bees were hurting. Unable to put away enough stored honey in the fall, even with supplemental sugar syrup, my bees simply ran out of food waiting for spring to arrive when nature offers fresh pollen and nectar from the willows and maples. If spring had been normal, my losses would have been my usual 10 to 15%.

Unfortunately, the only place I'm finding, "normal," is on the washing machine in the basement. There really is no such thing as "normal" in anyone's apiary, not any more. In reality, there is no reality and the only time I experience "regular" depends on my consumption of bran cereal as I start my day.

A secondary impact to the 2012 growing season was the unusual early start to the growing season before the drought sucked the life out of every living organism. One of my growers, on a farm where my bees pollinate his watermelons, said the 2012 season started exceptionally early. He was planting at the end of March, two weeks earlier than normal (yeah, I know, there's no such thing as "normal"), while the 2013 season was two weeks late...and that's a whole month's difference from one year to the next. No wonder we're all mixed up. Further, the early beginning to last year's spring urged the queens in my hives to lay eggs earlier giving the varroa mite a longer season to reproduce.

As I hunkered down through the drought, I'm sure my mite levels were quietly exploding, and as a minimalist beekeeper with "soft" chemical approaches to mite management, I'm sure mites were one of my issues to the worst hive mortality I've ever experienced. Still, I'm not complaining. I am one of the lucky ones.

Bees are dying, but there is some good news. In 2010, the agricultural census reported the number of managed beehives in the United States at 2.5 million hives, while in 2011 we had 2.6 million hives, a net increase of 100,000 hives. The good news is we are headed in the right direction, even if we seem to be taking three steps forward while incurring losses of two steps back.

So which of these steps does the media report? There's some good news on the horizon, but the media prefers the old mantra of, "If it bleeds, it leads." Bad news sells newspapers and keeps viewers glued to the television through the next commercial.

Unfortunately, most of our general public doesn't read the details beyond the headline and the general consensus of our population is the bees are in trouble. Which they are, but it's not time to turn out the lights and lock the entrance reducer, at least, not just yet.

Challenges Still Abound

I might add the beekeepers in trouble are not just the old, grey-haired, white guys. I see a lot of beginners losing their vigor, those who optimistically entered this profession hoping their efforts would turn the tide as they sought to "help save the honey bee."

I teach and speak at a number of conferences, especially those aimed at beginning beekeepers and those who wish to start keeping bees in their back yard. Enthusiasm runs high and optimism flows freely like chocolate syrup at the ice cream parlor.

I often entertain questions from people who have yet to buy their equipment about where they will be able to sell all the honey they intend to harvest. They ask how much honey I sell at the local farmer's markets, then quickly and apologetically assure me they'll be selling at a different market than mine.

Perhaps people like me make it look too easy, but these newbees act like it's no big deal to raise bees and make honey, let alone finding an opening at the local farmer's market to make a bunch of money selling all that honey.

I usually just smile and reply, "Let's get you through your first year and focus on learning about the bees." I might gently add the likelihood of harvesting a first-year honey crop is remote, though not impossible because every hive is different, every location is different, every season is different and every beekeeper is different. Some beekeepers actually have that problem of what to do with all that honey they produce in their rookie season, but they are the exception and not the rule.

Out of this ocean of first-year beekeepers will come a trickle of survivors that make it to their second year of beekeeping. And there are a plethora of reasons why beginners fail. First-year losses will cull the herd and even second-year beekeepers begin to drop like flies. An unsubstantiated statistic floats around the bee meetings and local associations that 80% of beginning beekeepers quit within two years.

Many of these newbees will be attempting "natural" or treatment-free approaches that won't work, largely due to their inexperience and *lack of knowledge* (which is a nice way of stating, "ignorance").

Natural approaches have merit when you understand honey bee biology and the seasonality of the hive and make the adjustments to your management practices to account for the problems. Natural approaches to beekeeping, while noble and notable, are no guarantee of success. Some days I wonder if it even makes any difference to go the natural route.

Thus, I'll also warn you that if you attempt a more natural approach, you're going to experience dead hives. Bees die. But the chemical beekeepers also suffer losses. There's an old saying that says, "If you raise livestock, you have to get used to dead stock." This notion of natural beekeeping is not fool proof, but in my opinion, it is a preferred method because you're not messing around with resistance and residues.

While I am not a strict, natural beekeeping purist, I tend to lean in this direction. But my goal of keeping bees is to keep them alive, and if need be, I will use appropriate measures to stay in business. I have no intention of keeping bees if I cannot keep them alive, nor will I unnecessarily consign them to a certain death just because they cannot fend off an infestation of mites as I arrogantly proclaim an uncompromising, treatment-free regime.

So on one hand we see a tremendous tsunami of beginners and their optimism washing over the landscape. Bee clubs and local associations are swamped with people, young and old, requesting beginner courses. The tide washes in, and then it washes out. Beginners lose interest or quit when their bees die. But next spring a new wave is building in the ocean of our humanity. They too will wash in, and then wash out. A few will fill the tidal pools and stick around.

Interestingly, I also find a lot of beekeepers with five to ten years of experience fading from the scene. I see more advertisements for used beekeeping equipment and beekeepers who lament, "I just couldn't keep ahead of the mites." Some say, "The moths got them." There's a lot of discouragement quietly mentioned from experienced beekeepers embarrassed by their inability to keep bees alive, searching for unexplained reasons why their bees died after several successful years.

To quote Greg Hannaford from Tulsa, Oklahoma, "We need more beekeepers and fewer former beekeepers."

At one local association meeting, a husband was complaining how, "There's no money in beekeeping," only to have his wife rather sarcastically, and publically chide him, "Well, not the way you keep them." It seemed he could not keep his bees alive, and any money from the little honey he sold was dedicated to purchasing fresh, replacement bees the following spring. I can relate to this.

These are challenging times and beekeeping is being contested and opposed by more than the usual suspects. When the surveys come out and we try and discern what kills so many hives, I am convinced a strong majority of our losses come from first- and second-year beekeepers who have not yet learned to manage their hives successfully, nor have they insights to correctly diagnose the cause of death for the surveys. I hate to use the words, "inexperience," and "ignorance," but that's a shoe that fits so let's learn to wear it.

And quite frankly, I lose hives. With some of these losses, I am perplexed as to what was the problem. I'm just as ignorant as the beekeeper over the hill.

I continually ask myself, "I thought I did everything right. What could I have done differently?"

Sadly, I'm often left guessing, asking questions to people who, like me, just don't know the answer. Part of my problem is my memory of how easy it was to keep bees several decades ago. One of my issues is the idealism that I can keep bees alive, and even losing one hive is a disaster. On the whole, I keep the greatest majority of my hives alive. But the challenges are increasing in their severity. It's just getting harder to keep bees and keep them alive.

Still, I persist. Call me a fool. Call me stubborn or stupid. Call me crazy, but I love keeping bees and I'm not ready to give up.

My intent of this manuscript is to share principles and explore methods that have worked for me, and hopefully, will work for you and keep you keeping bees. It's a challenging time with no real answers to those mysterious problems.

We're basically left to soldier on and bravely march into the skirmishes in the trenches and dodge the bullets on the front lines. Our best defense may be an aggressive offense. Our stubborn resolve may be the best way to break through the resistance until the reinforcements arrive.

And the reinforcements are coming, aren't they?

I liken my book to the idea of "sustainable beekeeping." Sustainable is kind of a trendy, "buzz" word tossed around these days, and not many people know how to define it, exactly.

No doubt, in a few years, we'll ask "paradigm" to share their previously private room at the vocabulary nursing home with this younger companion, "sustainable."

However, to me, to "sustain" is to keep going, and "sustainable" beekeeping is to find a way, or more than likely, <u>WAYS</u>, the plural vehemently intended, such that we keep on keeping bees in this demanding era. Dying bees from any cause is neither profitable nor enjoyable. We need ways to survive.

I hate it when I lose a hive of bees, especially if it was something I could have prevented. I even hate losing bees from those things I can't prevent. I hate losing a hive of bees for any reason, but in this day and age, my idealism is impractical. Bees are dying, and I don't like it. I want ways around this problem.

And in my discouragement, I am reminded how failure looks like the end of the road...until I make a new path. That's my hope; a new path in this age of CCD. A new paradigm for new problems.

The Greatest Challenge Lies With Us

Starting out keeping bees requires a large investment of capital, about $350 per hive at my last estimate if buying new equipment and a nucleus colony ("nuc" for short) of bees. Enthusiasm dims rapidly when our bees die and need to be replaced and we have to somehow explain to our impatient spouse regarding our wisdom of ignorantly entering such a challenging hobby at such a challenging juncture in time.

However, failure is only the opportunity to begin again...only the next time more wisely. (Henry Ford) I just don't want to give up too soon. I always feel I'm but one nuc away from real success.

To paraphrase a quote, the original version likely incorrectly attributed to John Wayne, "Beekeeping is hard, but harder when you lack experience and knowledge."

God bless you, if you are just starting out. The odds are stacked against you, don't pretend otherwise. They are stacked against all of us. I can only hope my trials continue to instill in me a sense of perseverance. I expect my perseverance to mature into patience, and optimistically, I anticipate my patience to give me character. May my character produce a hope such that I will not lose heart and give up. Yet there are days my wife assures me, "Thank God you have your day job."

And I am thankful for my day job, but I'm also thankful I am engaged in the most exciting hobby I can possibly imagine. As my good friend, David Burns likes to say, "Life is good this side of the mail box."

Life is good for me, as well. But it's also challenging. I want it to be better, but like Dorothy and Toto, I'm not in Kansas anymore. Welcome to beekeeping in the era of CCD.

My aspiration also includes sharing some of my tricks and management skills I've learned which keep me keeping bees, which to my mind I like to categorize as "sustainable" practices. And more than just keeping me keeping bees, I want to be profitable. The double-edged sword of profitability is to keep expenses low while working to maximize income.

However, if I'm buying nucs of honey bees every spring, I'm showing a negative cash flow. That's not my idea of sustainability. I'm also looking for some sense of self-reliance, reducing the need of depending on others who may not share my urgency, as well as minimizing my out-of-pocket expenses for outside inputs.

Sustainable beekeeping is ultimately about cash flow, even if you have no commercial aspirations. A positive cash flow is manifested by practices which keep hives healthy and productive.

I would also be remiss if I did not include this disclaimer that I do not know everything. Big surprise, right? I may sound really smart to some people, but I'm still learning and every year it seems the bees teach me a new trick or reveal the depth of my ignorance...I mean, my lack of knowledge. It's humbling, to say the least.

People ask me questions and my answer is increasingly becoming, "I don't know." And I continue to try and find really intelligent sounding ways of admitting my ignorance and failing wisdom.

Maybe I'd at least sound smarter if I paused, put my finger on my chin and prefaced my response with a contemplative, "Hmmmm...very interesting. I'm sorry, I don't really know."

As one of the national speakers is fond of saying, "The best teachers are the bees." I've lived by the axiom, "When the student is ready, the teacher appears." Unfortunately, I never feel ready and find myself in the position of a remedial student most of the time.

I started keeping bees in 1981 when life was much simpler and the science of keeping bees was easy and predictable. Every year throws me another curve ball. I would love to lay down a schedule that if I did "blah, blah, blah" on such and such a date, I can find "bim, bam, zoom" on this subsequent date.

It's not that easy. It's hardly that predictable. Beekeeping is much more "art" than "science," and the knowledge of how to keep bees is more "caught" than "taught."

Still, there are things I've learned on my journey to become a more self-reliant, sustainable beekeeper. Today's beekeepers are having a hard time with their own survival, let alone the bees they keep.

Much of what I write about can be debated and challenged, particularly because we live with the idea that all beekeeping is local, that is, what works for me in my area won't necessarily work for you in your area. But take this to heart: The methods will undoubtedly vary while the principles remain the same. There's a lot of adaptation and adjustment, so take my advice and modify my methods to fit your particular situation.

This manuscript is hardly the last word. I'm open to constructive criticism and improvement. We're in this fight together, irrespective if you are a conventional beekeeper or a natural beekeeper.

My writing coach, Linda Culbreth of www.bookdesignbylinda.com, has given me the Japanese word, "kaizen," which means, "always improving, getting better and better." I want my next season of beekeeping to be my best season of beekeeping, and the next season after that should be even better.

I hope to have the same desire that each subsequent season will be even better yet. I want to always be improving my beekeeping skills. These challenging times demand constant vigilance and improvement.

It's a quirky time to get into beekeeping. Desperate times may call for desperate measures, but tough times don't last while tough people do. When approached by someone who inquires about keeping bees, I hesitate to be too encouraging. There are easier hobbies with more enjoyment and fewer obstacles.

But if it is your desire to enter into this engaging enterprise, then buckle up, stow your luggage beneath your seat, return your tray table to the upright position...we're going to take off, and it's likely to be a bumpy ride.

Chapter 1

Sustainable Perceptions and Observations

*"You don't have to be great to start,
but if you never start, you'll never be great."*

"Why do we set our sites on the finish line, when the most important moment is the start, where we begin to dream, to climb, to soar? There is no finish without the most important part of the day, the start."

Not surprisingly, the greater beekeeping community is fractured into two "camps."

I'm going to use that word, "camp," to signify a loosely defined category, a gathering or group of beekeepers who share certain philosophies and management practices. Think of these camps as beekeepers who have an affinity for particular practices that set them apart and distinguish them from the other camp.

I'm also going to speak rather generally, using some broadly assumed stereotypes to illustrate differences between their respective philosophies that fall at the ends of a widely diverse spectrum of those who keep honeybees, and why they keep them in the manner they so choose. I choose to define the ends of this spectrum into a "conventional" camp and a "natural" camp.

Unfortunately, instead of working together and finding our common ground, we, like most human organizations, tend to drift apart to polar opposites on this wide spectrum of beekeeping practices and management objectives. And like most human institutions, we tend to point to the other camp and highlight all their problems, which is unfortunate as there is much each camp can learn from the other.

The "Conventional" Camp

One camp is the commercial beekeepers, largely basing their decisions on the use of pharmaceutical intervention to stop the mites and diseases. Management is focused on specific levels of production with intensive objectives, typically for financial profit. Even a hobbyist desires a positive cash flow, or at least their spouse wants a little return.

For the sake of our discussion, I'm going to call these beekeepers the "conventional" camp.

Conventional beekeepers, regardless of their size or intent, typically use the standard Langstroth hive and most commonly possess a desire to maximize their honey harvest, irrespective of how much they harvest or what they hope to do with it. Critics of the conventional approach to beekeeping perceive the colony becoming dependent upon the beekeeper for their survival, without such feeding and medicating, the bees are unable to survive.

This conventional camp is the majority of the beekeepers in the United States. The beekeepers in this camp implement an approach to beekeeping more commonly known as, "the dominant model," which I'll explain more fully in subsequent chapters. The dominant model is practiced without regard to the size of the conventional beekeeper. Most beginner classes taught by local associations promote the dominant model. It's the way most beekeepers keep bees.

We might even call this method "traditional" beekeeping, though there are some critics who pejoratively disdain these methods as "industrial" beekeeping with a "feed lot" mentality on a "factory farm" model, promoting toxic environments by greedy beekeepers who don't care if they kill their bees.

Really? I have yet to meet any beekeeper who doesn't care whether or not his, or her, bees live or die. This is a pretty strong charge. I was just kinda hoping we could, you know, all just try to get along. Perhaps in any camp, there are divisive extremes capturing our hunger for a negative stereotype.

The "Natural" Camp

The other camp is more natural, less chemical, significantly and intentionally less intensive in their management, and they have appropriated the name, "natural" to deliberately differentiate themselves from the conventional camp.

The natural camp believes their methodology is the best path forward to achieve sustainable beekeeping. At the extreme end, some natural beekeepers would like to think they own the concept of the "sustainable" approach

Given the number of conventional beekeepers who are calling it quits, unable to sustain their craft, from the large, multi-thousand hive, commercial beekeeper to the backyard beekeeper with but one hive, the natural camp is gaining traction and increasing attention.

It is not surprising how some beekeepers would tend to believe natural beekeeping equates itself to sustainable beekeeping. The old, chemical paradigm is falling apart, and we're discovering new chinks in its armor.

I tend to disagree that the natural camp is the only sustainable path forward, and I'll raise that point in a few paragraphs, but to cut to the chase, I think sustainable principles can bridge both conventional beekeeping practices and natural beekeeping practices. Sustainable beekeeping is something to be practiced, not owned and not collateralized.

But I digress, which I'm prone to do.

The natural camp focuses more on the needs of the bees rather than the products of the hive. The application of management practices honors the bees' natural inclinations rather than accommodating human convenience, while not striving to attain unnatural levels of production.

I don't exactly know what unnatural levels of production equates to, but I gather (and correct me if I'm wrong) that the hive is not manipulated or managed to the beekeeper's advantage. Whatever honey is produced is reserved, first, for the colony and its food requirements, and the beekeeper is allowed to harvest the surplus, if there is any surplus.

It is my opinion, based on my experience, that unless a colony is manipulated and managed for honey production, the likelihood of a surplus is reduced. Honey bees excel and respond favorably to human management. But human intervention, meddling, interruption, coddling, however you wish to define, "management," is not the priority of the natural beekeeping camp.

I continue to hear we need alternative management practices which are, "better for the bees." But I'm not sure how these practices are specifically "better" for the bees, nor do I have any idea how we can measure the benefit these practices offer.

The management objectives of this camp will likely be more passive, if not neglectful allowing the bee to be a bee. The natural camp is definitely non-commercial in their aspirations. They are the minority and might even be seen as "counter-cultural," sometimes even tossing around the words, "organic," "ecological," and "biodynamic."

So we have the conventional camp and their Langstroth hives, intensively managed by the dominant model on one extreme. These beekeepers tend to be rather obstinate and resistance to change. On the other extreme is the natural camp with Warre and top bar hives, passively managed, more than likely, in a treatment-free practice. These beekeepers tend to be rather zealous and righteous in their opinions about how to best keep bees.

Caught in the Middle: The "Balanced" Camp

I think there are many beekeepers who don't fit in either camp, neither the conventional nor the natural. And what I've described as both ends of this spectrum are kind of a caricature, a stereotype of the extreme.

But beekeeping is not really divided into two camps, and "us" and "them," but a wide-sweeping spectrum of everything in between. We forget the things we hold in common that both camps share and treasure. There are many people like me who bridge the gap between the two camps.

I am a conventional beekeeper in Langstroth hives with an emphasis on intensive management that results in honey production, but I am also a little squeamish about a routine, prophylactic approach to pharmaceutical treatments that result in mite resistance and chemical residues. I am not of the opinion, either, that leaving the bees alone to fend for themselves with treatment-free management works. I believe something needs to be done to keep the varroa population in check.

Further, as a conventional beekeeper, I don't fit neatly into the dominant model of splitting hives in the spring and filling winter dead outs from southern-raised nucs, packages and queens. I much prefer to work with locally-adapted stock that survives in my area.

Mostly, I'm trying to find balance. I want to work with the bees' natural ability to take care of themselves, hoping my management supports and nurtures the hive as a whole, living organism. I'm drawn to the ideals of treating bees to enhance their health, and their ability to defend themselves against pathogens and parasites, rather than treating them to develop chemical and pharmaceutical dependencies.

Still, I am a business man and I manage my bee hives with a profit motive. I will do what I need to do to keep my bees healthy and productive and I have not completely ruled out my options of resorting to synthetic commercial miticides, though such options would be my last choice.

However, I'm looking for sustainable practices that will keep me keeping bees, and keep my hives producing honey which in turn, keeps me making money.

Which begs the question: "Is it possible to keep bees in a conventional Langstroth hive, guided by a profit motive and intensive production goals, and still utilize balanced, sustainable practices and non-chemical responses that nurture and support rather than enslave and exploit?"

Can I have the best of both worlds?

I'm going to make the case for the affirmative answer to that question, though many adherents of the natural methods may disagree, that my only sustainable options are the less intensive, non-commercial venues such as the top bar hive or the Warre hive.

I may sound a little defensive, maybe even a little belligerent when I suggest the Langstroth design is here to stay, fits our modern agricultural model, produces quantities of honey our society demands, which I am able to market at profitable margins.

The Langstroth hive fits my purposes for keeping bees. One of the things beekeepers need to agree on is how each beekeeper is unique and we cannot foist our agenda upon another, just because we disagree on why each of us keeps bees. There are as many ways to keep bees as there are beekeepers.

Still, I think our common ground focuses on the bottom line of our privilege and our responsibilities of keeping bees, keeping bees healthy and productive, and finding the enjoyment of why we keep bees.

I'm frequently ask, "What is the right way to keep bees? Is there a right way?"

I believe there is a right way to keep bees. It's the way that works best for you, in your area, under your skill set, fulfilling your goals and purposes. Basically, each of us has to find the way that works for us.

And I can get kind of prickly regarding those beekeepers who stridently adhere to one way and promote and advocate how their one way is THE way. Or they may say, "Well, if I was you..."

I disagree. There is no ONE way other than what works for you, and you are not me!

People frequently send me e-mails asking questions, which is fine. I try and answer the best I can, given what they tell me, which isn't much, very often. But it makes me shake my head and roll my eyes when they add, "I read where some beekeeper said you should ALWAYS put marshmallows in the hive entrance just before dark when the temperatures drop below forty degrees."

What?

I have no idea where this came from. I don't think beekeeping has the universal, "ALWAYS," clause. Beekeeping is local and beekeepers are idiosyncratic. We all have our challenges provoking our best ideas. But marshmallows?

Which is why I may sound a little antagonistic toward the natural camp. Bear no mistake, I respect those who keep bees in that fashion, but I have different goals and purposes that will not, and cannot be met by keeping bees under their concepts of a natural management plan.

To push that envelope just a little further, what I perceive, what I hear, what I interpret and understand from the natural camp is an impertinence, inflexibility and intolerance that the natural way is the best way, the only way, or the way that is going to bring salvation and deliverance to the beekeeping community.

Sorry, I'm just not buying it. But I'll gladly concede the more chemical approach isn't the answer, either.

Can Sustainable Beekeeping be Profitable?

When I speak at conferences, I often state my goal is to make honey in order to make money, then intentionally follow up with the misquoted comment. So you'll hear me say, "I don't apologize about making money from my bees, though let us remember the Good Book says money is the root of all evil."

I can tell the biblically literate persons in the room when they correct me and say, "It's *the love of* money that is a root *of all kinds* of evil."

From here, we usually slide into a discussion on how money, in and of itself, is not evil. It's what we do with it that becomes subject to the criteria of being either good or evil.

Then, after the discussion, comments and questions subside and I feel like we can move on, I usually have some smart aleck who says, "I don't actually love money, but I sure love what it does for me!"

Beekeeping has been very good to my family. Through our honey sales at farmer's markets, we've enjoyed some things that would not have been possible if I choose to engage in a different hobby.

Sustainable production, beekeeping or anything else, is not really sustainable if it's not also profitable, able to produce a healthy income after paying the bills and support a good quality of life. If it's not profitable, it will have to be subsidized, which I think tends to negate the whole idea of "sustainability."

Sustainable practices in beekeeping lend themselves to smaller markets and local niches, i.e., farmer's markets, often selling directly to the consumers or within a local food system and a smaller, carbon-footprint. Sustainable beekeeping will also seek to increase the consumer's awareness of how wholesome food is produced, in general, and specifically why this honey is a superior product.

I make no apologies for making money from my bees, but my real point is how I want to work *with my bees*, colluding and collaborating with their instincts in rhythm with the seasonal fluctuations. Again, I'm looking for balance. I firmly believe I can effectively partner with the colony and manage it for greater production than if I ignored it and let the mites turn my hive into an all-you-can-eat buffet.

Yes, I am the recipient of the bees' hard work and they reward my responsible management skills. But don't fuss at me that I'm somehow abusing the bees as if they were "slaves" (a fitly chosen, racially-charged word to illicit an emotional response to deflect any rational intellectual conversation).

There is a commonly mistaken perception that conventional beekeepers exploit and bend the will of the honey bee to suit the beekeeper's selfish motives. We force them into square boxes with frames of unnaturally large cells and move them from monoculture crop to monoculture crop, then feed them an artificial diet the bees never imagined after stealing all their honey.

Many of these perceptions are grossly inaccurate, though may contain a grain of truth. Not all conventional beekeepers are on the same page, and as I said earlier, many of us bridge the gap between the two extremes.

The natural camp contends the best way to raise bees is an approach with less intervention or human "meddling," housing bees in vintage hive designs like the Warre hive, with less, if any emphasis on swarm prevention and less, if any concern with honey production.

It is true, that conventional beekeeping is built on finely machined, moveable frames (which often disrupt the design set up by the bees), in boxes which are often manipulated artificially for improved management and inspection. No doubt, it can be said it all ends up benefitting human beings at a detrimental disadvantage to the honey bee.

Moving frames around is like rearranging the furniture in my house where the dining room table ends up in the bathroom. Yes, this is confusing, but we can learn to make it work, and after some time, I learn to cook my breakfast in the bedroom because that's where the stove was relocated.

Hive inspections and manipulating frames is disruptive. Given the option, I would choose to keep my inspections to a minimum. Not only do they upset and disturb the harmony of the hive, I'm at a point in my beekeeping career where I just don't have the time. To a certain degree, experience has taught me there's much to discern by observing the activities at the entrance that, partially, tell me what's happening on the inside.

I'm not quite to the point where I feel my conventional practices are detrimental to the bee. I don't dump toxic and sub-lethal chemicals in my hives. I don't promote a hostile work environment of monoculture and I don't move my bees around. I like to think I use good, common sense which puts me in the position of a steward of these resources. I believe we reap what we sow, and any unsustainable practice will not produce the desired, long term benefits we anticipate.

With all the variables in location, it will be hard to narrowly define any single formula of what constitutes sustainability, and to a certain degree, sustainability is conceptionally-oriented rather than specifically method-driven. Which is just another way of saying, "Beekeeping is local."

Secondarily, not only does sustainable beekeeping resist a single formula, it is far more likely to be carried out through multiple management practices. Sustainable beekeeping is like a stairway, and unless you are Superman and can leap tall stairways in a single bound, you'll find sustainable beekeeping to be a series of smaller steps, that when you put one foot in front of the other, ascending to the next stair tread, and on to the next, you begin to see how sustainable beekeeping is more of a wholistic endeavor.

And yes, I know I misspelled holistic with the addition of the, "w," but I believe sustainable beekeeping takes the WHOLE hive into account as we manage our bees through the WHOLE year.

Besides, I told my spell-checker on my computer to add, "wholistic," to the list of "correct" words in my dictionary. We're all good.

The patron saint of the natural beekeeping camp is anthroposophist Rudolph Steiner, whose agricultural lectures are subtitled, "The spiritual foundations for a thriving agriculture." I will agree, there is an intriguing, underlying, mystic spirituality to keeping honey bees and the longer I keep bees, the more I respect what they do and how they go about doing it. Ironically, Steiner never kept honey bees but seemed to observe some qualities which he then turned into speaking points.

In 1923, Steiner predicted modern beekeeping practices (of that era, which hardly constitutes "modern") would create dire consequences leading to the demise of the honey bee within eighty years, which in turn, would impact our food production. He was pretty close, if you do the math.

However, I don't think Steiner had any idea of what we have been facing the past two or three decades, and there's no way he could have predicted calamities like global warming or the invasion of the varroa mite.

Personally, I don't put a lot of stock in Steiner's writings, but that's my personal baggage I've got to tote around. It does make for a nice coincidence to bolster the natural beekeeping methods.

Steiner is the father of a movement we also call, "biodynamic" beekeeping, which is heralded today by modern disciples like Gunther Hawke, David

Heaf and Phil Chandler. Though I may disagree with their thoughts and philosophy, make no mistake, I still value and respect their opinions. Biodynamic beekeeping has noble goals, some which can be carried over, syncretised and hybridized to benefit the conventional camp.

Some of these ideals may include,

- ✓ giving the bees their freedom to act upon their instinct,

- ✓ producing open-mated queens naturally through swarming and supersedure,

- ✓ allowing the bees to create their own wax comb with natural-sized cells,

- ✓ feeding on honey and pollen (not man-made, cheaper substitutes), and

- ✓ exploring a diversity of forage without being trucked all over from one monoculture to the next,

- ✓ without applying large doses of synthetic chemicals to combat other pests and diseases due, in part, to the perception that commercial beekeepers maintain an excessive concentration of hives in overcrowded apiaries.

These are not bad ideals. But the million dollar question becomes, "Are these standards practical to the bee keeper who wishes to produce and market honey for a fair return on their investment?" What about those of us who like to make a sideline income from our beekeeping endeavors? Must I apologize or somehow compensate the bees for my capitalistic desires?

I like those biodynamic ideals as they take great consideration into the welfare of the honey bee, but there is absolutely no concern for honey production. It turns honey bees into pets and honey production into an accidental coincidence.

Additionally, our modern agricultural practices work against our honey bees and only contribute to the challenges we face as beekeepers, whether you are natural or conventional.

However, conventional beekeeping has adapted to, and been groomed to work with modern agriculture, particularly in the migratory nature of the pollination of certain crops grown in a monocultural environment, of particular note, fruit trees and almond groves.

I'm not saying this is a good thing. It is what it is. This is how food is produced in our country to meet the demands of the consumer, and, yes, it's had a negative impact on how we try and keep our bees alive. But as I've already mentioned, the back yard projects of hobbyist beekeepers cannot meet our need to produce food for our hungry planet and an exploding population.

Maybe we need to reduce our population growth. Maybe we need to eat more low-end foods. The problems in beekeeping cannot be simplified to converting to Warre hives and allowing the bees to swarm. The situation with the bees dying won't be cured by totally giving up the conventional practices utilizing Langstroth hives with intensive management focusing on honey production.

If we are really serious about changing conventional beekeeping into a more natural management regime, we really need to change the ways we produce our food. Given the growing population of the world and the increased demand for high-end food (i.e., meat), I can't say much is going to change in the realm of intensive, production agriculture.

If people want to make a decent living from keeping bees, top bar hives and their limited production is not the answer. But neither is dumping all kinds of chemicals into the hives creating a toxic environment. Sustainable practices seek balance and longevity, which, in my opinion, are inherent qualities fulfilling the definition of sustainability.

Until modern agricultural and the increasing demands upon it change, the reality of what we are facing requires conventional beekeeping practices on a commercial scale. But these practices do not seem to be benefitting the honey bee or keeping the beekeeper happy and content.

Somewhere we need to find something of a sustainable model within the conventional beekeeping camp that synchronizes its livelihood with the reality of meeting the demands of modern agriculture, including honey production, while still meeting the needs and purposes of those who keep the bees.

So my intent, as I proceed in this manuscript, is to encourage you irrespective of which camp you belong. If you so desire to keep bees with low-level, less-intensive, natural management practices, I'll say, "More power to you! Good luck with that!" And I mean it.

But let's not pretend this back yard beekeeping model, with all its noble intentions, can possibly replace the need for pollination on the scale that modern agriculture requires. I cannot foresee the reality of our agricultural system changing, short of some apocalyptic catastrophe (and I'm not ruling that out, mind you).

Further, as modern agriculture attempts to meet the increasing demands of a hungry planet, beekeepers will have to adapt and live with a production system that continues to present, even creates apicultural challenges and environmental problems. Still, do not presume I'm blaming CCD on our modern production system of agriculture, as some members of the natural camp have alluded.

Keep bees any way you wish, but do it responsibly and successfully. Do it sustainably so you can keep on keeping bees. Respect the bee and what she is designed to do. Give a little latitude to your neighbors and the methods they choose for raising bees.

This is where I'm coming from as I put this manuscript together: In an age of intensive agricultural globalization and increasing urban sprawl, how do I maintain my bees and find a sustainable method to keeping my bees healthy and productive? How do I keep honey bees, which implies an objective to keeping them alive? To a lesser extent, how do I keep bees profitably, which presupposes an acceptable level of production?

I confess I'm not reverting to vintage hives and low, less-intensive management schemes. I am a conventional beekeeper. I produce honey for commercial, retail purposes. I like using Langstroth hives with moveable frames. I want to stay in this business and find ways to do it in a responsible, balanced, sustainable method.

Chapter 2

What constitutes, "Sustainable?"

"Seize the moment of excited curiosity on any subject to solve your doubts; for if you let it pass, the desire may never return, and you may remain in ignorance."
--William Wirt

There are basically three, distinctive types of beekeeping operations in the United States. There are, definitely, infinite numbers of the types of beekeepers and persons who keep honey bees, but we can wrap up their activities into three main areas of interest and pursuit.

To put it another way, there are three, primary categories in the world of conventional beekeeping that articulate and illustrate one's purpose for keeping honey bees. Most beekeepers tend to gravitate into one of these three categories as they follow their passion and carryout those respective activities in how they keep bees.

Three Types of Beekeeping Operations

The first type of beekeeping operation, perhaps the most popular, focuses on honey production. There may be differences in how and where that honey is produced and marketed, but your principle purpose, if this is your focus, produces honey.

If someone asks you, "Why do you keep honey bees?" the answer is self-evident when you hand them a jar of honey and say, "That will be $8.50, please."

Honey production is probably the most easily accessible beekeeping activity as it lends itself to the smaller beekeeper and those with less experience.

The second type of beekeeping operation focuses on raising queens, which, more than likely, also includes nuc production or package sales. The principle purpose is producing and selling bees.

The third type of beekeeping operation focuses on pollination, which will likely be migratory and include trucks and forklifts and hives on pallets. If not, then you have trailers, hand-carts and a couple of young guys with strong backs who have no qualms of working under the cover of darkness.

The principle purpose in this type of operation is obviously pollination and the likely revenue stream comes from renting and moving hives of bees.

I hear from a lot of beginning beekeepers who start keeping bees with the simple idea of merely providing pollinators for their garden. They are not interested in honey and they don't really want to, "mess with the bees," or manage the bees for any kind of increase. These beekeepers fall into this category of pollination.

These three categories of beekeeping activities broadly encompass the greatest majority of our reasons and purposes for keeping honey bees.

And, of course, I might reasonably expect some blending and hybridizing across the lines defining these three types of operations.

Many migratory pollinators, after the seasonal blooming cycle subsides for the production crops, haul their hives to the northern plains in Minnesota and the Dakotas to produce honey, before the hives are hauled to southern regions for the winter.

Pollination, however, is the prime purpose why these beekeepers keep bees, but honey production becomes an easy and complementary activity to migratory pollination, thus enabling a higher level of sustainability and cash flow.

Synergy Happens

In my opinion, a sustainable beekeeping practice intentionally hybridizes and blends and blurs the lines that set each type of beekeeping enterprise apart. Sustainable beekeeping finds ways these three types of beekeeping complement each other and "learn to play nice together."

I like the word, "synergy," to picture a collaborative effort or a planned, systematic integration of resources that builds up and benefits the bees and the beekeeper. Synergy happens when all things play nice together and complement other activities.

Synergy is one of my favorite, fifty-cent words which simply mean things work together for the mutual benefit of everyone and everything else. When synergy happens, the total effect is greater than the sum of all its parts. The beauty of synergy expresses itself as it only serves to add, never subtract.

And along with, "paradigm" and "sustainable," "synergy" may also be moving into the nursing home for old words. Nevertheless, I like it. Like the sweet old matronly resident who sits in the front lounge of the nursing home, she's still got some great stories to tell.

A sustainable practice seeks self-reliance by integrating different activities that fills the voids of vulnerability left by another activity. Synergy develops from assimilating various activities and resources, many of them you probably have at your immediate disposal, which you may be overlooking.

My purpose is honey production, but a few customers at the farmer's market requested pollen. I added pollen traps to a few hives and we broadened our customer base. A few requests for small quantities of bees wax inspired us to add eight-ounce tubs of bees wax to our table. I also make a very plain, unscented, bees wax, lye soap which complements our honey sales. These ancillary products attract customers and increase our sales and they don't detract from our main focus of producing and selling honey. This is synergy.

Even adding other activities, perhaps as simple as raising your own queens while your main focus produces honey, moves you in the direction of increasing your level of sustainability. Sustainable practices minimize the variables impacting our main focus.

My main focus is honey production. How can you tell? Watch my lips: "Here's a jar of honey. That will be $8.50, please."

More and more, I am refining my main purpose and creating synergy by raising my own, locally-adapted queen honey bees. I want to split my hives following my honey harvest and yet I've not been happy with mail-order queens. How can I step into a more sustainable practice and fill in these voids of vulnerability? How do I minimize the variables? How can I develop synergy in my management?

I integrated a small, personal queen rearing enterprise raising my own queens to meet my needs, in a timely fashion, without putting a dent in my cash flow. I maintain control over the genetics by selecting for locally-adapted bees that excel in honey production. I raise queens from the bees that work best for me.

Raising my own queens saves money, another benchmark of sustainability, and I have queens readily available when I want them. I'm not waiting or dependent upon the supply from a commercial queen producer due to weather challenges in other parts of the country. I do not subject my queens to the pressures of banking and shipping, especially during the heat of summer.

The time and energy to raise my own queens begins once my production hives are supered up for the nectar flow, right after Mother's Day. I raise my queens in a period of relatively low demand on my time and energy, and the key word is, "relatively."

The best time to catch me raising queens is prior to the next peak energy demand, my honey harvest, but it happens as I coordinate and allocate my personal resources between competing activities. Everything works together.

Your specific activities in beekeeping will vary with which type of operation you choose and how sustainable you wish to become. Your management style determines the goals and how you go about your business of keeping bees.

At one time, I imagined raising and selling queens to the local market of beekeepers, but two obstacles blocked this dream from materializing. First, raising queens is a lot of work. I found I can only, sensibly and realistically raise a small quantity of queens, pretty much what I need and not many more.

Second, most of my beekeeping buddies are still locked into the dominant model which acquires mated queens early in the spring to make early splits. With our fickle weather in southeast Missouri, I can't produce queens early enough to meet this market. Additionally, we don't have the drones for good matings. The dominant model requires southern-raised, mail-order queens purchased from commercial queen breeders.

Does Size Matter?

Further, aside from ascribing your activities to one of three categories, we tend to classify beekeepers based on the size of their operation. Roughly and crudely, if you keep 49 or fewer bee hives, we call you a hobbyist. If you keep from 50 hives to 299 hives, we identify you as a sideliner. Any beekeeper over 300 hives is deemed a commercial enterprise.

These figures are rather arbitrary. For a hobbyist, there's a huge difference between keeping a dozen hives and looking after forty-nine hives. And honestly, if you are keeping forty-nine hives as a hobbyist, what changes as you add one more hive to reach the level of a sideliner?

Really! What changes? Still, we seem to need some manner of keeping track of people, as if something mattered or as if we're trying to prove a point.

Diversification and Integration

Here's what I think is important and want to emphasize in this chapter: irrespective of what type of beekeeping enterprise you operate, without considering the number of hives in your apiaries, without taking into account your focus or what drives your motivation to keep honey bees, I am of the strongly held opinion you need to find ways to shift and adapt to a more sustainable model if you want to stay in business during these challenging times.

One key to being sustainable is hybridizing and and widening your intentions on the type of beekeeping enterprise you manage.

Joel Salatin, author and successful small farmer, advocates going with several "centerpiece" operations, to which several "complementary" enterprises are added. The key to this kind of philosophy shares some of the same overhead requirements, which lowers costs and distributes risk such that a producer does not "put all their eggs in one basket."

It reminds me of my father's upbringing on a diversified farm in southern Minnesota. His father, my grandfather, milked dairy cows, raised pigs, and grew corn, oats and hay in rotation, maintained a giant vegetable garden and kept an orchard of trees named after women.

If you were to categorize or classify my grandfather's farming operation, I would look to the centerpiece operation which was milking cows. We always identified my grandfather as a "dairy farmer." But the farm produced much more than just milk. The complementary enterprises, pigs, corn, etc., produced diversity and a synergy raising the profitability and sustainability of the farm. It also made for a lot more work!

This kind of diversity produces options, and options encourage flexibility in production as well as creating various avenues of marketing.

Diversity in marketing spreads out the cash flow. The diversity of production spreads out the labor demands. By-products, often overlooked as "waste," become valuable resources, i.e., straw from the oats for bedding, manure from the livestock to fertilize the soil, hay in rotation plowed under for organic matter.

Back in the "good old days," this kind of farming integrated various assets into the overall scope of the farm and synergy happened. Families prospered. The word, "sustainable," was not in their vocabulary, but the integration of these resources contributed to the overall production of the whole farm. I firmly believe these same principles are applicable to beekeeping.

As an example, I recycle my wax cappings and roll melted wax on my frames with plastic foundation. It's my wax and I know where it came from, and it becomes the resource the bees need to draw out plastic foundation.

I explain more of this idea in a subsequent chapter, but if it takes eight pounds of honey to make one pound of wax, and I sell my honey for $4 a pound, then my wax is worth $32 a pound (8 lbs. x $4). But if I sell my wax for cash at $8 a pound, I'm not sustainable. By recycling it back to my plastic frames, every pound of wax saves eight pounds of honey.

Further, bees are reluctant to draw out plastic foundation and the wax literally, seals the deal and gives the bees the green light to move forward and draw out that plastic foundation.

Over the years, the family farm in Minnesota slowly waned to the point where the livestock was gone and we leased the tillable land to a local tenant.

It was my father's recent lament, with the concentration of continuous row cropping, with monoculture and the intensive tillage practices, how the soil is no longer a living entity, but simply a neutral carrier for the seed and the fertilizer. With irrigation, even organic matter becomes irrelevant. Just give the plant somewhere to sink its roots and we can chemically deliver everything else it needs.

In the bootheel region of southeast Missouri, irrigation allows corn production in soil which is basically sand. The irrigation equipment is also set up to deliver liquid fertilizer, herbicides, fungicides and what ever else the plant requires, even water!

I see my beekeeping operation becoming more and more integrated and diverse. My centerpiece operation is still honey production, but my complementary enterprises include collecting pollen, raising my own queens and pollinating crops in a non-migratory operation that provides opportunities for producing honey. I'll add more details in a few paragraphs.

Sustainable Means Profitable

As I stated in the last chapter, your bottom line in conventional beekeeping will likely be the bottom line. I'm of the mindset that productivity does not have to conflict with sustainability, nor does sustainability take a back seat to profitability. As I think of the three main types of beekeeping operations, all of them share the ultimate goal of making money, though the methods and levels vary.

Conventional beekeeping hopes to be profitable, and even if you are just keeping bees as a hobby, most hobbyists want to, at the very least, sell a little honey to meet the expenses. Even your spouse may want to know the bees are paying their own way.

However, most of side-line beekeepers do not figure in our labor costs, at least I don't. My beekeeping enterprise is really a labor of love. It's cheap therapy. I could be fishing or golfing or watching television. I don't get paid for any of those hobbies. I choose to spend my time in the bee yard. I choose to ignore what I might earn if I did something else.

In an effort to become more sustainable, many beekeeping operations are becoming more integrated, blurring the definitions of these three types of operations. Even if you only have twelve hives as a hobbyist, you may adopt the philosophy of a commercial beekeeper and seek to make your hobby an income-producing venture, selling honey with a profit motive.

Even with twelve hives, you may already be looking at raising your own queens, splitting off a nuc and selling it to a buddy in the bee club, or keeping the nuc to replace one of your winter dead outs, saving a phone call to a southern nuc producer and the unnecessary expense of buying replacement bees.

Even with twelve hives you may transport your hives to your brother-in-law's yard to pollinate his apple tree while it's in bloom (wouldn't it be nice if that cheapskate shared some of those apples with you?)

Even with twelve hives, you need not apologize for making a little bit of money on the side selling your honey for market value. You should not apologize for making a lot of money on the side! Beekeeping is hard work!

I can remember the old days when people thought I should simply give them a jar of honey, for free, because my beekeeping was just a backyard hobby and the bees were doing all the work, right? Further, it's not like I incurred any cost in keeping bees, right? The bees work for free, right?

Sometimes these "customers" felt a kindred obligation to give me a couple of wrinkled dollar bills from their pants pocket to cover the cost of the jar.

Gee, thanks. I gotta remember to report this on my income tax.

The nicer folks brought their own jar for me to fill, and their consideration really warmed my heart. Still, a few bucks would be nice.

The habitual "drop-in" customer and the time they consumed by bending my ear over the weather, etc., moved me to set up a table in the driveway. Jars of honey prominently displayed a price sticker and I cut a slit in the lid of a coffee can for the customer's money. I never made myself available to negotiate a jar of free honey.

One of my "patrons" left me a large garbage bag of freshly dug turnips and a note in the coffee can suggesting he considered the turnips a fair trade for a jar of honey. I'm sorry he didn't sign the note so I could "thank" him for his generosity.

Maybe it's a good thing he didn't sign the note. I hate turnips.

Irrespective of which type of operation you run, the concepts of sustainability will improve your productivity, as well as your profitability, and help you become a better beekeeper.

In my operation, presently operating around 200 hives, I focus on honey production marketed on a retail level through a couple of farmer's markets. I also raise my own queens, mostly for my own purposes, and I've been known to sell a few queens to local beekeepers when they're caught in a bind and they only need one queen as soon as possible.

Most of these beekeepers who call needing a queen are some of the local, good old boys who helped me many years ago when I first started out keeping bees in Missouri. They don't want to pay the market price, claiming they're, "not in it for the money," perhaps implying they think I am.

And, of course, they are right; I am. But I want to return the favor of their previous help which they so generously and freely offered. So I dole out a few free queens to these guys every summer. There is a higher good to helping people, and doing good makes me feel good.

Additionally, I continue to believe in the theosophic, karmic kismet of paying things forward, or as my mother used to say, "There, but for the grace of God, go I."

By the way, that maternal entreaty is not found in any Bible, unless you take it upon yourself to write it inside the back cover.

I prefer splitting my own hives to repopulate my dead outs, choosing to split my locally-adapted survivor colonies. I've moved away from buying southern nucs.

For several years, I bought a trailer of southern nucs to resell to local beekeepers. I haven't done this for the past four or five seasons, in part, because I want to develop a line of locally-adapted stock.

Secondarily, I stopped reselling nucs as it just consumed too much time when my energy was badly needed in my apiaries. I was trying to manage my own hives and prevent swarming, while selling nucs and chatting for two hours in the driveway with beekeepers who have questions and like to pick my brain. Part of my problem is how I like to visit and talk to beekeepers and pick their brains!

My plan and purpose in those days was to buy a bunch of nucs, sell the majority yet keep several for my own needs to fill my winter dead outs or expand certain apiaries. The downside centered on the remaining nucs. After I sold the best nucs to local beekeepers, I was left with the runts of the litter. Reselling nucs was just not working for me.

One of the aspects of sustainability is to delete those activities that fail to benefit the whole operation, or suck up an inordinate amount of resources disproportionate to their contribution.

If synergy isn't happening, then the practice is not sustainable. If the practice doesn't complement your main purpose for keeping bees, it's probably a drain on your time and energy. Productivity cannot tolerate these kinds of distractions.

I own two, Nicot, non-grafting, queen rearing kits. The first kit I purchased a long time ago as I sought to raise my own queens. That's another whole story and I cover my queen-rearing trials and tribulations, and eventual success in my resource found at www.createspace.com/4542113

I bought one kit, then several years later, I added the second kit from a retiring beekeeper.

I answered a newspaper ad for used beekeeping equipment. I'm always interested in a deal, so I called the number and spoke to the gentleman, he said he had taken several calls and he was tired of talking to people who were always, "going to get back in touch with him," yet never did. He needed the space in his garage and if I was serious, I better get down to his place right away.

So I drove down and met this fellow. We hit it off quite well.

He told me he was going to make me a deal: I had to buy the whole lot. I was not allowed to cherry-pick his inventory and leave the dregs. It was all or nothing, take it or leave it. Since he was asking a fair price, I took it. I got everything, the good, the bad, and the high-grade kindling.

In the boxes of miscellaneous items, I spied a Nicot queen rearing kit. I pulled it out and said, "So you tried raising your own queens?"

He sighed and said, "Well, I tried. But I couldn't figure that dang thing out and it took too much time and I only wanted about a dozen queens, or so. It just wasn't worth my time and energy."

Bingo! That old man discovered what wasn't working and gave it up. There are many ways to diversify and build sustainability into your beekeeping operation. But if it, "takes too much time," and doesn't create benefits through synergy, it's probably best to give it up. If certain activities are nothing but an uphill battle, why fight? Why not go with the flow? Life does not have to be swum upstream all the time, unless there's a better destination upstream.

In the ministry, pastors are counseled to "pick their battles," that is, to wisely choose which ideals in the church are worth fighting for, and letting the minor skirmishes slide, even if the pastor disagrees with the minor activity. Unfortunately, some pastors lack this kind of wisdom, and even more lack discretion.

I meet many pastors who, "feel led," to take a stand for every conflict over every decision, even choosing which brand of coffee should be served in the fellowship hour. Yeah. For real. And such conflicts often denigrate into, "my way or the highway." Many of these pastors are now former pastors who tell me, "You can win the battle, and still end up losing the war...and your job."

It's no different in business or in beekeeping. I can choose to diversify, to integrate a variety of activities that broaden the scope of my beekeeping operation. I can attempt to be all things to all people. But I might also spread myself too thin to be effective. I might win some production battles, but in the end I really need to win the war. Some battles are just not worth fighting.

Marriage is a lot like this, too, and the decisions couples make, often involving compromise when one partner defers or acquiesces in favor of marital harmony. Not every decision has to become a battle, though I meet a number of couples, and divorced couples, who strongly believed otherwise.

When I first sold a few southern-raised nucs to local beekeepers, I could see potential profits if I expanded the numbers. So the following year, I ordered additional quantities. But reselling nucs simply took too much time. Yes, I made a couple of bucks to cover my costs and my time of providing a service and a convenience for local beekeepers, but this enterprise was becoming inconvenient for me. I could win this battle, but I could see the victory of the larger scope of the war slipping away from me.

Reselling southern nucs detracted from my responsibilities in the bee yard. I scaled back to simply ordering nucs for my own needs, but then I started thinking, and rethinking, what was I accomplishing by this activity? Nucs, while handy and darn convenient, were just not fulfilling my vision for beekeeping.

Sensing this conflict with my vision and ideals, I repositioned the future of my beekeeping operation on locally-adapted bees. When you raise your own queens, you shape the destiny of your apiaries through shrewd, sometimes lucky, genetic selection. But I was compromising those ideals of my main purpose. So I've quit buying southern nucs.

I continue to gravitate back to my thoughts about why I keep honey bees. What is my purpose? I remind myself to always keep the main thing the main thing, keeping first things first. My main focus, my centerpiece was honey production. Until this changes, everything I do in the bee yard belongs to this centerpiece.

So I made a choice. I could have switched my main purpose to the centerpiece of nuc sales. Instead, I recommitted myself to my main purpose which is honey production and I've let someone else in our area handle the sales of nucs. I shifted my paradigm.

I think we all need a sense of vision and purpose for why we keep honey bees. The beauty of beekeeping is the flexibility to choose which activities will fulfill our vision. Sometimes we need to keep bees a few years and let this sense of vision rise to the surface like the cream that rises from the milk. This flexibility is especially valuable to the new beekeeper who has not yet figured out why they, "want to get into bees," other than they think it's an interesting hobby. And it is!

But sooner or later, this kind of vague, non-committal attitude will be tested. Without a vision, these beekeepers become the casualties and the statistics of failed hives and incredulous spouses. I'll speak more to this in the next chapter.

I have traditionally been a minimalist, even a "natural" beekeeper when it comes to adding chemicals to my hives, or in my case, *not* adding chemicals to my hives. I have some hives that go treatment-free a few years, largely because they are so remote and my procrastination catches up with me.

I also trap feral swarms in pheromone-baited swarm boxes. I put my name on lists at the police station to retrieve swarms from harried homeowners.

I hive those swarms in my equipment. Those swarms surviving into the next season with my limited intervention become the genetic base for my queen rearing operation. I want to raise local honey from locally-adapted bees and continue raising queens from the bees that survive my minimalist and non-chemical approaches.

Trapping feral swarms replaces buying southern-raised nucs. These swarms are put to work producing honey, and this enterprise of swarm trapping complements my main purpose. It also complements my cash flow!

I also do some non-migratory pollination. A produce grower about thirty miles south of my home needed pollination and asked me questions about my honey bees and if I was interested in pollinating his melons and vegetables.

As we talked, I could see I did not fit the traditional migratory model of moving hives in and out (and I hate moving hives in and out), so I suggested a different version I could work with, and *voila!* A paradigm shift! He was open to my proposal.

I negotiated a fixed, non-migratory pollination model where I left my hives at the corners of his fields all year long, requesting 24/7 access. In exchange for placing hives on his property for pollination, I reserved the right to keep all the honey my hives produced.

Since I benefited from this relationship, we agreed I would not charge him for the pollination services my bees provided. We work wonderfully well together, a win-win situation focused on mutual benefits and results. The real beauty is I don't have anyone undercutting me for my pollination service and the honey production is high in this area. Best of all, I'm not wrestling those hives under the cover of darkness with handcarts and trailers as I don't have a couple of young guys with strong backs.

I am very concerned with the long-term viability of my beekeeping operation. I perceive the need for sustainable practices which enable this viability. My bees are important to me, not just financially, but socially as well. Beekeeping is a great diversion from the stresses of my normal work at my regular job. My main purpose of honey production brings in a little bit of extra money for some things I might not be able to afford.

Other Available Resources

In my beekeeping, I want to be sustainable, but what does this really mean? What does it look like?

Before we get too far adrift in that discussion, I want to share some other resources that may be of help to you, books I've written that describe, in detail, many of my hopes and dreams and how I go about keeping bees.

If you have a vision for turning your interest in beekeeping into an income-producing endeavor, or just expanding your hobby into the germinal stages of a semi-commercial enterprise (or maybe just a "hobby on steroids" as how my wife refers to my dalliances in the bee yard), then I recommend one of my books entitled, "**Beekeeping with Twenty-five Hives.**" You can find the details, along with a full description on the Internet at this web page (www.createspace.com/4152725).

If you desire to maximize your honey production, which is my ultimate purpose for my beekeeping operation, then check out my resource entitled, "**A Ton of Honey: Managing Your Hives for Maximum Production.**" (www.createspace.com/4111886)

If you want to raise your own queens, I have another resource entitled, "**Nicot Queen Rearing: The Non-Grafting Method For Raising Local Queens.**" (www.createspace.com/4542113)

I raise my own queens from locally-adapted stock that survives my incompetence and procrastination, along with my busy schedule. Of course, I'm also looking for hives that have the potential to produce a ton of honey!

Some people think raising their own queens will save them a bunch of money, which it will, but I will tell you this: the real value of raising your own queens tunes you into the rhythms of the seasons and educates you in the art and science of honey bee biology. Queen-rearing made me a better beekeeper.

Raising your own queens is not a practice left up to the "experts." Anyone can learn to do it, even without learning how to graft.

A new paradigm is rising in the local associations, promoting small scale, back yard, queen-rearing initiatives for a number of reasons.

Here in southeast Missouri, we are becoming aware of the potential of importing the Africanized Honey Bee (AHB) genes with our purchase of southern-raised queens from areas of known AHB infestations.

Likewise, if you are looking to capture and retrieve local swarms of feral bees -- the basis of my stock selection -- here are two resources:

"Free Bees!: The Joy and the Insanity of Removing and Retrieving Honey Bee Swarms," (www.createspace.com/4107714)

"Keeping Honey Bees and Swarm Trapping: A Better Way to Collect "Free" Bees," (www.createspace.com/4106626).

A full listing of my books can be found at http://grantgillard.weebly.com/my-books.html.

And don't get me wrong. I sure don't claim to possess the exclusive answer to many of our bee issues or retain the ONLY way to raise bees, but I have been around the block a couple of times and this is not my first rodeo!

I enjoy sharing ideas and providing information on how I do things. I'm always refining what it means for me to call myself, "a beekeeper."

Setting Out to be Sustainable

But back to our task at hand. What do we mean by sustainable? As you might expect, definitions and expectations vary. It's a problem asking *four* beekeepers a simple question and you receive *five* answers because one beekeeper cannot make up his mind.

Beekeepers are also quite creative and inventive, and as soon as someone offers, "Here's how I do it," another beekeeper, eavesdropping on the conversation feels obligated to add, "Yes, but have you tried this other way which is more natural and promotes the environment?"

I still maintain the position that two beekeepers can hold diametrically opposed methods and both of them may still be right...or both wrong. But there's no need to make it complicated.

Back many years ago when I first started this wonderful hobby of beekeeping, I advanced a lofty and noble set of ideals defining a viable model for keeping honey bees. By our definitions today, what I had in mind was a sustainable method, but that word, "sustainable" was not yet part of our vocabulary and not associated with our traditional paradigm of beekeeping practices.

When I shared my lofty goals with other beekeepers, many of them responded incredulously, saying, "Now just why you want to go and do something like that for? That just sounds like extra work, to me. We know these chemicals work and if you just put these strips in the hive and leave them until spring..."

Mind you, the dominant model of beekeeping was THE way to keep bees and it was THE way we all did it...but it wasn't exactly working to my satisfaction.

As I set out to be sustainable, my primary goals in beekeeping became 1) to develop self-reliance and resiliency to the outside forces that work against my goals, 2) to find ways to resource myself and not depend upon others, and 3) to negate the variables due to fluctuating, outside conditions.

I also think sustainable practices ought to synergize our efforts and integrate our resources that we are never left with excuses why we cannot be successful beekeepers. Sustainability generates efficiencies as different activities work together.

As I developed my beekeeping operation back in those days, still just a part-time, income-producing "hobby" supplementing my full-time, regular job, I was distraught over the inconsistent quality of mail-order, southern-raised queens. I didn't want the expense and labor applying chemicals to defeat the varroa mites, and further, I was growing leery of suspected chemical residues.

I hated losing hives, especially with my only option of turning to southern package producers and nuc sellers who gladly accepted my money in order for me to fill my winter dead outs each spring. There was nothing in my operation but a negative cash flow.

Now bear in mind, I have nothing against my southern brothers and sisters in the business who supply packages, nucs and queens. It's a business that serves a vital market in our industry. But these products and services were not meeting my expectations, failing to sufficiently perform for me in my geographic location, and further, the volume of the national demand these producers sought to meet was not satisfying my level of quality/ anticipation.

Looking at Sustainable Perspectives

Maybe I was too fussy, maybe too frugal, but it seemed the money I made from my honey sales this year was being spent on packages and nucs in the next year. Of course, I was still expanding, but my growth was not internal. This model was not working for me and it was not the way I wanted to continue. It wasn't sustainable. Something had to change.

Here are two quick thoughts. First, I like the definition of insanity that tells me this: insanity is doing the same thing over and over and expecting different results. I wanted different results which meant I had to do something different, something sustainable. If I was going to keep on doing what I was doing, I was going to keep on getting what I was getting. That's insane!

Second, I like the philosophy of the "Serenity Prayer" which, and I paraphrase, informs me there are a) things I can change and b) things I can't change. The prayer demands my courage to change what can be changed and my humility to accept that which cannot be changed. But the real power of this prayer requests the wisdom to recognize the difference between what can be changed and what cannot be changed.

Denis Waitley says it more succinctly, "There are two primary choices in life: to accept conditions as they exist, or accept the responsibility for changing them."

In order for me to develop a sustainable beekeeping practice, I had to figure out what I could change and then take responsibility to change those things. I also had to discern what things remained outside the realm of my control which I just had to accept, irrespective of whether or not I like it. When I look at things that cannot be changed, what needs to be changed is often me, my attitude, and my approach to how I keep bees.

For example, I'll listen to you gripe all you want about the weather, but your complaining simply isn't going to change a thing. However, if you accept what weather comes, if you make plans to account for the weather and how it impacts your beekeeping operation, and if you make the appropriate adjustments, I'll guarantee you a better mindset and a more productive afternoon.

Sustainable practices will self-sort, that is, what works will survive and what doesn't work will fall by the wayside. If top bar hives and Warre hives prove to be sustainable, then Langstroth hives will begin to disappear due to their unsustainablility. If top bar hives are nothing but a fad resurrected from the ideals of Rudolph Steiner, they, too, shall pass.

At one time, fogging food grade mineral oil (FGMO) into the bee hive was the next "silver bullet" against varroa mites (and it was "natural" as well). It quietly died an appropriate death, though there are still a number of faithful adherents who maintain its effectiveness.

There is an element of survival of the fittest to sustainable practices, and it seems like the old traditional practice of synthetic, chemical intervention is witnessing its own demise. But what will take its place?

Sustainable practices evolve as we discover and discern what things in our beekeeping operation can be changed, and what things cannot be changed. At the heart of sustainability is that wisdom to recognize the difference between those two things.

A Little History How I Developed Sustainability

My desire for sustainability didn't happen overnight. I cut my apicultural teeth in the traditional methods of conventional beekeeping, but it was my frustrations with what wasn't working that motivated me to look for a better way. While I had no idea how to spell, "sustainability," or even how to go about becoming sustainable, the intuitive rationale of its necessity resonated in my soul.

In my early years, I was part of what was then known as the "dominant" model of beekeeping. One of the signs of this model was the purchase of southern-raised stock through packages and nucs. This meant more out of pocket expenses resulting in a negative cash flow.

Our demand in the early spring could not be met with raising our own, local queens and making our own nucs. So we'd order southern nucs and packages to restock our dead-outs, or we would simply order new, southern queens and we'd split our surviving hives.

Characteristically, these nucs and packages came with a new queen and sometimes the bees accepted that queen and sometimes not. Another frustration.

These bees were typically raised on medication and miticides so we had to follow those protocols or the bees would succumb to the mites. But since we had these wonderful chemicals, we gladly used them to save our colonies from varroa. Still, these strips were expensive.

Because these hives were re-established in the spring, their honey production was far below my hives that survived the winter with an established queen that started laying several weeks before the package or nuc arrived.

This was one of the insights that came to my awareness, a definite, no-brainer: Overwintered colonies out-performed any purchased nuc. Since I was in the honey business, this was a critical observation into my adaptation of sustainable practices. I really began to observe and discern what it takes to successfully overwinter a colony of honey bees in my area.

So I still had to buy a few nucs to replace my losses and I accepted harvesting average crops of honey. I'd medicate and treat my hives then wonder how much of the chemical was hurting my bees, after all, we're putting chemicals in the hive "to kill bugs on bugs."

How selective was this poison on the respective bad bugs and how much was hurting my honey bees? How much residue was being absorbed into my comb? How much of this chemical was leeching into my honey? Yes, I had concerns. And most of all, I wanted a wholesome product in the honey I produced. Could I stand behind it with integrity to its content and purity?

The following spring some of these treated hives would survive, some wouldn't. So I'd begin my annual call to my southern colleagues for packages and nucs. One of the drawbacks of being a small hobbyist beekeeper is finding myself coming to the feeding trough too late. All the big beekeepers were ahead of me and buying up the availability of queens and packages. There was nothing I could change here unless I became one of those big producers, but that wasn't going to happen anytime soon.

By the time I recognized my needs for replacement bees, the nuc and package supply was dwindling and availability of bees so low that I was put on a waiting list and my order was left to the end of the spring season. Basically, I was buying bees that were installed too late to make any significant honey. My only hope was they survived to the next year when they would be strong enough to catch our early honey flow. Another frustration.

I ventured into treatment-free regimes and bees seemed to randomly die just like they did with the chemical treatments so I began experimenting with "natural" treatments. Some of these, like making patties of vegetable shortening (Crisco®) and sugar are not really natural, that is, there is nothing "natural" about vegetable shortening in a bee hive!

But these methods did not leave chemical residues nor did they create any negative side effect that endangered my honey. Still, I was losing some of my hives every winter.

I hate losing hives and it makes me feel like a failure. Plus, in every dead hive I see the lost production that could have been sold at the farmer's markets, not to mention the cost of refilling that hive with a purchased nuc--now that's a double blow! I'm a grouch after my spring inspections when I find winter dead-outs. Something had to change.

I began using Integrated Pest Management methods (IPM) to discern what problems required treating as the industry began to observe how routine, even indiscriminate, prophylactic treatments were breeding resistant mites. That was another concern for me.

So I added Screen Bottom Boards (SBB) to my hives and sticky boards to count mites (there are better ways, i.e., the alcohol wash method to assess mite loads, but they take more time and a little more expertise).

Still, keeping bees alive from one season to the next proved to be a challenge and it didn't seem to make any difference if I used chemical treatments or not. My preference was to be chemically-free and all-natural, but my losses were about the same when compared to my colleagues and peers, both chemical beekeepers and natural, treatment-free beekeepers.

Every spring someone from our area would drive down south to pick up a load of packages or nucs and sell them upon their return on behalf of our local bee club. It wasn't cheap, but it was easy.

Observing how they were making a little extra money bringing the nucs to our area inspired me to look into doing this activity myself, but at this stage in my beekeeping career, I was still figuring things out and I had not yet made connections with southern nuc producers. I shared how that ventured evolved a few pages back.

Thanks to a video offered by Brushy Mountain Bee Farm, I began experimenting with pheromone-baited, swarm traps. One of the delights of catching swarms is watching how intent they were in terms of drawing out comb and even making a honey crop! They seriously out-performed those expensive packages...and they were free for the catching!

Thus began another shift in my beekeeping to finding my own local supply of replacement bees rather than buying someone else's chemically-treated stock from the southern states. Not surprisingly, my survival rate using locally-adapted feral stock went up and my winter losses decreased. I felt like I was on to something innovative.

I wanted to move into raising my own queens from these feral swarms but the notion of grafting scared me to death. So I bought a "Nicot" non-grafting, queen rearing kit from Mann Lake Bee Supply for about $80 which I considered cheap given the quality and price of mail-order queens. It wouldn't take long before the unit would pay for itself.

I will tell you, in all honesty, the Nicot queen rearing unit has benefits but it also has some drawbacks. It's not perfect, but it starting working for me *once I figured out how to make it work.* It also took me a couple of years to scale the learning curve as one really needs to understand honey bee biology to raise good queens. So I saved money raising my own queens, but experience comes with a price of time and energy.

Since I gave up buying southern queens, and the best time to raise the highest quality queen is when the nectar and pollen are flowing, I found I couldn't raise my own queens until May or June. And our nectar flow is early, so the idea of making spring splits was not feasible with my own home-grown queens.

Thus I began a shift from spring splits to late summer splits, using my own queens rather than buying southern queens. This shift improved my cash flow. Big surprise, right? Rather than sending money to someone else, my money stayed home. I was becoming more self-reliant and sustaining my beekeeping enterprise, but I still had not yet put all the pieces together on how to become sustainable.

Now splitting hives is a very effective means of retarding or even redirecting the swarm impulse in a colony. The dominant model at the time was to order southern queens and make early spring splits from the hives that survived. This was a good way to fill my winter dead outs, but I ended up with two marginal colonies that were not quite strong enough to make a decent crop of honey.

The quality of the mass-produced, southern queens remained a random variable and their acceptance was often a roll of the dice. Still, this is how we rolled with the dominant model, and splitting in the early spring was our method of preventing swarming.

I knew, from experience, that swarming reduced my honey crop and I was discerning my main emphasis focusing on honey production. I had to find other means to keep my hives from swarming other than buying southern queens and making splits.

Thus I began a shift to "checkerboarding," a wonderful, swarm prevention technique developed by Walt Wright of Elkton, Tennessee. It keeps my hives strong and productive. Utilizing other techniques like the DeMaree method or the Snellgrove technique also worked to keep my hives from swarming without negating a honey crop.

Since the nectar dries up around the 4th of July, in a "normal" year, I find my honey crop is all in by the middle of July and ready to harvest. Because of this timing, I could make summer splits after my honey harvest without any worry of reducing my honey crop. These bees were all done making honey as we entered a summer dearth. In Southeast Missouri, our fall flow is so fickle I never count on it for harvestable honey, and if we get a flow, I leave that honey for the bees (mostly golden rod and aster, anyway).

With summer splits, I would raise my bees in preparation for the following spring. I coined my new approach, "Biennial Beekeeping," like a biennial flower you plant one year when it puts out nothing but foliage in preparation for the magnificent display of flowers blooming the following spring.

My queens were established in the summer of the first year and laying early in the early spring of the subsequent year. I would later learn this practice was in line with the philosophy of Brother Adam at Buckfast Abbey. Things were falling into place.

Now bear in mind, I still lost some hives during the winter months, but making more splits than I reasonably needed for the following spring helped me survive the normal attrition that so many of us experience. I go into greater depth in my later chapter entitled, "Is Beekeeping a Game of Attrition?"

It was out of these experiences, and my penurious frugality, that I developed my concepts of sustainable beekeeping.

While neither definitive nor fully exhaustive, here are some of the features I think an approach to sustainable practices should, or could, entail.

- ✓ An independence from needing to purchase outside supplies (queens and nucs)

- ✓ A freedom from seasonal variations of commercial vendors due to weather or price

- ✓ An education to assemble and create the resources I can supply to meet my needs

- ✓ An opportunity to enhance my positions without worrying about the fickleness of external forces and the uncertain availability of what I need, when I need it

- ✓ A capability of supporting my hopes and dreams and achieving my goals, and not depending or relying upon others who may not share my sense of urgency

- ✓ A support to provide the necessary inputs to accomplish my goals and fulfil my responsibilities

- ✓ An endurance to survive the variables we cannot otherwise control, including availability and price, by providing for contingencies

- ✓ A harmony that does not inflict undo distress upon the local economy or the environment, or impinge on my fellow beekeepers from reaching their goals and desires

- ✓ A shift from being beholden to others keeping them from their respective, busy schedules

- ✓ A balance and renewal of resources that does not restrict others in my field

- ✓ An ability to function from an abundance mentality rather than a scarcity mentality, to have what I need when I need it, rather than hoping someone else can meet my needs

- ✓ A refusal to subject myself to the idiocy of someone else's procrastination or well-intentioned promises of, "Well, I was planning on doing that"

While many of these attributes of sustainability sound a little "preachy" or stilted in their formality, I wanted to try and cover the gamut of possible applications.

As I stated earlier in this chapter, my goals in moving toward a sustainable beekeeping practice is 1) to be self-reliant and resilient to the outside forces that work against me, my plans and my goals, 2) to find ways that I can resource myself and not depend upon others and their inconsistent availability, and 3) to negate the variables due to outside conditions like weather and price.

It's also my belief that sustainable practices synergize our efforts and integrate our resources, such that we are never left with excuses why we cannot succeed at beekeeping.

Nothing infuriates me more than going into a store to buy a product I need, only to have the clerk act as if I didn't matter and my needs were no big deal, or worse, they have no idea what I'm talking about and have no knowledge of what product will work in my situation.

There is one, big-box retailer in particular, that when I ask a clerk where I might find a certain item (because they are constantly moving merchandise to different locations in the store), they initially stare at me with a blank expression, then passively say, "I'll need to find a manager." Then they disappear and a manager never shows up. Unfortunately, this big-box retailer carries everything, including many common items the local, mom-and-pop stores can't seem to have on hand, so I find myself shopping at this store, almost against my will.

Sometimes these clerks know exactly what I need and they don't have it, but they'll gladly back-order what I need, yet have no idea when it will arrive. How does this help me?

My desire for sustainable beekeeping has an element of anger to it, that I will not be thwarted from my goals by someone who can't find what I need, when I need it. Or I find an item I need today when everybody else needs it and demand outstrips supply so the item goes on back order. Why did I not see this coming? Why did I procrastinate?

One year, I was complaining to some church members how the time just flew by, and before I knew it, Christmas was upon me and I wasn't ready for it.

One of my more laconic church members came right to the point, "I don't know why Christmas took you by surprise. You had 364 days to prepare for it."

Yep. Guilty as charged. One thing I learned that day was the need to be careful who I complain to as not everyone is as compassionate as we hope. I also learned there really was no legitimate excuse, and any compassion on her part would only enable my procrastination. Sometimes the best lessons are learned when we're forced to face the music.

We know spring rolls around and we're going to be busy. We know swarm calls will be coming in or our hives might swarm. So why do you call me and complain, "Gee, Grant. My hive swarmed and I don't have any extra foundation to put in my old frames and I don't want to lose the swarm."

There's a national comedian who so often and wisely observes, "You just can't fix stupid." Ah, there, but for the grace of God, go I.

I always have to go back to the idea that procrastination on my part does not constitute a crisis on your part, but like everyone else, I, too, find myself unprepared. There is no excuse, though I may try and convince you with some really slick talk to kindle your empathy.

Thus, I am reminded so often how we need to make our own breaks, and "if it's going to be, it's up to me." I began to ask in earnest, "How do I control all these variables? How do I minimize my exposure to the uncertainties and make contingencies to cover my risks?"

Thoughts of autonomy and independence fuel my desire to be sustainable. I detest subjecting myself to the mercy of someone else's incompetence, especially my own incompetence, laziness and inane procrastination.

My basement workshop looks like a beekeeping supply business. I have unassembled frames, unassembled hive bodies, boxes of foundation, boxes of craft sticks for foundationless frames...all at my access so I have them when I need them. I spend my winter months fixing and rehabbing frames, for I know when spring comes, I'm too busy to mess with this tedious work at that time.

I believe in keeping extra supplies on hand so they are available. My still wife wants to know why I have so many cans of different colored, mis-tint paint under the steps.

Because I might need them some day, dear.

Then she asks why I have a million scraps of odd-shaped lumber in the garage. I offer the same reasoning of maybe, no, probably needing it some day. She counters by asking, "Well, doesn't the lumber yard and the big-box, home improvement center sell wood, every day of the year?"

Well, it does. But why throw out what can be used some day, and besides, I have this wood available and I don't need to waste time, gas and money driving to the lumber yard to get more. It's right there waiting for that golden opportunity.

You remember what I said about this genetic defect handed down through my family tree? I am married to an absolute saint. She has the patience of Job, if I don't send her to the loony bin before too long.

My loving wife assured me when I die, she's going to make two phone calls. The first call is to any company who can deliver a dumpster that afternoon so she can clean out the garage. The second call will be to the funeral home to come and get my body.

There is no real excuse for being caught short. Somewhere along the lines we have to realize what variables we can control and which variables are out of our control. Some we can change; others we have to accept. But the real secret to being sustainable is discerning which is which.

Do you know the worst time to order wax foundation? Early spring. Not only does everyone need it, the weather is too cold to safely ship the foundation.

Better yet, have you considered foundationless frames and allowing the bees to draw out their own wax comb with natural-sized cells?

Sustainable practices are important to me because they will help me overcome the short-term bumps in the road that I may enjoy the leisure of a long-term journey, watch the scenery out the window and continue to keep bees as long as I wish. Sustainable beekeeping forces me to be responsible when it would be easier to blame someone else for my shortcomings.

However, I have learned I can have either excuses or results, not both, and it's better to create the resources for the results, rather than manufacture the excuses why someone else is to blame. Given the choice of excuses or results, I want results.

Further, results put bread on my table; excuses simply leave me hungry.

I've learned to follow a smart little bit of advice:

Never complain; never explain.
Don't tell me what you're gonna do; just do it.

My simple definition of sustainable beekeeping is to take responsibility for what I need, when I need it, that I may experience the results and fulfill my goals without enduring the variables and fickleness of the availability when dealing with outside resources.

Okay, that definition isn't that simple.

However, in reality, this definition works whether you are a natural beekeeper or a conventional beekeeper, plumber, pastor, nurse or nuclear scientist.

Mostly, I desire control over the variables in my beekeeping future to insure my operation is productive and profitable, keeping my bees healthy and alive, continuing my participation in this wonderful endeavor, growing in my appreciation of, and gratitude for, their tireless work. That's the simple part!

Okay, my apologies. That definition's not that simple, either.

Chapter 3

More Practical Thoughts on Sustainable Beekeeping

"Replace excuses with effort; replace laziness with determination, and everything else will fall into place."

I pastor a Presbyterian Church and belong to a national denomination known as the PC(USA) or Presbyterian Church in the United States of America.

Like many once-flourishing, mainline Protestant denominations, we are presently declining in membership and resources.

Did I say, "presently?" I should have used the adverb, "rapidly." Our decline is in freefall mode. I'm wondering if there will even be that proverbial request, "will the last person left please turn out the lights?"

Churches of all denominations are closing and merging due to financial problems of aging congregations attempting to support full-time pastoral leadership. Even part-time pastoral leadership is expensive for the smaller congregation. Finding pastors willing to serve in more rural settings, for less compensation, with limited growth potential, not to mention, few vocational opportunities for their spouse...yeah, times are changing.

Further, many of today's seminary graduates enter the field burdened with a ton of student loan debt.

Additionally, PC(USA) congregations are leaving for other denominations due to the polarizing, politically-charged theological stands taken by our national denominational leaders. To add insult to injury, we're having a hard time attracting young people.

Our membership is in such decline that some people project the day when the PC(USA) will cease to exist. Calculating the trend of our current losses, a consensus estimates the church cannot survive beyond the year 2046 (which is not that far away!).

In a nutshell, we are not sustainable and we don't have a clue how to reverse this trend. Even when ideas are brought up, we exhaust valuable time studying the issues, binding ourselves up in, "the paralysis of analysis." We think we're doing something because we form a committee and ponder irrelevant questions with motions to form another committee.

Rather than change, we prefer to "rearrange the deck chairs on the Titanic." We haven't been able to bring in younger members and families to replace the dying generation, nor have we attracted any sizable group that identifies with our liberal, ideological stances. We are dwindling away.

Did I say, "dwindling?" I should have used the word, "eroding," though it's more like a landslide or avalanche.

We cannot sustain ourselves under this present decline. So why do I stay? That's a topic for another day, but to tip my hand, I've pastored this church in Jackson, Missouri, for the past twenty years. We've got a lot of history. I really love these people. If I were to leave, I'm not sure where I would go. And so I stay.

It's time to get off my soapbox.

My thoughts shift to sustainable beekeeping, with the declining bee population and the demographic of aging beekeepers as a parallel to the PC(USA). Sustainable beekeeping, especially the practical applications, has to do with two things.

First, how do we replace our aging demographic and attract young people to this profession? And I don't mean the millions of back yard enthusiasts who keep a couple of hives for a couple of years. We need younger beekeepers who have the commitment and the vision for larger-scale operations, and who develop the resources to meet the demands of today's level of agricultural production.

If you want to read a humorous parallel, humane shelters are filling up with chickens from the suburban homesteaders who thought back yard chickens and all those fresh eggs would save society. Can you perceive the day when feral chickens run amok from all the well-intentioned folks who simply turned out the chickens to be the ultimate, free-range bird they were meant to be?

Critics suggest, tongue-in-cheek, how back yard chickens are the, "gateway livestock" to worse addictions.

Ah, but I seem to be in a "foul" mood, today. I need to get back on track.

The back yard apiaries, for all their wonderful intentions, cannot meet the demand for pollinator-dependent crops. We need more commercial beekeepers coming up through the ranks. Where do these people come from? How do you spark an interest in this kind of lifestyle? Who is willing to step up and do this kind of laborious work?

Second, how do we cover all these losses of bees? We are losing millions of colonies of bees annually. Someone like me, a small-scale producer, can split my surviving hives. I raise my own queens and trap feral swarms. But there is a limit of how many hives I can manufacture from what survives. There is a limit as to how many swarms a guy like me has time to catch. And then some of my bees die every year.

Yes, I can always buy more nucs and more packages next spring to replace this year's losses, and if I sold enough honey to make enough money to replace those bees, then I might think of myself as sustainable.

But I'm not selling honey just to buy more bees. I'm not keeping bees just to have them die. This model is more subsistence beekeeping, as opposed to sustainable beekeeping. I think a sustainable beekeeping operation should keep bees from dying, but that reality does not seem particularly realistic these days.

And this idea of simply looking to our colleagues in the south, many of them aging, retiring commercial beekeepers, asking them to supply nucs and packages for the rest of the country has lost some traction recently. We're searching for a better solution, and maybe with a better solution we can attract more serious, committed, professional beekeepers instead of the short-term hobbyist.

I want a beekeeping operation that is profitable, that is the output (honey sales) exceeds the inputs (purchased nucs). My idea of the practical side of sustainable beekeeping prefers to raise my own bees to replace the ones I've lost, a self-sustaining model. But I also want to become such a beekeeper that I don't have to worry about covering those losses. My idea of keeping bees is keeping them alive.

I asked my highly respected friend, John Timmons, President of the Missouri State Beekeepers Association (www.mostatebeekeepers.org) about his thoughts on sustainability in beekeeping. John preaches a message of sustainability and supports beekeepers interested in Warre hives and top bar hives in the St. Louis, Mo., area.

John writes, *"Sustainability to me means working within a beekeeping model – no matter the size of operation – whereby there are no resource dependencies outside of a geographical region. In other words, any beekeeping resources required to sustain a successful* beekeeping operation, no matter the size, year after year, are provided by the resources of the local region.

Examples of beekeeping resources include:

> ➢ Queens for growth and replacement

> ➢ Nucs and packages for growth

> ➢ Nucs and packages for hive loss recovery

All resources should be locally produced, utilizing local genetics.

The question arises as to my meaning of "regional". A beekeeping region could be limited to the boundaries of a beekeeper's backyard. However, it would certainly be a geographical region defined by common climate and biodiversity conditions. As an example, if you move my bee hives fifty miles to the south, I doubt they will know the difference. However, if you move them a thousand miles to the south or north, they would be in a totally foreign climate with significantly different food sources, and pest conditions.

As I've considered this "sustainability" model over the past couple of years, I've become convinced of the necessity of "local community" to provide true sustainability. It's highly unlikely that twenty individual beekeepers in a given geographical region will each have all the skills necessary to be "self-sustainable". However, within the group, some will be good at producing nucs, while others will be good at producing queen cells or *mated queens. Collectively, the group, working together, is sustainable.*

It strikes me that a locally sustainable beekeeping community is very similar to a sustainable hive, with each individual providing a unique skill in support for the "whole". This concept reinforces the value of local beekeeping clubs to maintain regional sustainability."

I love John's insightful perceptions on sustainability, which is probably why we pay him the big bucks to lead the Missouri State Beekeepers Association.

You'll note in John's comments a specific emphasis on a community of beekeepers, how any one beekeeper may not be able to produce what is needed, yet in a local association, individualized, specialized production by several respective members may likely meet the needs of the whole group.

This is the beauty of collegiality and collaboration. As I think of my local association, the Jackson Area Beekeepers, we are friends and colleagues, first, and competitors, last, if at all. We strive to work together for everyone's benefit. We have no fear of someone else succeeding. We realize the market for local honey is so large not any one of us can fill it all. There is room for all of us, and we work to help others succeed.

Traditional definitions of sustainability often overlook the value of the collective wisdom of the local associations, not just for sharing information, but meeting the needs of local beekeepers from regional sources. John does not specify the parameters of what constitutes a geographic region as that would vary from region to region, and may, in fact, be a rather arbitrary designation.

One might question, "Can a limited region produce and supply all the needs for the beekeepers in that area?" Case in point: mated queens in early spring.

The answer is no, not under the traditional, dominant models of commercial beekeeping where early spring, mated queens are required to make early spring splits. Early spring queens must be imported from points south where the season starts earlier and drones are available.

Thus, sustainable beekeeping must also include an adaptation to the local patterns of seasonality. If early spring, mated queens are required than one option is to raise summer queens the previous summer and overwinter them in nucs. The early spring queens could be sold and the remaining bees from the nuc combined with another nuc or hive.

The key is adaptation to the local patterns of seasonality. We cannot raise bees like our grandfathers by ordering southern queens and nucs without some kind of negative consequences. There are many people who question whether or not the bees know the difference in climate or length of seasons as any overwintered bees in the south are soon replaced by a new generation as the queen kicks into gear and increases her egg laying.

While the new, freshly emerged bee may have no knowledge of the colony's mild winter in Texas, the imported colonies or nucs originated with bees that prospered in that region. They may, or may not acclimate to my location further north. I will confess, in the days when I bought southern nucs, some of them performed marvelously well in southeast Missouri and some of them did not. Still, I'm a firm believer in raising new queens from colonies that adapt and survive in my area.

I turn to another beekeeper in southeast Missouri, an up and coming queen producer specializing in treatment-free, hygienic stock named Cory Stevens of Dexter, Missouri.

Cory writes with regards to sustainable beekeeping, *"Sustainability is the capacity to endure. To endure in the beekeeping industry definitely takes an iron will, persistence, a good understanding of honeybee behavior and biology, fetching a good price for bees or honey to keep the operation profitable, as well as superb stock selected for disease resistance and production.*

If you're not profitable, I assure you sustainability will not be accomplished. Without those characteristics, you are as they say "peeing in the wind." I'm of the mindset, the more "needs of the operation" you can control, or create yourself, the better the chance you have of being sustainable. By not relying on outside parties, you can control the quality, and your costs which directly affect profitability, and your reputation.

Queens are the foundation our empires are built upon. Everything we can control about the characteristics of our hives lie in the DNA of the queens we choose. We must focus on what we can control (genetics), and not focus on what we cannot (weather). Rearing quality queens for your operation is a must in sustainable apiculture. Queens are increasingly costly, and are decreasing in quality. This is probably the most important aspect you must control for sustainability."

I note, in Cory's comments, the element of control, namely, controlling costs and quality, not to mention availability of resources. And as a queen producer, Cory's bread and butter, he notes the necessity of good quality queens.

Cory is one of my inspirations for raising my own local queens. I relate many of his attributes and insights in my non-grafting, queen-rearing resource which can be found at www.createspace.com/4542113, if you are so interested in raising queens from your own stock, as well.

Both John and Cory write of the freedom from outside variables, that growth and maintenance come from within, and if not from within, resourced from a local community.

Inherent in both John's and Cory's comments is the subtle idea of a wholistic concept of beekeeping. This idea of wholism takes into account the whole spectrum of beekeeping, that beekeeping is not just the sum of all of its "parts."

What I mean by this, is beekeeping is more than just winter management, added to swarm management, added to honey harvesting, added to requeening objectives, added to purchasing packages every spring. It's more than all of these things when you put them all together.

Wholistic beekeeping strives to look at the big picture, how these individual concepts (requeening, swarming, etc.) work together, and how management integrates and incorporates all the seasons of the year into one philosophical entity I like to call, "sustainable" beekeeping.

As an example, we encourage beekeepers to requeen annually keeping a young queen in the hive. Young queens reduce the urge to swarm and young queens lay more eggs than an older queen. Bear in mind, swarm prevention takes more than just a young queen. When swarming is alleviated, your colony stands a much better chance of producing surplus honey. More eggs laid means more foragers which translates into a larger honey crop.

But requeening with young queens won't work unless you have them in place before the hive starts to decline due to an aging queen. My nectar flow is early, so I really need to have my young queens in place before winter. But if my hive is overrun with mites, requeening won't have the desired effect I'm looking for.

It all works together, or it doesn't work at all.

I think beekeepers forget how all of these aspects of management play into, and off of, one another. We mistakenly seem to think of swarm management as one thing; queen vitality as another thing; mite treatments as yet another thing.

A wholistic concept strives to incorporate all these "things" and integrate them into a whole, like covering my whole year with a large umbrella of my management. My management is then divided into seasons when certain management systems must be put in place, and if not, then I mess up my next management system down the line.

I try and encourage beekeepers who call me up and simply say, "Not much happening in my hive. I need to requeen. Do you have one I can come by and pick up?" I ask if perhaps the colony swarmed, in which case not much is going to be happening. I ask if they are sure the mite treatments are working, that is, have they checked for mite loads? Most my buddies shrug and say, "Dunno. The bees were fine last fall. I just need a new queen."

Sorry. Throwing a new queen into a hive that has swarmed won't do you any good as there is likely a new swarm queen running around and the colony will likely kill the replacement you're trying to introduce...unless you realize the colony has swarmed and you kill the new virgin running around preparing for her mating flight.

If mites continue to be an issue, a new queen won't help too much, either. If your hive picked up some pesticide from a local farmer, then you've lost a bunch of foragers and there won't be much nectar or pollen coming in.

All of the functions of the hive have to work together. Everything has to be firing on all cylinders for the hive to be successful and sustainable, working in concert, integrated into a collective whole. The coordination of that integration is what I like to call, "management," (and that's you and me!). You can have sustainable practices, but management is responsible for coordinating them together.

To borrow a few concepts from other production venues, sustainability is usually measured in a) economic profitability; b) social sustainability and benefits to the producer and the community, including a quality of life; and c) environmental sustainability and the conservation of resources, including a wholesomeness of the product.

To put it another way, to be sustainable is to find long-term solutions to problems instead of short-term treatments of symptoms. There will be a diversity that lends itself to stability. Stability creates perpetuity. And perpetuity takes a wholistic approach.

When this happens, you are a sustainable beekeeper.

Chapter 4

Are you, yourself, sustainable?

*"If you don't think you're a winner,
you don't belong here."* -- Vince Lombardi

*"It's not who you are that holds you back;
It's who you think you're not."* -- Denis Waitley

I consider it the highest honor and privilege to list Robert Sears in my circle of special friends. Bob lives in St. Louis where he serves as the president of the Eastern Missouri Beekeepers Association (www.easternmobeekeepers.com).

He's an exceptional, uniquely-gifted person and a knowledgeable beekeeper. He leads with an uncompromising commitment to excellence. After spending five minutes with Bob, you can't help but learn something new about beekeeping or feel so inspired you want to reach for loftier goals and become a better beekeeper.

Bob is the kind of guy that commands my respect and loyalty. If Bob said to me, "Grant, I want you to go out to my truck and bring me a hive tool. My truck is on the far side of the parking lot. There's not a cloud in the sky and that blistering sun is at high noon turning the parking lot into a steamy oven. Not only that, I want you to crawl on your hands and knees across the scorching asphalt which happens to be littered with broken glass, bent nails and assorted small stones. Can I depend on you?"

If Bob asked me to do this, I'd have only one question: "Is your truck unlocked?"

Not that I expect Bob to request such a ridiculous task of anyone, but Bob's the kind of guy where I wouldn't think twice of anything he needs or asks. I'd return with the hive tool in my hand, blood on my knees, a smile on my face asking, "What's next?"

Bob excels at getting new beekeepers started in this wonderful hobby and keeps them going with educational workshops and lining up new beekeepers with knowledgeable mentors. His passion is infectious. Bob is one of the reasons I continue keeping bees as his friendship and encouragement, along with his accountability, keep me sharp and focused on what I need to be doing. He brings out the best in others.

Bob notes there are countless first-year beekeepers, but far fewer second-year beekeepers, and he finds this disconcerting, as do I. This means there's an incredible attrition rate between that first year and the following season.

This also means there's a lot of used bee equipment sitting vacant or even neglected from well-intentioned "wanna-be" beekeepers who found they didn't have the time or the inclination to withstand all those stings (yeah, both of them) that one time they opened the hive.

And I can relate to this kind of intimidation. Opening a hive used to cause my breathing to become rapid and shallow and I had to summon great amounts of courage just to lift the initial frame from the hive body. I was so fearful I was rolling my queen, even as I started on the outside of the brood box.

Bob once said that if he could keep someone keeping bees for 60 months (yes, five years), that person would be a beekeeper for life. But five years is a long time, and a lot of things can happen during those sixty months.

I think the first year is the hardest for a new beekeeper, but the second year is also fraught with new challenges unique to that second season. Along the way, every new beginner finds it's not as easy as the books make it out to be as it seems the bees are reading a different set of books.

Could you last sixty months? How many of you, after six or seven years, are still in your first or second year of keeping bees because you had to start over two or three times? What do you do when you've invested upwards toward $1,000 in a couple of hives (new equipment, nucs with bees, plus the attendant accessories) and you still have no honey to show for all your efforts?

What had you promised your spouse in terms of your expected production (implying a return/income) and don't some books suggest an average harvest of 60 pounds? How close did you come to five gallons of honey? How many of your relatives are still bugging you for free honey as Christmas presents? How many of them have questioned your beekeeping abilities, asking, "for crying out loud, it's just keeping bees in those white boxes. How hard can it be?"

Well, it's hard, but not impossible. Still some people get it and others do not. I often ponder whether a person is naturally born with the inclination toward beekeeping or can one be taught to keep bees? Or is it both? From my personal perspective, beekeeping isn't something I do; it's what I am.

When I consider the discouragement many first year beekeepers endure, I confess I'm at a loss for any legitimate rationale why they should continue. Beekeeping is hard. I want them to give it another try, hoping they're not ready to give up so soon. But I also acknowledge some people just don't understand the dynamics of the hive. They just don't have the knack for beekeeping. There are days I, too, wonder what the heck I'm doing. It's easier to give up, move on and do, or be something else.

I took years and years of piano lessons when I was young, but I couldn't really play very well. I had a tin ear, two left hands and no sense of rhythm. Any ability to successfully hit two keys together was largely mechanical, if not accidental. There was little enjoyment. I had no knack for the piano. I just didn't get it, but my parents thought it was a good idea to take lessons, perhaps hoping I'd catch on. I never did.

Today I marvel at people who can play the piano, and I just about crap my pants when I watch people sit down and play by ear. They don't even watch their hands and fingers. I'm convinced not everyone, especially me, is cut out to play the piano. I've heard it said, "If it were easy, everyone would be doing it."

And I think the same philosophy fits beekeeping. Not everyone is cut out to keep bees. But that's not much of a consolation when you've got another dead hive to refill and you're still trying to capture a little honey from all your hard work. I wonder if I'm doing a person a favor by selling them another nuc knowing they stand a pretty good chance of losing those bees, and their investment, as well.

What would be your next step, as you follow all the advice from all the books you read, and you come out of the following winter with dead bees? Are you ready to pony-up another $125 to $150 for replacement nucs for each dead hive? Are you ready to quit? Are you hoping to sell your hives to your brother-in-law? Will you give it, "one more year"...then one more after the next dismal year? How many times will you say, "Maybe next year."

No one thinks of these issues when they start out in their first year, and even if we mentioned them in any beginner course, 99% of the students are going to say, "Well, that's the other beekeepers, but not me."

Richard Taylor, in one of his many books and columns published in the old *Gleanings in Bee Culture*, once said new beekeepers are like comets. They streak across the night sky lighting everything up with their enthusiasm and passion. Everything they talk about centers around their hard-working bees and the natural qualities of honey. They fill every zealous conversation with their brand of apicultural evangelism. And then suddenly, in a quiet "poof," they flame out and disappear from view, never to be seen or heard again. What once illumined the night sky suddenly grows dark and silent.

At the farmer's market, a youngish woman approached my table and shared how her husband tried his hand at beekeeping and much to his disappointment, and hers, he was not successful. He followed the conventional advice and started two hives. In our conversation, his wife made it quite clear she was more than surprised how much it cost to start keeping bees. I agreed. It's an expensive hobby to start.

I've found many people mistakenly think something "natural" ought to be inexpensive. However, it costs quite a bit of money to start from scratch and buy all new equipment and bees, and pay for the shipping. As a side note, once you get started, there are less expensive alternatives but their proper application comes with experience.

Sadly, both of his hives died that first winter, and toward the following spring, he was thinking of trying it again.

I was tempted, in my conversation with this wife, to quote Yoda from the Star Wars franchise when he said, "There is no try; only do," but I refrained as I could see she had an agenda in this conversation.

For some reason, he didn't follow through and his hives sat vacant. I think we all know the return on an empty investment is zero. She suggested I call her husband, without mentioning her conversation with me, that perhaps I could buy all his equipment and they might get some of their money back.

I think she was hoping he'd give up this dream of keeping honey bees that was nothing short of a nightmare from her perspective. I guessed this wife, like many spouses, thought there was a better place to spend/invest that money other than buying more bees to fill empty bee hives. She gave me his phone number.

I made the call, playing ignorant and not mentioning the conversation I had with his wife, respecting her wishes. He was adamant he was not interested in selling, that he was <u>definitely</u> planning on getting back into bees one of these days, some day when he wasn't so busy, some day when things settled down, some day when the baby was older...some day...some day...then he shifted the conversation asking me questions about beekeeping, culminating in the request, "I know I was supposed to find a mentor. Will you mentor me?"

I wondered how angry the wife was going to be with me for not getting her husband OUT of beekeeping, but I agreed to mentor this hopeful new beekeeper with the admonition, "When you are ready to move ahead and get some bees, give me a call and I'll mentor you through the process of getting established." I even offered to give him some swarms when I caught them the next spring so he would not have to worry about unnecessary expenses getting restarted. I offered my honey house when it came time to extract.

I have yet to hear from this fellow. He never followed up on our conversation and far be it from me to push someone where they don't want to go. Maybe "some day" had not yet come. I didn't want to sound like a nag. Maybe he sold his equipment to his brother-in-law, and I'd give the brother-in-law the same deal if he called and asked me to be his mentor.

As I write this manuscript, it's been probably ten years or more since I had that conversation. I haven't seen her around at the markets, either. Maybe they moved away. Many unsuccessful beginning beekeepers just quit too early. They fail to learn from their mistakes or they neglect to temper their unrealistic idealism about their chances for immediate success. Some are still waiting for "some day."

First-year beekeeping is like a flip of a coin. You either win or lose, and there are so many variables you have yet to learn, that entering this sacred profession and surviving is sometimes a stroke of luck, like the flip of a coin; heads your bees live; tails they die.

And if you start with two hives, a recommended practice for beginners, one of those hives will survive and produce a first-year crop of honey while the one right next to it dies without any explanation. What if you could only afford one hive and it was one that died out?

If this happened to me, I'd be pretty ticked-off at the fellow that sold me those bees, thinking there was something wrong with the one nuc. But many suppliers who sell nucs only offer the "tail-light" guarantee, that is, the bees are guaranteed until he loses sight of your tail-lights as your drive home. After that, you are on your own.

The investment to get started, when you buy all new equipment, is staggering, especially to those who have no idea what it costs. Still, I get those phone calls and they say, "Yeah, I was thinking about getting into bees this year. Saw you at the market and thought I'd like to do that, too."

When I mention the cost of getting set up, around $350 per hive, which includes bees, there's a long pause on that other end of the phone line. I can almost detect the four-letter expletives whispered beneath their breath as if I'm taking advantage of their desire to keep bees.

Few people make it past the "thinking about it" stage. Often they say, rather evasively, "Let me get back to you," but they seldom call back. Sometimes they stay on the line and the conversation switches to used equipment, as if I might have some hives for sale.

At this point, let me politely say, "No. No ever living way will I sell you, or anyone, my used equipment. I don't sell used equipment. It's not going to happen, and that's my final answer."

The explanation why I won't is far too lengthy for our time together, and I get way too whiny when asked. Call it a hard lesson learned or once-burned-twice-shy but I'm never, ever selling anyone any of my used equipment. Period. Yes, there is plenty of used equipment sitting around if you can find it, and I may help you find it, price it, even help you pick it up and bring it home.

A lot of one-year old bee hives sit vacant, quietly tucked away, either in embarrassment or in the hopes of "some day" getting put back into use. There's also a lot of really old equipment sitting in sheds full of mouse nests and wax moth webbing.

I go into detail how I got started with vacant, used hives in an era when I had more time than money in my book, **"Beekeeping With Twenty-five Hives,"** (www.createspace.com/4152725), but we seldom encourage beginners to start with used equipment.

When asked about getting started, I'm a little embarrassed to tell people what it costs, and in most cases, we insist beginners buy new equipment. If you're handy, and you think you can make it yourself, you'll find plenty of free plans all over the Internet. All you really need is a simple table saw and you can make all the boxes, tops and bottoms. Most of us think it's better to buy the frames, but if you have more patience than me, frames can be cut out and assembled, as well.

Yes, used equipment is cheaper, and it's definitely easier, but it's also riskier for a lot of reasons. We're trying to eliminate the unmanageable risks. And if you can only afford used equipment, it helps to have a mentor who can guide you on pricing and what equipment you need and how to avoid the junk you don't need. If you find some used equipment for sale, I will gladly and joyfully guide you, even accompany you through the process, but my stuff just ain't for sale.

It takes a level of commitment to sustain oneself to keep investing in something that seems like a roll of the dice. My uncle Charlie was a farmer in Minnesota. When the state legalized the lottery, someone asked my uncle if he liked to gamble. His stoical response was, "I farm for a living, don't I?"

Beekeeping is just another form of agriculture, prone and susceptible to many of the uncontrollable variables, the largest one which is weather. Just because you keep bees on a small scale in your back yard does not exempt you from the same risks facing the large farmers. Beekeeping is a gamble and there are no guarantees in life, not at the casino, and not in the bee yard.

Sometimes you can do everything right and still suffer lost hives. I had a beekeeper buy sixteen nucs from me one year. The next year he was asking if I had another thirteen nucs for sale. I responded favorably and intimated that he must have had a good year to be expanding so aggressively. On the other end of the phone, a long sigh followed a protracted silence. Of the sixteen original hives he started the previous summer, only three survived.

When I asked him what happened, he wasn't sure. He said, "We were hoping to go about this beekeeping venture in an all-natural fashion and the bees just died. I thought it would be easier than this."

Do not kid yourself. There are huge hurdles to overcome in these challenging times. On one hand, philosophically speaking, obstacles present themselves to test us, to signify how bad we want something, to refine our intentions of why we want to continue keeping bees. Some people say, "Try, try again," and others will say, "Quit before you look like a fool."

It boils down to asking, "What do you want? What do you want more than anything else in the world?"

I complimented this fellow on his fortitude and his resolve to give it another try, but I could hear the pain in his voice and his tentative weariness of basically starting over. Thank goodness he had regular employment to pay the bills and some disposable income to buy more bees, not to mention a supportive spouse.

The late-Johnny Cash, a man well-acquainted with trials and troubles said this,

> *"You build on failure. You use it as a stepping stone. Close the door on the past. You don't try to forget the mistakes, but you don't dwell on them either. You don't let failure have any of your energy, any of your time, or any of your space."*

Success does not come easily in beekeeping. Beekeeping is a challenging hobby and these are excruciatingly difficult times. Despite that incredible line from the movie, *Apollo 13*, "Failure is not an option," failure in beekeeping is more common than we'd like to admit.

Herman Melville said, "Failure is the true test of greatness." Okay, thanks, buddy. Maybe I don't need to be that great. What's the true test of sustainability?

If you experience such failures, relax. You're in good company. But take heart; we live in a culture which makes you believe your failures speak louder than your successes. We just need to find the successes to celebrate, even the small ones, and then we can tell our failures to shut the heck up and take it somewhere else!

Kent Williams, a phenomenal beekeeper from western Kentucky, spoke in St. Louis about options when bees die. First, he acknowledges that bees die. That's a fact. Bees die in nature and they die in managed bee hives. Even nature knows bees are going to die and that's why a colony will swarm to perpetuate the species in that area. Bees die, simply put. The average life span of a colony is only three and a half years, but in the course of that duration that colony will have thrown off several swarms. Swarming is nature's way of insuring the honey bee colonies will continue to survive.

So what can you do when your bees die? Kent says you have two choices. First, you can learn how to manage bees and raise your own replacement bees, or second, you can buy new packages every spring.

Then he blew me away when he said, "The only way to stay in the bee business is to not quit." Then he added, "There will always be beekeepers who sell bees." But he goes on to strongly suggest beekeepers should learn how to manage bees and raise our own replacements.

That statement, "The only way to stay in the bee business is to not quit," really struck a chord with me. I was instantly reminded that my future in beekeeping lies within the power of my choices. I am in control of my future, even though the deaths and destinies of dozens of hives is beyond my control.

That was an eye-opening, hit me across the head with a two-by-four moment for me. When I realize I am in control, I am empowered. I have options and options give me choices.

Of Kent's suggestions, the former (learning to raise bees) mirrors my sustainable hopes and the latter (buying more bees) is a drain on my bank account and creates a negative cash flow.

Jamie Ellis, Associate Professor from the University of Florida, says, "You learn how to keep bees by killing bees and sticking to it."

Sounds kind of morbid, doesn't it? But you keep on keeping bees until you learn how to do it, or like the old proverb encourages, "The master has failed more times than the beginner has ever tried."

Somewhere along the way, we learn how to manage our bees and raise our own replacements.

Losing bees is part of the business. I don't like it, but it is what it is. It is the reality we have to accept these days. How does one continue time after time, season after season, year after year when bees die?

I love that old admonition that, "If you are going to fall, try to fall on your back so you're looking up. If you can look up, you can get up; then never give up."

If the only way to stay in the bee business is to not quit, then I want to be the John Cena of the apicultural world.

John Cena, professional wrestler inspires me with his statement:

> *"I will not quit. I have tasted victory and have been stung by defeat but I WILL NOT QUIT!! I have been knocked down, knocked out, busted up, busted open but I WILL NOT QUIT!! I've often said a man's character is not judged after he celebrates a victory, but by what he does when his back is up against the wall. So no matter how great the set back, how severe the failure, you never give up. You never give up. You pick yourself up. You brush*

yourself off. You push forward. You move on. You adapt. You overcome. I haven't backed down from a fight in my life, and I won't start tonight. You can't erase me. I'm gonna make you taste me. My road to [success] starts right now. I won't be stopped. I can't be stopped."

There are sustainable practices, but one of the primary things we need to sustain is ourselves mentally and emotionally and intellectually.

- ✓ How does one keep going amidst the frustrations of bees that die and need to be replaced?

- ✓ Where does one find the money to buy new bees every spring if the bees cannot survive the winter?

- ✓ How does one scale the learning curve to raising replacement bees, even locally-adapted queens?

- ✓ How do we withstand the ravages of unpredictable weather and other factors beyond our control?

✓ Most importantly, when the mistress of misery comes calling, as she always will, what will keep you in the game of beekeeping?

Vision

My answer to this heart-wrenching, back-breaking dilemma is *vision.*

Everything starts with vision. Even as you start your day, you mentally prepare by rehearsing all the things you need to get done, the people you need to see, the appointments you need to keep, etc. You kind of plan it out, mentally. That's vision.

Beekeepers need vision. Even if you are starting out and told someone, "Yeah, I'm thinking of getting into bees this year," that's a vision, though a poorly developed vision. Everything starts with vision.

Vision is like asking, "What do I want out of beekeeping? What do I want to do for me? What's possible? Where do I want this hobby to take me?"

Unfortunately, most of us operate out of our personal history and our memories. We limit our vision based on what we're already done. We need larger visions of what we want to experience and to believe such visions are possible.

In southeast Missouri, we like to fish. We adhere to that old saying, "Give a man a fish and he'll eat for a day. Teach a man to fish and he'll spend all day in a bass boat drinking beer and telling stories."

I went fishing with one of my church members, so you can probably guess we weren't drinking beer. We were telling stories, however, unaided by the embellishment of alcohol.

This church member had a nice bass boat and we went out on a small lake west of Cape Girardeau. I was catching some small fish and tossing them back, into the lake. Then I caught a nice fish that I decided to keep and put it into the live-well. As I was unhooking my fish, I notice the church member catch a nice fish as well. I watched him unhook the fish, then to my amazement, I watched him gently slide it back into the water and release it.

When I went to put my fish into the live-well, I noticed he had kept all the smaller fish. Curious, I asked him, "So what gives? You've been keeping all the small fish and I just watched you release a really nice fish that I would have kept."

He shrugged and said, "My wife only has a small frying pan and I have to catch the fish that fit."

Really? C'mon, man! You just need to buy your wife a bigger frying pan. And so it is with our visions. Since most of us, based on our experience, only have small frying pans, we only have small hopes and dreams. We need big frying pans and start believing big things are possible.

Vision takes imagination. Ponder for a moment, and suspend reality, that if you had no obstacles and no limits, what are the things you might imagine doing? What could you do that you are not currently doing?

Imagination is future-based, transcending the limits of the present. I love that guy who called me up and wanted to start beekeeping. He was looking to purchase forty hives. I didn't have forty hives to sell him. So I asked him what he had in mind, after all, starting out with forty hives is a little aggressive, not to mention, ambitious, especially for someone who had not experience.

He had been reading about beekeeping on the Internet (and that should have raised the first of several red flags). He told me he wanted to start keeping bees. He planned to start this year with forty hives, and by mid-summer split them all and make eighty hives. Based on what he read on the Internet, he figured by next spring he could split all eighty hives and have one hundred and sixty hives.

He told me he was going to requeen half of them, sell eighty at a profit and grow the other eighty and split them later in the summer for one hundred and sixty hives.

Now that's a vision pouring out of his imagination, transcending the limits of the present...and reality for that matter. But this is the power of vision: it moves you out of where you are to where you want to go. Vision does not worry about the cost or how to arrive at that destination. It paints us a picture of what we want.

When we struggle, vision is like the harbor lights guiding us home when we're still awash at sea battling the waves. Every day should start with our vision. To really be successful, it has to own you, possess you as it drives you forward.

When I started keeping honey bees in 1981 on the family farm in Minnesota, I was fresh out of college, full of youthful, impractical enthusiasm, and consumed by an optimistic, totally unrealistic vision to become a commercial beekeeper. I had all the answers, totally ignorant of the real questions. I wanted to keep enough bees to make a living at it. Never mind I had no idea how much work it entailed, *this was my vision.*

I had, in the back of my mind, a verse from the Bible, Proverbs 29:18, "Where this is no vision, the people perish." (KJV) Other possible compilations include, "without a revelation, the people cast off restraint and give up on their dreams" or "where there is no guidance or revelation, the people have no idea where they are going and they do whatever they want."

Without a vision, you probably won't survive in beekeeping. You might make it through a couple of seasons, but push through the frustrations, you need a vision. Having a vision does not guarantee you success, but your chances greatly increase when you start imagining what's possible and dreaming a creative future. Vision paints a target to shoot for, and even if you fail to hit that target, you'll be further ahead than if you blindly fire into the sky.

To have a vision is to know where you want to go. A vision is not necessarily a complex concept. When I talk to people about a vision for their work or their hobby, I rephrase the question by asking, "What are your hopes and dreams? What will things look like when you have reached that destination?"

The battle for achievement of success is half won when one knows definitely what is wanted. Which again, begs the question: What do you want?

A good way to have a vision is to start with the end in mind without worrying how you're going to get there. Where do you want to go? What level do you want to reach? Where would you like to be in ten years? Five years? Next year? Everyone, perhaps even secretly, has a vision, an idea, an inspiration...but these are lofty words. Sometimes we give them different, more mundane names like hopes and dreams.

Everyone has hopes and dreams. These hopes and dreams are typically idealized desires, but they keep us going in troubling times. We're told to never give up on our dreams, and the best thing we can do in troubling times is to keep moving forward toward seeing that dream become a reality, which is our vision of where we want to go.

We all need hopes and dreams, but do not forget a dream does not become a reality through magic. It still takes sweat, determination, and hard work. But when you believe in the dream, you are much more willing to put in the hard work to see it come through.

Dreams still need the proper direction and methodology, trusting in those subtle, intuitive nudges. Intuition seems to know what we truly want, even those things we're afraid to admit to ourselves. Do you trust your intuition?

I'm a strong believer in writing down one's vision. I like to put my goals in writing as if my conscious list tells my sub-conscious mind that I'm serious about this stuff.

So every winter, when it's cold and ugly outside, I stoke the wood stove and sit quietly, pondering and dreaming of my plans when the weather moderates and the bees awake from their winter confinement. I ask myself, "Where do I want to go? What do I hope to accomplish this next year? What do I want?"

I keep written notes on all my bee yards. During the summer season, I like to jot down ideas that come to my mind. Some of these ideas are new things that make my apiary more productive; other ideas remind me how some experiments were not worth the time to mess with and did not give me the results I hoped.

One of the best ways I've found to sustain my vision comes when I'm done working a bee yard. I have a notebook for every bee yard, and when I'm done working the hives, when all my equipment is secure in the truck and I have everything loaded up, I sit on the tailgate with my notebook and a pen. Before I leave to move on to the next bee yard, I ask myself, "What do I want to do with this bee yard? How can I improve this bee yard, given its location and how often I visit? Where do I want this bee yard to take me? What's possible?"

I am amazed, surprised, perplexed, even blown away from the insights I garner just sitting and pondering my dreams, my hopes, my vision for this one bee yard. Then I write it in my notebook.

Come winter, I cannot possibly remember all the stuff that happened during the summer, so I go back and review my notes and ponder the possibilities of this next year.

Remember this: you don't have to write down the whole vision all in one sitting. There's nothing more intimidating than a blank sheet of paper staring back at you when your brain is just as blank and empty.

So I jot down notes on little pieces of paper as I go through my day. I may be in the middle of a meeting with my mind wandering as I struggle to keep track of the speaker's line of reasoning and these stray thoughts about a troublesome bee yard keep popping into my head. The best thing I can do is write the ideas and thoughts down on paper, capture them at that moment, then later incorporate them into my greater vision.

There is great power in a written statement of where you want to go! And, according to something ascribed to Yogi Berra, "If you don't know where you're going, you'll end up somewhere else."

Do not trust your vision to memory or the vague feelings of "being a better beekeeper with more hives." Quantify your goals. Remember, as well, no one else is going to read your vision statement. Don't feel embarrassed. Write!

A vision is not set in concrete, but remains flexible to adaptations. I have not yet achieved my post-college vision of beekeeping as a full-time profession, but as a part-time side line, it remains a significant part of my life and I make some nice money at it.

I continue to torment my church congregation, threatening to retire to keep bees on a full-time basis. Then good things happen and I realize how much my congregation loves me and how much they appreciate my ministry.

Then my wife reminds me I better not quit my day job if the bees, like any agricultural enterprise, are so susceptible to fickle weather patterns and death. Still, I wonder...

My vision is to keep bees and do so profitably. I once explained to my congregation that my vision for beekeeping is to make honey, in order to make money, in order to pay for my son's tuition at Mizzou (the University of Missouri in Columbia, Missouri).

Beekeeping has been very good to my family and provided some financial perks that would otherwise not been attained. I am exceedingly grateful. My vision is to make my hobby an income-producing enterprise with a positive cash-flow that expands each year.

When I keep my vision in front of me, especially if it is written down, my vision keeps moving me forward. As I mentioned earlier, this past winter of 2012 into 2013 was one of my worst. The drought of 2012, the long winter, the late spring of 2013 all took a toll on my bees. With dying hives that made it through the winter, right up to February before biting the dust, it took a toll on me, mentally, emotionally and physically.

I hate losing hives. I hate losing more than I love winning--and there's a difference. I'm the kind of beekeeper that plays to win rather than playing not-to-lose.

We often hear, "It's not whether you win or lose, but how you play the game." I can guarantee that was said by someone who lost the game. Vince Lombari said, "Winning isn't everything; it's the only thing!" So is keeping my hives alive.

One of my church members, John Lysell, offered this keen insight, one cold Wednesday morning about 6:30 am: *"I don't think I can learn to win until I have learned how to lose."* I know that feeling of losing. I hate it. Losing propels me to work hard. The bitter taste losing leaves in my mouth makes me hunger for winning. Both winning and losing sharpen our vision.

On the positive side, I learned a lot through this experience about keeping bees and I continue learning new things every year about what it takes and what I might expect. I also learned how to handle what I never saw coming. I learned to prevent what I can; deal with what I can't. I could have given up. I could have sold all my remaining live hives. I could have done a number of things.

Instead, I hunkered down and made a special effort to put up extra swarm traps. I got an earlier start on raising my own queens. I pulled special hives to split and requeened the slower, non-productive hives. I kept my vision in front of me and my vision kept me going.

In 1959, when Cecil B. DeMille was directing and filming the great movie, *Ben Hur* with Charleston Heston in the starring role, it came time to film that wild chariot race in the coliseum.

Heston approached DeMille and said, "I'm sorry, Mr. DeMille, but I've never raced chariots before, especially in such tight quarters as this coliseum. I don't know if I can do this and win the race."

DeMille just smiled and said, "Don't worry about a thing. Just stay in the race and I'll see that you win!"

Sometimes, as beekeepers, we need just enough vision to stay in the race and keep on keeping bees, especially if the only way to stay in the race is to simply not quit.

Focus

Along with vision, you need *focus*. If vision keeps us in the race, focus provides us a picture of the track that leads to the finish line.

Focus is a narrowing of the vision, breaking the larger, big-picture vision into smaller, seasonal goals. The next step, after you have clarified your goals, is to write down smaller, more detailed objectives on how to accomplish the goals.

It's like that philosophical question about how to eat an elephant. The answer is, "One bite at a time and with a big appetite."

The vision is to eat the elephant. Focus moves us to think in smaller goals, which, in this case, is to cut the elephant into bite-sized goals. Goals then need the smaller details which we call objectives which might include finding a sharp knife, some barbeque sauce and making sure we skipped breakfast so we're really hungry.

And let's face it; looking a large vision in the eye is terrifying. A vision should be a wide-screen, mountain top vista of great things. Focus brings things into perspective, and with goals, moves us forward. A vision motivates, but focus empowers, and goals tell us how we're going to get the vision accomplished.

Passion

I've also been sustained by an old classic book entitled, *Think and Grow Rich* by Napoleon Hill.

Now don't let that title seduce you into thinking there is nothing you have to do but sit around and simply "think." The title should be revised to, *Get Off Your Backside and Work Hard in Order to Get Rich.* But that's not what the author intended.

The premise of the book is to think, to dwell, to ponder, to keep a vision in the forefront of your mind that consumes your daily consciousness. It's like we eat, drink and sleep beekeeping. It is to be obsessed with what you want to accomplish and where you want to go. And they have a word for this kind of obsession: it's called *passion.*

At the time when I was writing this manuscript, Nick Saban was the head coach of the University of Alabama Crimson Tide college football team. He's won national championships, currently holding the #1 ranking and he flat-out wins football games.

People ask, "Why does Nick Saban win so many football games?"

The answer is, "Because he **obsesses** about winning football games." That's passion. Passion is energy. Energy is fueled by desire.

Passion turns dreams into reality. I've observed a key character trait commonly held by successful beekeepers. They are the ones who possess a high level of passion for what they do. This is especially necessary at this time when beekeeping is challenged on every side.

If you don't love what you are doing, if you're not having fun doing it, if you have no passion for beekeeping, you would not be able to persevere when times get tough. And this is what happens to most people. Who would continue and put up with this stuff? It's always easier to quit.

Successful beekeepers possess a high level of passion. They continue where any reasonable, rationale person would give up without the slightest regret. As I said earlier, beekeeping isn't something I do; it's who I am.

And some people think I'm crazy. Who in their right mind goes outside, on the sunniest day, in the heat and humidity of the afternoon, to put up with stinging insects, to say nothing about the ticks, the chiggers, the snakes and spiders, the poison ivy and the thorns? And then on top of that, these lunatics tell you they enjoy it and wouldn't want to be anywhere else but under those hot, white overalls.

That's passion. Either that, or insanity. But as a beekeeper, I understand this energy that fuels our drive. It's crazy.

You cannot have passion without a vision. Focus empowers the vision and passion ignites the desire to see the vision fulfilled. Passion sustains my beekeeping.

When we have passion, we have momentum that washes up and spills over our problems, steamrolling them into submission. Passion makes a huge difference, and we find it by dwelling, even being consumed with thinking about our situation and challenges.

Purpose

When you combine vision, focus and passion you create a *purpose* for why you are keeping honey bees.

Purpose is about "why" you are keeping bees, but it won't necessarily tell you "how" to keep bees. The "how" will follow once you know the "why."

When you know the "why" you can find the way to "how." In fact, if you have a "why" to live for, you can overcome any challenge to the "how." Further, if you can sell the "why," you'll be more apt to buy the "how."

But it starts with a vision that is refined by focus, then fueled by passion. Without either vision, or focus or passion, you'll not have a purpose. With no purpose, you'll struggle asking "how?" With no purpose, you'll give up and surrender the minute the wind switches direction or your hives die out.

Faith

Faith is simply the belief that you can do this. Faith wraps up the vision, the focus with its goals and objectives, the passion with its energy and desire, and your purpose for why you want to keep bees.

Faith is like the icing on the cake. You need faith to believe all things are possible. Faith believes you can do this.

Finding Your Way Forward

Vision, Focus, Passion, Purpose and Faith now become the foundation to move forward. Together, they set the stage for action and execution of your plans. I'm a fan of professional football and coaches are always talking about executing a play, carrying out the intended plans.

There's an old story about three frogs sitting on a log. One decides to jump. How many frogs remain on the log?

The answer is three, because the one who decided to jump didn't follow through with his plans. He didn't execute his idea and take action. He only decided to jump, and until he actually followed through, three frogs remained on the log.

The ideal time to start beekeeping is in the spring. Every year, usually when the weather warms up and nature blooms in her full glory, I get a number of calls from people who tell me, "I'm thinking about getting into bees."

My response usually runs along the line of, "That's good. When you are actually ready to make the jump and get started, let me know. Until that time, there's several good places to find information. Call me when you're ready, or send me an e-mail and I'll help you get started."

It's the whole Yoda thing again, the idea of, "There is no try; don't think; jump, do." I seldom hear back from them. In the early days when I was significantly more eager to help these fence-sitters who were perennially stuck in the "thinking" mode, it bothered me they never called back. In this day and age of fickle, short-attention mentality, I don't lose any sleep. If you really want to keep bees, you'll get back in touch with me.

Vision, Focus, Passion, Purpose and Faith will propel you through some tough times. And I think I'd be remiss if I didn't warn you tough times will come. There is no end to the amount of knowledge it requires to raise bees. There is no end to the amount of potential snares and pitfalls that await you and your bees.

But when the mistress of misery comes calling, as I know she will, what will keep you in the game? How will you find your way forward?

I have found value to this idea of quieting my mind and meditating on my challenges. Meditation, sometimes just sitting quietly, opens my mind to new possibilities. It's like thinking on certain things, dwelling on certain problems, rolling dilemmas around in my mind as I drive from one appointment to the next.

Sometimes I ask questions of other beekeepers, not to debate, but to listen to their insights, to glean their wisdom, to gauge their commitment and weigh their struggles, then I inspire myself to become obsessed with finding a way forward that works for me.

One of my favorite church members, Joe Mathews, has said, "There is always a way; all we have to do it find it."

There is one other little element to surviving in these challenging times and that's what I like to call, "the hunger factor." How bad do you want it? How far are you willing to go to pursue your dreams?

Based on dealing with a lot of people from all walks of life, I've come to the conclusion that if something is important to you, you'll find a way. If it's not important, you'll find an excuse.

Finding the way forward often takes a lot of mental rumination. We like to apply the over-used cliché, "Thinking outside the box." Sometimes I have to literally, physically, "get outside my box" to put my brain in a different setting to stimulate a new idea or refresh my vision.

Sometimes it is as easy as taking a walk in the city park or taking a day off from work. I've been inspired sitting on the bank of a farm pond watching my idle bobber, waiting for the fish to bite. But in reality, I'm waiting for inspiration to strike.

Sometimes I need to burn off some energy to clear my mind. I might mow the grass, whether it needs it or not, but it usually does. I might nail some frames together, some tedious, mindless work to free up my creative processes. I may go to the health center and run the treadmill if the weather keeps my confined to indoors.

When I am vexed by a certain problem or stymied over finding a solution to a difficult dilemma, I find the best thing I can do is go somewhere else, to physically move to a new location that dislodges my presumptive consciousness. The social scientists call it a "spatial release," meaning you give yourself some space and move to a new location.

In a different environment, your brain shifts gears. You look at this same challenge but roll the problem around differently in your consciousness as your senses are bombarded by different stimuli. New insights come to your awareness. You see things differently, from a new perspective.

A different location is not just to seek new solutions, but to give you the opportunity to see your problems differently and in a new light. You jot down possible solutions without qualifying them or evaluating them. You allow your brain to be free to think outside the box.

I like to go to low-end restaurants, the old-fashioned "greasy spoons" where the flirtatious, aging waitresses wear grease-stained aprons (sans "bling") and call me, "hon," and "darlin," as they constantly warm-up my coffee to cultivate a better gratuity.

These are the fertile places where I can occupy a booth, breathe in the second-hand smoke from the other patrons, and amid the clatter of dishes and coarse conversation, ponder a different reality to a seemingly unsolvable problem.

I find these places inspirational and a plate of eggs, bacon and toast, with coffee, only runs me about five bucks...more if that waitress keeps my coffee warmed up. Even more if she gently rests her hand on my shoulder as she leans in real close and coyly offers, "need a warm up, hon?"

You bet. Warm me up!

Maybe it's the comfort food that stimulates my mental processes, maybe it's the constant stream of caffeine from all those warm ups, but a different environment sharpens my senses to see things differently.

A different environment moves me out of my normal way of thinking and my conventional method of fixing problems. Mostly, my problems no longer seem so large and I begin to develop a sense of hope. I begin to see options, and with options come choices. With choices, I am empowered.

In the television show, "Cheers," Norm, one of the bar's patrons, is challenged to come up with a decorating scheme for a young couple's apartment. He makes the claim that, before he goes to sleep, he programs his brain to dream about their apartment. The young couple buys his line, which is total baloney. Somewhere, Norm picked up the eye for design but no one believes he can just do it. So he shares his secret with his potential customers, this plan to "program" his brain and they think he's a creative genius.

In this same way, I've gone to bed thinking to myself, "I just have to sleep on this problem. When I wake up I'll be refreshed and I will find a new solution." This relatively innocuous affirmation relaxes me that I actually get some sleep rather than tossing and turning because I don't have the answer.

Early in the morning, sitting on my patio with a fresh cup of coffee, I'll contemplate my situation in the crisp coolness of the pre-dawn grayness and watch the sun come up. Just sitting still, to be still inside and out, engages my creativity. I do well to have a pen and paper as ideas come faster than I can retain them in my mind. It's a magical time. But I have to <u>make</u> the time rather than <u>find</u> the time to do this. It has to be intentional. Nothing important merely happens.

Acquiescing to the Dominant Model

In years past, my most common method of replacing winter dead outs was simply ordering southern raised nucs. Over the past five years, southern nucs were running $100 to $125, the cost of which I could recover with an average honey harvest. And like most yards, I had some nucs that made honey; some that did not.

As I shared in an earlier chapter, it was my custom to bring up a trailer load of nucs, selling some to local beekeepers and keeping a bunch to replace my dead outs. Then I shifted to just buying nucs for me and not bothering to resell. Then the past couple of seasons or so, I've really sought to convert my entire operation to local bees.

At best, buying nucs was a break-even proposition, but I'm in the business of selling honey and there's no way to manufacture honey other than from bees. Buying nucs was a sound option, but I kept thinking there was a better way. Instead of pursuing an alternative option, it was always easier to simply order more southern nucs.

Having gone through this experience for several years, I learned to order nucs early in January, and order extra nucs for I had no idea how many I would need to cover my losses when I started opening hives in March. Even though my intent was to keep the nucs for myself, I learned any nucs above my needs were very saleable to other beekeepers who also lost their hives over the winter.

I tried to balance my needs against some of my buddies who only needed one or two nucs. By the time they opened their hives and discovered their needs, it was too late to order more nucs. I strive to help those in need, as I think we all should.

But since I am in the business of making honey, there was no such thing as an unneeded nuc. I always have room for more bees. While I bought some to sell, I really wanted more bees to make more honey. This, of course, was simply hanging on to the dominant model of beekeeping.

After one of my discouraging visits to a bee yard in the spring of 2013, I walked about a hundred yards to the top of a hill overlooking the fence line and underbrush that sheltered my bee yard. I simply sat down on the ground and asked myself, "How am I going to get through this?"

Many of my contacts on the Internet were already talking about losses more severe than mine. Nucs would be in short supply due to an expected high demand. I started counting my losses and calculating how much replacement nucs were going to cost, provided I could find nucs available. I would be coming to the table a little late.

It was at that moment, on a chilly day in late February, sitting on the top of hill that I received my inspiration. I resolved I was NOT going to buy into that old habit and purchase southern nucs this year. I resolved to rise to the challenge to catch more swarms. Swarm trapping would be my method of replacing dead outs. I would stick to my vision of keeping local bees in my apiaries. That was my vision.

Then I focused my vision: I would establish the swarms in my northern yards, likely harvesting an average crop of honey. Then I'd move those bees south to catch the southern flow where I would have a much better chance at producing a honey crop.

This revelation, if you want to call it that, came when I intentionally sat down, quieted my mind to ponder where I wanted to go. I asked myself, "What is the end I have in mind? What do I really want?"

In mid-March, I noted more dead hives. Spring was not on schedule and I was getting nervous. The weather was still cold and I was irritable. In a typical winter, it's usually my weaker hives that die. This past winter, it was my strongest hives that died, mostly due to starvation, though I think my minimalist mite treatment and the long summer the previous year set up a lengthy mite breeding period which likely also contributed to the deaths.

When the weather finally warmed up and the survivors emerged, I had lost around 25% of my hives--my worst winter ever. Yet as I held my vision in the forefront of my mind, as I continued to think, dwell and meditate on my vision of a viable, profitable beekeeping business, I found the perseverance to carry on.

I remembered and hung onto an old piece of advice: "Don't worry about what's lost; give thanks for what's left."

This past summer, 2013, was a rebuilding year. I felt a measure of satisfaction in my refusal to buy more southern nucs and shift my energies to catching more swarms. Because of favorable weather, my honey crop was exceptionally good. I'm back up to 200 hives and some nucs to overwinter.

I continue to keep my vision in the forefront of my consciousness. I think about what it means to be profitable as well as sustainable. I think about these things, and when I intentionally take time to ponder my problems and options, I find creative solutions to my challenges.

Asking the Same Questions in New Areas

On one of my professional retreats for ministers, we were at Columbia Seminary in Decatur, Georgia. While still in the classroom, we read scripture passages and shared our thoughts on their meaning. We were all pretty mainstream and conventional in our interpretations.

In a surprise move, the professor said, "Okay. Let's take a little field trip."

We carpooled into downtown Atlanta to the county hospital. We broke into small groups, spending twenty minutes just watching the people come and go, enter and exit, sitting wearily at the bus stop, pushing their carts, looking for some hopeful sign. Then we read the same scriptures from the classroom to one another. We asked, "How does the reading and interpretation of this same passage change as we moved to a new location, viewing the possible interpretation through different eyes?

We were instructed to read the passage aloud, one more time, then sit and ponder the plight of humanity for another hour. This covered a shift change at the hospital. We were then instructed to remain silent as we headed back to the seminary. When you don't waste energy on inane conversation, those mental images linger in your mind and begin to consume your consciousness. It's hard to let go of the situation. That's the value of silence.

While at dinner back at the seminary, during our meal, the silence was lifted and our conversation was confined to what we observed that afternoon. Several people were instructed to stand and read the same passages aloud as the rest of us continued to eat our dinner.

We were later instructed that the last thing we were to do before going to bed was read the passage again, aloud, in our room to ourselves. The first thing we were to do upon waking was read the passage again, aloud.

After breakfast the next day we gathered in a group to share our insights. It was remarkable what new revelations came from the intensive process of keeping the passage in the forefront of our consciousness, even as we pulled a "Norm!" unintentionally programming our brains to dream about the passage as we slept.

The more we contemplated, pondered and meditated on that passage, the more it became real and relevant to us. New applications and new meanings from these ancient words came forth. It was a remarkable, literal and spiritual, out-of-the-box experience.

As I apply that same lesson to beekeeping, I am often thwarted and frustrated by my losses. I still cling to an unrealistic idealism of not losing any hives at all. I want every hive to survive!

But in the wake of my losses, I think about what I did and what I failed or forgot to do. Why did something work in one hive but not the other? What could I have done differently? What am I missing? Is there another way? Yes, there is always another way. All I have to do is find it.

Greg Hannaford is quick to add, "When working on your goals, you need a plan B, and a plan C, and a plan D, and a plan E, because you never know what is going to work and what isn't going to work.

Blake Shook, a young Texas beekeeper, encourages beekeepers to have a back up plan, then have a back up plan to their back up plan, and a back up plan to their back up plan to their back up plan. Then a...well, you get his point. We need multiple back up plans. I call them, "contingencies," something to fall back on when we run into a brick wall.

What both Greg and Blake preach is having options. When you have options, you have choices. Having choices is empowering.

Have I mentioned that already? Yes! The reason I repeat it is wake you up. In my cranky old age, I'm getting really tired of people who come to me and say, "I had this really bad thing happen and I don't know what I'm going to do."

I just want to slap them. Use your brain! Use your creativity! Think through your options! You always have options.

People should learn to stop asking whiny questions of cranky old people like me.

And the times I get suckered into their problems and, at their request, I offer advice. Most times, well, they never take it. Why waste my time if you're not going to do anything but wallow in your helplessness? Wake up!

We are not powerless! We have options. I can only hope the realization of this fact, that we are not powerless, is significant. Do not let any problem paralyze your thought process or seize your problem-solving abilities.

Just pondering a back up plan stimulates my mind to thinking about my problem or challenge in a new light. Which way is my best way? When that doesn't work, what's the next best way? When that comes up empty, what's my next option? Is there someone I might consult or run an idea passed? Is there ultimately a better idea than the one I'm working on, even if it's working?

I ponder these questions and meditate on possible solutions. I purposefully consider how to best take care of the bees that take care of me. Meditation is a lost art in our hurry-up, harried, electronic world.

Most times we are in such a hurry that we simply fail to stop and think, pause and listen.

And this whole idea of getting up early and sitting in stillness just sounds loony. When I suggest it, most people complain, "C'mon, man! I don't have time to just sit there and meditate; I need to do something!"

It's so easy to be distracted in today's electronic world. Instead, I need to be still and listen. What are my bees telling me? What did I miss because I'm so quick to jump on the computer and use social media to squander my time? Have I kept written records on what I observed? Am I pondering my problems or piddling my time away texting on my cell phone? Have I taken the time to sit and be still or am I off to tackle another project on my endless to-do list?

Opportunities abound, but unless we have the mindset to observe them, they tend to slip away from us. What do I have to do to see them? As much as they say, "Seeing is believing," so is, "Believing is seeing." Believe in the vision and you'll begin to see the opportunities.

And on a side note, when the Mr. Hill wrote *Think and Grow Rich*, he also concedes that "rich" does not always equate into money. There are many things in life that make us "rich." Having a vision that sustains my efforts is a very enriching gift. Keeping bees has enriched my life in more ways than I can count.

When I talk with discouraged beekeepers, and in these challenging times there is much to discourage us, I like to ask, "What was your vision when you started keeping bees?"

Many beekeepers are reluctant to articulate that vision for they see themselves as a failure, unable to fulfill that vision. I tone down the level of my vocabulary and ask, "What were you hoping to accomplish?"

When they share their hopes and dreams of what they wanted to accomplish, I shift the conversation from what was (a bunch of dead hives) to what is yet to be (a thriving hobby). Reframing of the situation often stimulates their sense of vision to find new, creative solutions, if not the mental resolve to give it another try.

Bees die. They've been dying and they will continue to die. You can worry about what was lost or you can give thanks for what is left. There will always be beekeepers who sell bees. You can always split your surviving hives. There will always be a way to continue on, all you have to is find it.

Some good advice I got was, "So when in doubt, press ahead blindly and pray for luck and God's delight in the reckless." Sometimes we find success just by showing up and putting our shoulder to the wheel.

Newton's first law of motion states, and I paraphrase for simplicity, "An object at rest will remain at rest. An object in motion continues in motion." This law is often called "the law of inertia." This means that there is a natural tendency of objects to keep on doing what they're doing. All objects resist changes in their state of motion.

Another key to sustainability is to keep moving, even in the wake of disappointment and frustration. Shut up, show up, and don't give up. If you really desire to keep on keeping bees, then get more bees to keep. Keep that momentum going.

My intention in writing this manuscript is to find ways to keep my operation sustainable by keeping me sustained as I try to find some way to level out all the variables that discourage my success. Above all, I need to sustain myself and avoid the emotional roller coaster of good seasons and bad.

If you give beekeeping an honest shot and it doesn't work out for you, that's fine. I'm not saying you have to be a beekeeper. Beekeeping is not for everyone, nor is everyone cut out to be a beekeeper. One of the longest roads a person can travel is the journey from, "I'd like to..." to, "I am doing..."

Something to remember is that:

Good things *come to those who* <u>*believe*</u>*;*
Better things *come to those who are* <u>*patient*</u>*; and the*
Best things *come to those who* <u>*don't give up*</u>*.*

When asked what makes him tick, one of my mentors in the ministry had this to say, regarding his formula for success. He said it was simple and we only needed four things:

"The <u>*power*</u> *to get it done, and
the* <u>*patience*</u> *to see it through;
the* <u>*faith*</u> *to believe it, and
the* <u>*will*</u> *to make it happen."*

Further, he challenged me to say, "As I see it, you have two options; you can continue to talk about it, or take action and make it happen. Action maintains momentum; momentum creates massive success."

Beekeeping is no different.

If I were asked what one thing would make all the difference in the world to your success or failure keeping honey bees, I would have to say written goals. Put your goals in writing. Even if you have nothing more than a list of bullet points or a grandiose "to-do" list, you are going to be five times more successful than the beekeeper who does not write down where they want to go and what they want to accomplish.

I think we grossly underestimate the human side of beekeeping. We're so wrapped up in what's happening in those little white boxes that we completely ignore the vital functions taking place between our ears. Sustain yourself, first.

You want to know the secret of keeping bees and what it takes to keep on keeping bees? A sustainable beekeeper is one with vision, focus, passion and purpose, and the faith to believe it can be done. You need all of these characters before you even light up your smoker if you want to keep bees for the long haul.

The value and benefit of sustaining ourselves is to find the joy in beekeeping. After listening to a grumpy, old man complain about a number of topics, I challenged him and asked, "Where's your joy?"

He said, "Under the kitchen sink with the rest of the soap."

We may not be here for a long time, but we're here for a good time. If beekeeping isn't fun for you, quit. If you're miserable keeping bees, everyone around you is probably miserable, as well. Misery does not love company. Give it up. Sell your hives to your brother-in-law and quit this incessant line of, "Yeah, some day..." unless you really intend to get back into bees. But don't keep fooling yourself and lying to us. The rest of us want to help those who are willing to help themselves.

When you discover how to keep bees and keep them sustainably, your hobby becomes a labor of love, and in reality, if it's something you enjoy, it's not really work. It still takes effort, time and energy but it's not really work as we think of "work."

People see me work hard at keeping bees. Some of my lesser successful beekeeping buddies have told me, "Man, it just takes too much work. I don't have your sense of commitment." And that's okay. We're not all cut out for this line of work, if that's what you want to call it. I enjoy working my bees.

Getting back to my analogy of my years of piano lessons and the frustration of not getting it, I remember a story that was told about the great American, classical pianist Van Cliburn.

Reportedly, a woman approached him after a concert and said, "Oh, that was so wonderful. I wish I could play the piano like you. Why, I'd give half my life to play like you."

Van Cliburn, totally unimpressed, replied, "Well, I gave my whole life to play like that."

Having counseled a number of beekeepers, having mentored a handful of local beginners, having taken a billion phone conversations from all over the country, I come to the conclusion that if you can't sustain yourself, the rest of your beekeeping efforts just won't fly, either.

Sustainable beekeeping begins with your attitude and your level of commitment to a very challenging endeavor in a very challenging era. If beekeeping was easy, every body would be keeping bees.

You have to have a Teflon® exterior, and may it always be said that your **vision** remained resolute, your **focus** endured, your **passion** persisted unabated, and you held unswervingly to your **purpose** because you had the **faith** to believe you could make it all happen.

And never let anyone tell you beekeeping is easy.

Chapter 5

The Queen -
The Heart of Sustainability

My wife spent several years working for a hospice agency. Hospice work concerns itself with end-of-life-issues with a non-intervening, palliative care (relieving without curing).

In short, hospice care acknowledges the body's inability to sustain itself and seeks comfort and an existential purpose for living rather than finding a therapeutic remedy to curing the ailment or disease. Hospice gives hope and comfort for what time remains.

My wife noted, that despite the problem or disease facing the patient, the ultimate cause of death was always cardiac arrest, that is, when the heart stopped beating and it no longer pumped blood throughout the body.

One can make a case for cancer as the cause of death, but in my wife's opinion, as long as the heart was still beating, the patient was still alive despite any conflicts caused by the cancer.

I began thinking of other causes of death like accidents or starvation or drowning. I concluded that irrespective of what life-threatening trauma we put our bodies through, as long as the heart is sustained by the other organs (lungs for oxygen, colon for nutrients, etc.) we possess life. When we wonder if someone is alive or not, we always check for the pulse. No pulse, no life. When a person collapses and basically dies, the first thing we do is chest compressions to get the heart going again. The beating heart equals life.

My 83-year old father died in St. Mary's Hospital in Rochester, Minnesota in late July of 2012. In the last hours his life, an intubation tube hooked up to a respirator "assisted" his breathing. In reality, it was breathing for him. An oxygen mask furiously forced oxygen into his lungs to keep the carbon dioxide levels from becoming toxic. The previous days were marked by his objection to the oxygen mask as he fought the nurses and had to be restrained.

On that last day of his life, my father was not consciously aware of anyone's presence. When my brother and sister arrived, the doctors and nurses called a family conference with the staff. They demonstrated they were ready, willing and fully able to continue medical assistance as long as the family desired. They graciously offered to do just about anything, and everything we asked. They also added, since my father had not really eaten much during that last week of his life, their first priority would be to surgically implant a feeding tube for liquid feeding.

One family member asked, "If all of this assistance was kept in place, including the feeding tube, how long will he continue to live?"

The irony of such question was more for information as my father had expressed on many occasions throughout his life how he had no desire to be kept alive by "artificial" means. From his perspective, this was not his idea of "living." We all knew that it was not our idea of living, as well.

The doctor answered the question factually in measured tones, that if the intubation tube was left in place, that if a feeding tube was installed, my father might continue to live another six to eight weeks, maybe twelve weeks at the outside, but he conceded no one really had any idea.

I asked the doctor what would happen with respect to his health, pondering, "Would my father ever regain consciousness? Would he be able to come home? Would he spend the rest of his life in a skilled-care facility?"

The doctor was straight-forward and clinical as he said the likely scenario would be a continual, though slow, decline in health to the point where the heart would eventually, and finally wear out, ceasing to function, at which point, my father would "pass."

There was very little hope for any improvement. With respect to the hospital, the doctor intimated the hospital would not keep my father too much longer and we would have to locate a longer-term, skilled care facility.

The key was the heart. As long as the medical staff could continue to assist the other organ systems that supported the heart, my father would live. To make a short story even shorter, knowing my father's objection to all this assistance and his desire for a quality of life rather than a quantity, and taking into account his faith and our faith, we, as a family, unified in purpose and in spirit, told the medical staff to begin removing all the devices that were keeping him alive. That was our decision, and we believed, with certainty, these actions were in line with my father's wishes.

The doctor, in response to our request, bluntly stated that it would be only but a few minutes before the heart would cease to beat for lack of support from the other organ systems and our decision would be the ultimate end of his life. I was momentarily put off by the doctor's attitude, as if the doctor thought we should agree to this continued support of a situation that was, clearly, not sustainable.

We were confident and resolute in our decision, and with all due respect, we did not see any quality of life that was in line with my father's desires which he so adamantly articulated on so many occasions as he lamented the demise of many of his peers.

Once the medical staff removed the assisting devices from my father, the process of dying took about twenty minutes. The fundamental and ultimate cause of death was cardiac arrest. As long as the other organ systems were supported mechanically by artificial means, the heart continued to sustain life.

The Significance of the Queen

In the bee hive, the queen is the heart of the colony. As long as the colony's heart is beating, the hive is alive, sustaining life. If a queen is present, there is always hope for the future. When something happens to the queen, the colony's future is threatened, and the workers will take action if viable options are still possible. If not, then the colony either wanes and dies or becomes subject to a laying-worker. Neither of these scenarios is sustainable.

The queen is the heart, yet the other half to this equation is the "support systems" that keeps the queen healthy, happy and fed. However, when mite infestations overpower the support staff, i.e., the workers, and the viruses begin attacking the developing larvae, the queen cannot carry the load and the colony will dwindle and eventually die. But as long as she lives, the colony has hope. The key to the queen's viability is the health of the workers.

I receive frequent calls from local beekeepers needing a queen. I often wonder if they really need a queen or perhaps there are other problems in the support system that keeps a colony going.

Some of these callers tell me they don't have much brood, but in reality, if a hive is suffering under a crushing load of mites, the worker bees will not be healthy enough to feed and tend to the duties of raising larvae.

Further, a colony that is hurting from disease will not have the foragers to bring in fresh pollen and nectar to feed the larvae and the queen will be forced to scale back her egg laying numbers.

The two forces go hand in hand. You need a queen but you also need a healthy support system to keep her going. To simply requeen a failing colony is to delay the inevitable demise of the hive.

In my opinion, the foundational core of sustainable beekeeping lies with the queen honey bee. The queen is the repository of all the genetic material needed to survive, including the genetics that her successor will possess. The genetics reflect the colony's ability to defend itself from disease, to show grooming tendencies or exhibit hygienic behavior, to overwinter on marginal stores and when to start laying eggs in the spring or shut down during a nectar dearth.

But genes are also governed by the environment, and non-genetic cues received from the environment. How a gene is expressed is called "epigenetics."

Genetics + Environment = What We See

Epigenetics is the fancy word we are using today in the selection of queens, and how the offspring of those queens behave, given the local environment. I want bees that function in my area, and thus I'm going to look at my bees and how they perform, then choose the queens from those colonies to raise new queens and requeen my failing or marginal colonies.

The ideal in raising my own queens is to find stock that is locally adapted, that is, suitable to my part of the country. Every successful colony originates from the ovaries of the queen, but the local environment gives those genes permission to express themselves in different ways.

Epigenetics is the expression of a particular gene triggered by an environmental cue. To put it another way, a honey bee has a wide variety of genetic material (which we call the genotype). It shows up to our naked eyes in a certain behaviors or physical characteristics (which we call the phenotype).

However, there are environmental or non-genetic signals which may prompt the genotype to be expressed differently. There are things that happen to a hive which inform the genetics to start or stop a particular behavior. These signals may be stress, nutritional deficits, even environmental toxins.

When I speak of environmental toxins, there are two which come to mind. External toxins would be pesticides sprayed in the fields where the bees forage. Internal toxins would be the crap and garbage beekeepers intentionally put in the hive to combat mites, namely the synthetic miticides like fluvalinate and coumophos. These sub-lethal doses have a profound affect on how the hive functions.

But don't get all high and mighty with respect to "natural" or even "organic" treatments. They, also, profoundly affect the environment of the hive. Thymol products and formic acid products, even essential oils, mask the aromatic communication processes in the hive. Bees communicate through their sense of smell.

In human beings, for instance, there is a theory suggesting we all have the genetic code for cancer. So why do some people get cancer and some people don't? The theory suggests there is something in the environment or something we do, or don't do, to our bodies (smoking, pollution, diet, exercise, fiber, excessive calories) that holds the power to turn that cancer gene on...or keep it off. Epigenetics tries to explain how this happens and encourages us to make healthy choices in how we treat our bodies.

As a child, I was always told, "Don't smoke; you'll get cancer." Yet as I matured, I discovered hundreds of people who smoked and did not have cancer. Then I came across stories of non-smokers who came down with cancer. It made no sense to me, though I felt non-smokers coming down with cancer was a horrible injustice. The randomness of disease seemed to be a roll of the dice, but we have concluded there is something that causes a normal cell to grow abnormally into a condition we call cancer. We just don't know what triggers the growth that initiates the cancer.

Epigenetics is not a clear science as a strict cause and effect relationship because our bodies have zillions of alleles (combinations of genes) that combine to control the visible phenotype to varying degrees. Further, while we are still wondering what turns the genetic code on or off, we know something flips the switch.

When it comes to bees, we are asking questions that fit into this realm of epigenetics. For instance, does the introduction of certain miticides (i.e., fluvalinate or coumophos, two of the popular chemical miticides marketed as Apistan and CheckMite+) change the ways the bees are resistant to, or are susceptible to the viruses the mites carry?

Such an irony that we put something in the hive to kill the mites only to shut down the bee's resistance to a virus! (Now I don't know if this is true, so please don't quote me, but I use this as a hypothetical example of how epigenetics work, i.e., a miticide that could possibly suppress the bee's immune system.)

Or is the opposite true, that if we remove the application of Apistan or CheckMite+ from our arsenal of mite treatments, will our bees have their genetic switch flipped to fight the mites and the viruses they mites carry?

The push for more natural beekeeping practices suggests by removing the chemical treatments, we might have healthier bees that can legitimately fend for themselves. All we have to do is breed queens from the survivors of our treatment-free methods.

But can we stomach all the hives that will crash and die through this natural selection process? Has our use of our present miticides only perpetuated a host of honey bees that cannot survive without treatments? Can we live by consigning some of our hives to a certain death? Is it a good thing to eliminate these susceptible genetics from the gene pool? Are we not also allowing the demise of other beneficial traits by their deaths? These are hard questions, and obviously hypothetical.

I think we need to step back and take a larger, longer perspective. We are not simply choosing queens to lead our hives. We are selecting the carriers of certain genetic traits which transmit the desired characteristics to the work force of the colony, and hence the survivability and the productivity of the hive.

We also have to agree our environment, and our management style that alters the environment, governs the expression of those genes. This is not as easy as my seventh-grade biology course and the red/white sweet peas grown by Gregor Mendel. (By the way, did you know Mendel started his genetic research with honey bees?)

Beekeepers often use a treatment marketed by the name Fumagilin-B to treat for a disease we call nosema. But we also know this treatment messes up the gut and the bee's ability to digest protein. With poor protein absorption, other ailments come into play. I'm caught trying to figure out what's worse, the nosema (which is triggered by stress) or the poor nutrition the bees have to endure until the stress is relieved and they overcome the effects of the nosema.

With poor nutrition, the bees cannot function normally (like foraging, feeding larvae, cleaning the hive, fending off small hive beetles, etc.). Nosema doesn't usually kill the colony, but it makes the bees in the colony feel so poorly that the whole morale and health of the hive declines until something else takes them out.

We are now questioning the feeding of high-fructose corn syrup (HFCS). We also know sucrose has a higher pH than honey. What do these optional, replacement food sources do to the bees?

And if the source of the HFCS comes from a GMO crop source, now what? Is there something in a GMO crop that turns certain genetic switches on or off? We don't know, but there are crowds of people who love to speculate the causes and effects and rail against the large agricultural corporations.

Anecdotally, I know of a handful of people, which is a very insignificant sampling, whose health improved by switching to a gluten-free diet, or a vegetarian diet, or a grass-fed beef diet, etc. While I have no solid medical evidence other than to suggest a possible correlation, I think beekeepers ought to consciously monitor their management practices that may be causing undesired consequences that, of course, we'd much prefer to blame on something, or someone else, like large agricultural corporations.

Epigenetics: The Study of Side Effects

As I ponder the problems understanding epigenetics in the bee hive, I see a parallel problem in humans. A typical person has a problem and they go to their doctor. Their doctor says, "This is no big deal. Just fill this prescription for pharmaceutical "X" and we'll have you back on your feet in no time. But I will warn you, pharmaceutical "X" has been known to have a side effect, but if it becomes a problem, come back and see me and I'll give you another prescription for that side effect."

So the patient starts taking pharmaceutical "X" and suffers the expected side effect. The patient reports to the doctor and the doctor prescribes pharmaceutical "Y." But pharmaceutical "Y" also has side effects so the doctor prescribes pharmaceutical "Z" to combat the side effect from pharmaceutical "Y" which is addressing the side effects of pharmaceutical "X." The patient ends up taking fifteen different pharmaceuticals because everything has side effects.

Think of epigenetics as the study of side effects. We put something in the hive to address a problem and there is an unintended side effect, i.e., susceptibility to a virus. The pharmaceutical triggers something else by switching the genetic code on or off.

Or think of it another way. Again, suppose we refrain from putting commercial miticides in the hive and the bee's genetic code learns to turn on the genetic switch for hygienic behavior or grooming which reduces the mite load. The removal of a chemical that alters the environment produces a positive side effect. Epigenetics works both ways.

Our management practices are also a study of epigenetics. Since my main goal is honey production, I do not want my hives weakened by swarming. I have a zero tolerance for swarming and do what I can to prevent it.

And to be certain, honey bees are genetically predisposed to swarm. It's in their DNA to reproduce and create new colonies of honey bees in the area because, as I mentioned earlier, even nature knows that bees die. Swarming is nature taking a deliberate precautionary step toward perpetuating the species.

But I don't like swarming. I like harvesting a honey crop. We know there are several cues in the hive that trigger the swarming impulse. We know that swarming does not happen overnight and colonies do not swarm without solid preparations. Any preventative measures on my part need to take place prior to the construction of swarm cells which indicate the colony has already decided to swarm.

One of the preventative solutions to swarming is to cut out those swarm cells, but if you understand what has already happened, cutting out all the swarm cells, particularly if they are capped, may leave your colony without a queen. Those swarm cells contain future queens, and if they are capped, the original, old established queen has likely already left. The hard part is not knowing how long those swarm cells have been capped. It is still possible the original queen is still in the hive, or not.

When the original, established queen leaves, we call this a "prime" swarm, and any subsequent swarms are called, "after" swarms. There is one prime swarm, but the colony may cast off several after swarms, depending on how many swarm cells the colony has made.

The hive, at this point prior to swarming, is likely pretty crowded with bees (though mere crowding does not trigger swarming). You may have found a queen, but unless you mark your queens, you have no way of knowing this queen is your established queen. If she's marked, you've successfully prevented a swarm from happening. If you don't mark your queens, you may have found a virgin ready to leave with an after swarm.

By the way, I am a HUGE proponent of marking your queens, and if you buy queens from a reputable queen producer, I insist you pay the extra dollar or two and have them marked. The purpose of marking your queens helps you find them easier and you also know the age of the queen as each year is marked by distinctive colors.

There is a generalized complaint among beekeepers that mail-order queens are becoming more and more susceptible to supersedure, which in itself, is a side effect of another problem. Several theories abound, but unless you buy a marked queen, you'll never know if they do supersede her, and if you don't mark your own queens, you have no idea if that queen is old or new.

When a hive starts to decline, the workers will start the process to supersede the old queen. This behavior is genetically programmed and triggered by a non-genetic environmental cue. The new queen emerges and begins to lay eggs following her mating flight. But there is a lag in time that creates a brood break, or at best, a decline in the brood production. Even as the new queen takes over, the colony will look puny and run down.

You come along, open the hive and, "OMG! This is a bad queen. There is hardly any brood. I need to kill her and order a new queen through the mail."

So you ignorantly spend money on a mail-order queen to replace a perfectly good new queen that just hasn't yet had the opportunity to fill up the comb with brood.

So a few days later you kill off the supposedly "old" queen and wait twenty-four hours, and introduce the new, mail-order queen. Then the hive rejects your new queen and you complain vociferously about those horrible people who raise bad queens. I'm telling you, save money; mark your queens.

Better yet, don't let your colonies swarm. Even better still, requeen your colonies annually instead of forcing your bees to supersede a poorly producing queen because you were too lazy to know this queen was old. And in today's apiaries, even young queens play out. Good management knows which hives have good queens. Mark your queens.

And if those queen breeders were kind enough to mail you one queen (probably on very short notice), I think a little gratitude is in order...but that's just me thinking out loud.

Back to our swarming dilemma. If you cut all those swarm cells, you'll have to return in ten days to cut out the next bunch of swarm cells, if your original queen is still present. Note: she may not be present!

It seems once the colony decides to swarm, it's going to swarm. If the existing queen is present, the colony will rebuild all those swarm cells. However, if you cut out all those swarm cells and the original queen has left, you might not have any other eggs or viable larvae from which the colony can make a new queen.

So now you have a choice. You can break up the colony into nucs so each nuc has a queen cell, or you can cut out or squish all the swarm cells but one and leave the colony in tact, hoping to recover some semblance of a honey crop. But good luck with that idea.

I have found exceptional results to reorient the swarming impulse by using the checkerboarding method promoted by Walt Wright of Elkton, Tennessee. You can find many of his articles all over the Internet though he has changed the name of his method to "Nectar Management." Additionally, the Snellgrove method and the Demaree method, older versions that accomplish the same objectives can be searched on the Internet.

What I'm getting after here is the notion that management impacts the expression of the genetic code, turning the genetic switch on or off, for better or for worse, as the colony exhibits the phenotype (the physical expression of that gene).

Checkerboarding expands the brood nest, relieves congestion (not the same as crowding) and reorients the colony into raising more bees rather than separating and creating more colonies through swarming. Successful swarm prevention techniques change the behavior of the gene that dictates the swarming event.

One noted exception, the natural beekeeping camp believes the swarming impulse is not to be suppressed or redirected. If bees are in a hollow tree and existing on their own, their genetic code compels them to divide and create new colonies to live in other hollow trees.

My managed bees living in square boxes also have the genetic code compelling them to divide and create new colonies. I, on the other hand, will work to prevent swarming, presenting me with the opportunity to harvest my honey crop, then allows me to split the hive to make new colonies. The end result is the same: more colonies. I just go about it in a different manner and take responsibility to manage the colonies to make a honey crop.

I trap a lot of local, feral swarms and if you are interested, there is a resource I put together at www.createspace.com/4106626. Southeast Missouri, particularly Cape Girardeau County, has a plethora of feral swarms. It's always hard to tell if the bees are truly unmanaged for multiple generations or if I'm catching a swarm from someone's hive in their back yard. Never the less, I've got some free bees!

When I gave a talk on how to trap feral swarms, a little old lady questioned the value of this practice. "Aren't you just catching bees that like to swarm and will likely swarm on you?"

First, I commended her thinly disguised disdain for swarming. Nearly all of us conventional beekeepers want to prevent swarming.

Second, I mentioned that all honey bees have that genetic switch to swarm. It's in their DNA. All honey bees are bred to swarm and all they need are the right physical conditions to trigger the behavior. There are some races of bees (Carniolans and Russians) that seem more prone to swarming because they tend to sit back and build up slowly in the spring, lulling the beekeeper into thinking nothing is happening, then with a sudden urgency, the queen goes to laying eggs. The cells become congested with incoming nectar and BANG! They swarm, which in my bee yards is followed by weeping, gnashing of teeth, and a profusion of profanity because I procrastinated and now I'm paying the price!

I believe the key to swarm prevention lies with management and not blaming certain races of bees for this problem. Management has to learn to manage the swarm impulse and we do it through our knowledge of epigentics. Epigenetics asks, "What makes the bees do what they do, and what is the triggering mechanism?"

Third, I pointed out to this older lady, that when I catch a swarm, and if I give them the right amount of room when I place the swarm in a hive, they are not likely to even think about swarming until the next spring, provided they survive the winter.

So where am I going with all this information? To cut to the chase, I think we need to find a race of honey bees that works for us in our unique locale, and is adapted to our individual management skills (or incompetence) and I firmly believe we need to raise queens from that stock that thrives under our management and survives our environment, inside and outside the hive. Whether we choose to dump all kinds of toxic miticides in our hives or go treatment-free, a key to sustainable beekeeping is to raise queens from the genetic stock that works for us and works with us.

This is a point where I differ greatly from the natural camp. Raising queens from the stock that works for me in my area is all about *ME!* The natural camp would rather pull me aside and politely inform me that beekeeping isn't about me, it's about the bees.

And here I get back to one of my earlier points: can we keep bees conventionally, still honoring who they are and how they are "wired" genetically, doing no harm but harnessing their industry and work ethic to pollinate our agricultural crops and produce a surplus of honey?

Obviously, I think the answer is yes, it's possible. More than anything else, however, managing honey bees and respecting the power and potential of epigenetics gives us the proper perspective to keep honey bees and keep them alive through our selection of which hives to create new queens. Are not hives full of living bees a good thing, even though I benefit from keeping them healthy and productive?

And remember, management and environment possess the ability to turn those genetic switches on or off. We want bees that respond favorably to our management levels.

To put it another way, our management skills are going to make some bees function better than others, literally expressing their genetic code with a positive behavior that responds to the way we raise our bees.

My Stock Selection

So how do I go about doing this? First, I select hives for breeding stock that thrive under my management. My idea of sustainability is a bee that survives under my soft-chemical approach. I like using powdered sugar dustings over the brood area, and you have to realize that it takes multiple dustings to shed the bees of the mites, and it is best used on screen bottom boards.

I will use formic acid, an organic treatment that requires a great deal of care in the application. Some applications of formic are temperature sensitive so it cannot be used in certain time periods. I use an alcohol wash to count mites, and a 1/2 cup of bees (roughly 300) should show between six to ten mites per wash. That's a 2% to 3% threshold to dictate the severity of the mite load.

Sticky boards do not give an accurate assessment of the severity though they are a whole lot easier to use than an alcohol wash. I'll have more to say about sticky boards in a later chapter, but if you are using a sticky board to measure a threshold level, you are better off using a ouija board...and you'll probably get more accurate results.

I keep Randy Oliver's advice in mind to never let the mite load reach high levels where you need to kill the mites, but rather work to keep the mite levels in check by several, frequent treatments. And I have to remember that certain treatments are not permissible during the time the honey supers are on the colony.

Which is why I like the powdered sugar dustings. I take down the honey supers and dust the brood area where the mite infestation is going to be concentrated. Powdered sugar doesn't interfere with my honey production. Supposedly, the new formulations of formic acid can be used with honey supers in place but I prefer to wait until the honey is off.

I've used drone trapping, mostly as an indicator of the presence of mites as mites prefer to reproduce in the pupated drone cells. Using a cappings scratcher, I can pull out a sample drone pupae from their capped cells to inspect for mites. A lot of the time, I do not find mites in my drone cells.

If I find mites, I will follow the protocol for drone trapping, which entails putting the whole drone frame in the freezer to kill the drones and any mites that may be present in those cells. If not, I leave the drone frame in the hive to hatch out. I like to keep drones around to mate with my queens.

Some people will put a shallow or medium frame in the brood area. The bees will draw out that bottom half of the frame, typically with drone cells. Once those drone cells are capped, the beekeeper simply slices off that drawn drone comb and puts the frame back in the brood nest for another round of drone comb.

The slab of capped drone comb can be fed to chickens, if you got them. I don't, so I tend to see this kind of drone trapping as wasteful of the metabolism it takes to draw out the drone comb and feed the drone larvae. Still, it works to draw the varroa mites to these cells rather than to the worker cells.

I continue to trap feral swarms. They seem to do quite well with the brood break that suppresses mite reproduction for a little while. I also believe my midsummer splits create an artificial brood break.

I'm pretty lean with my mite treatments, and if my alcohol wash showed a high level of mites, I am not opposed to treating colonies with commercial, chemical miticides to keep them alive. I don't believe in neglecting a colony, basically giving it a death sentence merely because they show a susceptibility to mites or reveal a high mite load. They may, in fact, be good honey producers.

These colonies still have the right to live, and I don't buy into the idea that I'm perpetuating an inferior line of bees. I'm not normally going to use those bees in my selection of queens to rear, though they certainly produce drones which may mate with my desired queens. I will keep that colony alive to produce honey, or split that colony and use its brood for mating nucs to raise new queens from my resistant lines.

This brings me to my second part about epigenetics: raising my own queens. The first part is to identify those colonies that show the physical characteristics to produce honey under a minimalist approach to combating mites. It's not exactly a survival of the fittest, but it's an identification of the colonies that thrive without chemical assistance in my area, under my management.

I mentioned my buddy, Cory Stevens, a treatment-free queen producer in Dexter, Missouri. Cory does not use treatments because they mask the bees' ability to function and fend off the mites. Cory calls treatments a "crutch." He wants the pure genetic material to be fully expressed without any treatments covering up a genetic deficiency of susceptibility to the mites.

When I hear people wanting to start keeping bees and go the natural route, they often overlook the genetic component of why bees survive without treatments. Cory is quick to note, that if he did not have the appropriate genetics to support and defend the colony, he'd be crazy to try beekeeping treatment-free.

However, some beekeepers, mostly beginners, think all bees are suitably bred to be raised treatment-free, provided the beekeeper is but wise enough to know treatment-free beekeeping is the best way to raise bees. Unfortunately, not all bees are suited for this method, but if this is your choice, you certainly are free to allow a natural selection process to winnow out the susceptible bees and you can then work with the surviving colonies that respond to this avenue of management.

In my opinion, you need something to combat the mites, and I recognize the genius of Cory's approach by utilizing the bees' own DNA instead of suspicious chemicals. Genetics is one way to combat the mites. You can find all kinds of advertisements in the trade publications on queen producers who specialize in treatment-free queens and queens that produce bees with special traits such as hygienic behavior. If you desire to go treatment-free, be sure you have the right kind of queen, with the right kind of genetics, heading up your colony.

Crazy as it may sound, I know bee clubs in Missouri that ship in southern-raised nucs with the purpose of selling them to beekeepers who want to raise bees in an all-natural, treatment-free environment. Which works if you have the genetics, but if you don't, you're likely to lose a good portion of your colonies to preventable diseases and mite infestations.

Thus Cory is comfortable going treatment-free. He has the genetic stuff to go treatment-free, and it starts with the right queen. He meticulously counts mites and chooses the best of the best of the best.

I'm not quite so bold in my production hives to go completely treatment-free, but I'm looking for bees that fit my minimalist management practices and excel in my area with their honey production. Once I see how my colonies perform, I'm ready to select the colonies from which I'm going to raise my own queens. Once I've selected the colonies for queen rearing, I stop the treatments as the final criteria for the selection process. I also want to avoid any conflict with the treatments, even "natural" treatments in the development of my queens.

It's difficult to be too precise in selecting known traits in my queens. It seems as we select a specific trait we may unselect another trait. I go with what works for me, works with me, produces honey and survives the following winter. With the unknown variations in genetics, I take a skeptical view of my ability to pinpoint specific traits. My queens are also open-mated to feral drones so I've lost all control with choosing drones.

Further, I'm selecting queens based on the phenotype, the expression of the genotype that interacts with the environment. And I cannot control the environment except to choose my apiary locations away from pollution, pesticides and contaminants. But good luck on this idea. Mostly, I'm basing my queen selection on performance. I can live with this selection. So can my bees.

Oddly, I favor the darker queens over the more yellow varieties. I had my feral stock genetically tested and my hives represent a divergent variety of races and strains of honey bees. Diversity is a good thing. And the bees that survive make good queens the next season.

Surprisingly, very few beekeepers raise their own queens. But as I've been raising my own queens for many years now, I have a good idea how much work it takes and I am no longer surprised why only a few beekeepers raise their own queens. It is definitely easier to pick up the phone and purchase a mail-order queen from any one of the hundred of commercial queen producers. But I'm approaching my beekeeping from a position of sustainability, and buying queens is not high on my list of priorities to be sustainable.

The most common method of queen rearing is called the "Doolittle" method which involves grafting. Grafting is the physical transfer of day-old larvae from the brood comb to cups initializing the building of the queen cell.

They say it takes three things to successfully graft larvae: good eyesight, a steady hand, and good lighting (I usually only have two of the three at any given time). As soon as I mention grafting to someone, it's not long before I see the eyes glaze over and their resistance builds. A lot of people do not want to graft larvae, and even more do not want to even learn how to graft. I am one of these glassy-eyed non-grafters, and no, I don't even want to learn how to graft.

The good news is you can raise queens without grafting. I use a plastic contraption called the "Nicot" system in which I transfer cell cups with newly hatched larvae. Technically, I am grafting, but I graft large cell cups and not the tiny larvae.

I started raising my own queens because I was receiving what I deemed "inferior" queens from commercial queen breeders. But here's the rub: were these queens really inferior or were they merely unsuitable for, and not adapted to my management practices and a southeast Missouri environment? Costs for queens were going up and shipping options were becoming more risky. I also thought I would save money raising my own queens.

Well, if time is money, then I didn't save anything. Further, experience is expensive. There are no shortcuts in beekeeping, only trade-offs. While my out-of-pocket costs were being reduced, it took a lot of time to learn how to raise my own queens. The process is not difficult, just tricky...and you must stay on a schedule and you cannot allow vacations or procrastination to sidetrack your efforts.

I think everyone ought to raise their own queens, which is a pretty broad, sweeping generalization. Some of you won't have the time; some won't have the inclination; some of you only need a couple of queens. But we're all good, here. I'm not laying a guilt trip on anyone.

But as the custodian of the genetics that thrive under my management skills, I want more queens just like the one that gives me a great honey crop and didn't require high-priced, synthetic chemicals to beat the mites. If I don't raise these queens myself, where do I get more queens like them? Wal-mart?

The alternative is to buy queens from several different commercial queen producers and see which producer raises queens that work best for you. Then give that producer all your business.

I wrote another manuscript about the Nicot, non-grafting, queen rearing system and how I use it. It's not the only way to raise queens; it's not the perfect method, either. Many bee clubs and local associations are offering classes in queen rearing, and if you don't raise your own queens, find a local beekeeper who will raise a few local queens for you.

You can find my Nicot, queen-rearing resource at www.createspace.com/4542113

There are many ways to become more sustainable in your beekeeping enterprise. Having purchased a number of commercially-produced queens, some that worked for me, many which did not, I wanted to end this hit-or-miss aspect of my beekeeping. I shifted to raising my own queens.

Ironically, some of the queens raised from my efforts work out, some don't...but I'm not creating an out-of-pocket expense and a drain on my cash flow. When I've ordered a $25 queen and I come back to find her dead and the colony bordering on becoming broodless, I think I could have just as well burned that $25 in my smoker. Or bought my wife a nice dinner.

But when I raise my own queens, I can raise ten queens and choose the top five queens, kill off the five inferior queens (or even give them away to a buddy who needs an emergency queen) and combine the mating nucs. These queens might not be "inferior" but I'm going to choose the best of my best. I'd hardly dare do that with ten queens I purchased for $25 each!

Or I can keep all ten queens and see what they can do. I do not have any shortage of bee equipment or locations to place hives. It doesn't take a lot of honey to break even on a home grown queen in one of my splits.

Also, locally adapted queens fitting my management schemes create colonies which are more productive than a colony requeened with an out-of-state queen. Part of being sustainable is taking the guess work out of which queens work and those which I hope will work out.

When I choose to raise my own queens, I get to choose the genetics (more or less), and allowing my queens to be open-mated to the drones in southeast

Missouri gives me great confidence I'm not picking up the genetics of the AHB (Africanized Honey Bee). I'm not dependent upon the early spring weather delays or on the busy schedule of the southern queen producer when I was buying mail-order queens to make splits under the dominant model.

It is estimated that the ten top queen producers in the United States produce half of all the queens that are ordered by beekeepers like you and me. That's a pretty narrow genetic base. We have a stake in good queens and queen breeding is too important to be left up to a handful of mass producers.

In reality, we are all queen producers. Some of us are inadvertent producers via swarms and supersedure. I choose to be more intentional in my efforts as I seek to become more sustainable.

And just as a kind of "addendum" to this chapter on queens, several surveys have been taken on hive mortality and the reasons why colonies die. The results were somewhat surprising.

The list fares out in this order:

1. Poor queens

2. Starvation and nutritional issues

3. Varroa and the accompanying virus

4. CCD

5. Pesticides

6. Unfavorable weather

When this list became public knowledge, I was shocked. I thought CCD would top the list and pesticides would be second. But knowing the top reason colonies failed fell on poor queens motivated me to take my queen rearing opportunities seriously.

The hand that rocks the queen cell is the hand that rules the apiary. I have a factor within my control toward my sustainability.

And I have to drive home the point that poor queens are not the <u>real</u> problem but rather a symptom of a greater problem, which may very likely be the residues and residual chemicals in wax comb or environmental toxins playing havoc with my epigenetics.

I continue to remind myself that sustainable beekeeping is not about treating the symptoms but fixing the root causes with long-term solutions to the problems. Still, a question that desperately needs an answer is, "Why are we experiencing such poor queens?" What is the real problem?

The queen is the heart of the colony. If you want to take a large step toward sustainability, find those queens that work <u>for</u> you, work <u>with</u> you, and succeed in your neck of the woods. Work with a local beekeeper who will sell you locally-adapted queens if you choose not to raise your own. Do not underestimate the value of a good queen. She can make or break a hive's productivity and longevity.

Brother Adam of Buckfast Abbey thought the best queens were those raised in the summer of one year, and allowed to overwinter into the subsequent year. It was the subsequent year when they would be most productive.

Underlying Brother Adam's conclusion is a key to sustainability: keeping young queens at the helm of our production colonies.

Chapter 6

Frames and Foundation - The Womb of Sustainability

If the queen is the heart of the colony, then the comb is the womb. Or the pantry. Or both! It's in this precious and costly structure the bees raise their family and store their food. In a sustainable model, I think more respect is due to our frames, foundation and drawn comb.

Protecting Drawn Comb

Let's start from the back end, the protection of drawn comb. Somewhere in our beekeeping history, or maybe from our apicultural lore, someone came up with the idea that it takes eight pounds of honey to produce one pound of wax.

We have no verifiable confirmation, anywhere, that this statement is true. Perhaps someone guessed and we've told ourselves this story so long we all believe it. I can't say for sure if it is true, but on the other hand, neither can I argue against it. What I can tell you is bees have a high metabolic investment in their drawn comb. It takes time and energy to draw out wax, so staying with the convention, let's assume it is true.

I sell my honey, on average, for around $4 per pound, give or take size and quantity of the containers. Accepting the formula as truth, eight pounds of honey makes a pound of wax worth $32, and yet I sell my clarified, melted beeswax for $8 per pound. That's simply bad economics.

It would be better for me if I worked harder at protecting my frames of drawn comb, and when extracting, go easy on cutting away the cappings before I put the frames in the extractor. But some beekeepers are prone to say, "Why worry? The bees can just draw out that comb again, right?"

Yes, conceivably, you could force your colonies to draw out all new frames every year, but is that a sustainable practice? I don't think so. Yet it baffles me to no end why beekeepers do not protect their drawn comb once it comes off the hive. Seemingly smart beekeepers follow foolish and lazy practices and they allow the wax moths to needlessly destroy a lot of the bees' time, energy and work.

The late George Imirie used to say in his "pink pages" that drawn comb was the beekeeper's greatest asset, and yet he observed, in so many beekeepers, a carefree spirit when it came to appreciating and protecting this asset. He could not see the wanton neglect, even downright abuse of drawn comb and was not bashful in sharing his opinion.

Protecting combs is easy, but it seems when beekeepers get lazy, wax moths find their way in and destroy a lot of the bees' hard work. The simplest, and most cost effective method of protecting frames of drawn comb is to freeze the comb for 24 hours which will kill all the bugs, eggs, larvae, whatever. If you can keep them frozen until you are ready to thaw them and put them on the hive, so much the better.

Otherwise, thaw them to room temperature and place the comb in plastic trash bags in a protected area free from moths and mice like a basement. Garages might work if the plastic bag is sealed, and if you live in an area where it gets cold and stays cold. Many of the large, home-improvement stores (i.e., Lowes, Home Depot, Menards) sell giant trash bags for construction debris. These bags are large enough to hold a short stack of supers and still have room to seal the top.

I might also add you need a supportive spouse and a freezer with enough room to freeze your supers. A basic chest freezer will only handle about six to eight supers at a time if there is nothing else in the freezer. Unfortunately, we use our freezer at our house for food...imagine that!

If you run a little larger operation, there is a biological control in which you spray each frame with a solution of Bacillus thuringiensis (Bt) of the strain "aizawai" sold under the commercial name of Xenteri. While it is NOT licensed or labeled for beekeepers, it works on wax moths. The larvae begin to chew on your frames and get the biological agent in their intestines and they die.

Since this strain is specific to certain larvae, it does not affect the honey bees in any way that we know. There is no known human concern for it, either. This is an organic, biological control. Garden stores carry a small spray bottle of Certan which will do the same thing. Likewise, it is not currently labeled for use on honey bee comb as the registration for this use ran out, and since no one was making any money on this product there was no motivation to keep the registration current.

This method is quite labor intensive, but I've used it with great results. I simply pull my frames from the hive bodies and lay them out on my concrete driveway, edge to edge, like a quilt. Using a common, 2-gallon garden sprayer which I dedicated to this purpose of spraying Bt, I spray the frames with a fine mist until they appeared to be substantially "sweaty." Then I carefully flip the frames (gently, so I would not rattle or shake off the solution) and spray the other side. The frames are lightly handled and placed back in the hive bodies to air dry, then stacked and stored.

The solution is pretty thin. It only takes three teaspoons per gallon of warm water and I can cover about a dozen to fifteen supers/hive bodies with those two gallons.

If you get quite large and don't have the time or labor to spray your entire set of frames/comb, there are chemical means of protecting comb. It's very easy and quite effective and uses a very specific kind of moth crystal, sometimes sold as moth balls. If you choose this route, please read the fine print on the label and **do not** use the moth balls made from naphthalene. These moth crystals or moth balls are available from any hardware or discount department store.

Choose the moth crystals made from paradichlorobenzene, sometimes abbreviated as PDB. These PDB crystals are legally registered for protecting drawn comb in storage (never use in the bee hive). There is a huge difference between PDB and the naphthalene products, and often they are packaged in similar containers. Read the label.

Those who use PDB typically stack three or four brood boxes and insert an empty super. Across the top bars, lay a sheet of newspaper and deposit a small pile of PDB, then stack three or four more brood boxes and repeat the process. The PDB acts like a fumigant to kill eggs and larvae that may still be lurking in these hive bodies.

In the spring, you'll find the moth crystals have evaporated but you'll need to set the supers or hive bodies out in the sunshine to "air out" for a few days before using. It always seems a residual smell lingers. And you have to realize, if you can smell the faint odor of moth crystals, it must certainly have an effect on the bees and their desire to live in a hive with that lovely aroma.

One last thought, PDB is a known carcinogen and one might consider if this is a viable option.

You can always simply store your supers in a criss-cross pattern, alternating the boxes so light can penetrate (moths hate light). Many beekeepers have done this telling me it works. It has never worked for me and I usually end up quietly complaining, under my breath, about those other beekeepers who recommend it. Maybe they criss-cross their supers in their freezer...and that's why it works.

I also use black-light, electric bug-zappers inside my honey house, in a far, darkened corner. Moths frequently fly into my honey house where I store my supers and hive bodies thinking they are going to find plenty to eat. Then they are diverted from my hive bodies by this alluring light and zap!

There is one more way to deter moths. I take a plastic milk carton and fill it with water about 1/4 full. I add a 1/2 cup of sugar, a 1/2 cup of apple cider vinegar and a banana peel from one, nicely ripe banana. Putting the cap on the milk jug, I shake it until all seems dissolved. Then I cut some holes above the fluid line.

The mixture will ferment and attract moths and hornets. I hang a couple of these from tree limbs in my bee yards. Not sure if they really protect my hives, but they soon fill up with moths and other insects. When the summer ends, I usually just put the jug in the trash and bid them farewell. The fermented goop gets pretty nasty.

So more than anything else, let me state without reservation, "Protect your drawn comb." The bees put a lot of work into it. Honor their work. When wax moths destroy your comb, it's a mess to clean up. Don't spend your own time and energy cleaning up frames and replacing foundation because the wax moths got into it, or rather, that you didn't do anything and basically invited the wax moths to come in. Sustainable practices honor what the bees have done.

Choices of Foundation

Which brings me to my next subject as long as we're on the topic of frames: Choosing foundation. Basically, you have three choices when it comes to foundation, which is our language for that sheet of embossed material which the bees use to create the comb.

One choice is wired or unwired wax foundation. The second choice is plastic foundation, which may come as plastic sheets to snap into wood frames or it may come as an all-in-one, molded, plastic frame and foundation. The third choice is to go to a foundationless frame and allow the bees to build the cell size of their own choosing, kind of like the top bar hives or Warre hives.

Let's start first with the wired or unwired wax foundation available from almost all of the major supply houses. Many options abound as there are several options with wooden frames. I highly encourage you to use the wired foundation which is supported vertically with crimped wires, then I'm going to strongly suggest you buy the tinned wire and wire the frames horizontally. Some beekeepers use high-tensile monofilament fishing line.

Do something to support the foundation horizontally, even if you have no plans to extract these frames. The wires, both vertical and horizontal, will keep your wax foundation from sagging from plain, old-fashioned gravity. Sometimes the wax will warp in the summer heat and lean over to one side. Then you have a mess on your hands as the bees draw out one side really deep and the other saggy side really shallow.

One of the drawbacks to wax foundation is the contamination issue. Since the large commercial beekeepers supply the wax to the wax mills, testing has revealed residues of all the major miticides, including some which are not legally registered, as well as residues of PDB from the control of wax moths.

If you want to purchase commercially prepared wax foundation, contamination is an issue you cannot avoid. Still, many of us continue to buy this contaminated foundation to use in our hives as if it were no big deal. More and more, I think it's a big deal.

The second option, which is my favorite, is plastic foundation. These are stiff sheets of molded plastic with the outline of the hexagonal structure embossed on the frames. As I said earlier, you can buy the one-piece frame/foundation or buy sheets of foundation that snap into the wood frames. I use both and love both.

This foundation option usually comes with a thin, almost microscopic layer of wax sprayed on from the factory. It is often hard to even detect as it is nearly invisible. So I go ahead and melt my own bees wax in a crock pot on "high." Using a simple, 4" foam paint roller available at any paint department, I "paint" on a visible layer of wax.

This wax becomes the beginning resource the bees will use to start constructing the drawn comb. They will chew up whatever I paint on and use it to draw out the foundation. Without this added wax, bees tend to be a little reluctant to draw out the plastic, even downright balky.

Further, it takes a strong colony and a strong nectar flow to successfully draw out plastic foundation. If you place a frame of undrawn, plastic foundation between two frames of open brood, those nurse bees will draw out that plastic foundation without so much as a whisper of complaint.

I hesitate to recommend plastic to a beginner, especially if the beginner is starting the hives with packages. It takes some experience to manage plastic foundation, yet for some unknown reason, many of the beekeeping suppliers sell beginner's kits with plastic foundation. In my opinion, that's a recipe for disaster and frustration, a precursor likely contributing to the 80% of beginners who quit keeping bees.

If there was a drawback to plastic foundation, the plastic is supposed to be giving off some fumes, a process people call, "out gassing." I have no idea if this is accurate as I have no knowledge of injection-molded plastic. I have no idea if this is a problem to the bees or an urban legend by people who do not trust plastic in any shape or form, for any function. I have no idea how long it takes to finish the process of "out gassing" if it ever ceases, at all.

It has also been suggested that plastic foundation interferes with communication because it doesn't "vibrate" like wax foundation. There have been discussion about thermoregulation and how plastic interrupts this vital process. And there are those who say, "Plastic just isn't natural."

I've heard many arguments against plastic, mostly on the honey bees' reluctance to draw it out, but it seems to work for me when I add the extra coating of melted wax from my own cappings. In the essence of sustainability, I can simply scrape off the old comb or wax moth damage, recoat if necessary, and reuse the plastic foundation over again. Plastic foundation is moth-proof, resistant to mice and can be reused. I'm a big fan of plastic foundation.

There is a third option and that's to use foundationless frames. This option is gaining traction and I like it, as well. A foundationless frame is a wooden frame, usually, but not always, wired to give the comb support. In place of the sheet of foundation, some kind of guide is required. "Popsicle" sticks are commonly glued into the top bar to give the bees a straight line. Often times beekeepers feel the need to add some kind of wax coating, but it isn't necessary.

Any hobby store or craft department will carry these sticks and market them as "craft" sticks. They come in the size for popsicles and a size for tongue depressors (which is the size I prefer). Maybe if you have a good check up at the dentist he'll give you a box of them instead of that pack of sugar-free gum.

The bees will draw out their own foundation, as they would in nature, using the popsicle sticks as a guide...mostly. If you put ten foundationless frames in a hive body, the bees frequently migrate horizontally from one frame to another and you lose the benefit of your moveable frames without tearing up their work.

You also need to have your hives level or the bees will draw out the comb like a plumb line and migrate vertically. In reality, you should have your hives level, anyway. This just goes without saying.

But here is the main benefit of this option: the bees chose the size of the cell they desire. They do not follow the prescribed embossed cell size the manufacturer forces the bees to adapt because there is no mandated size or pattern. Bees are free to choose.

You may notice different sized cells chosen by the bees, and it may concern you just how much drone comb is built. Foundationless frames allow the bees to choose, and generally drone comb is not built unless the hive is strong and feels the need to produce drones. Don't obsess about what the bees do; you've given them the choice. Follow their lead.

The "natural" sized cell is the selling point for top bar hives and Warre hives, and you can see how you can capture that same benefit in a Langstroth hive. What I really like about foundationless frames is the cost I don't have to incur buying a sheet of wax or plastic foundation.

The beekeepers who like to practice natural methods or treatment-free beekeeping like the idea of foundationless frames, and as a conventional, Langstroth beekeeper, foundationless frames are my concession to a more natural approach to my conventional management.

However, to best draw out a foundationless frame, stick it between two frames of brood. The bees will jump on that frame and draw it out as straight as an arrow. Screen bottom boards impede the foundationless frames from being drawn all the way down to the bottom bar. But this isn't much of a concern to worry about.

Again, I am drawn to concede foundationless frames give the bees the opportunity to do what they do best. I have to accept their methods and not worry excessively about their failure to fulfill my expectations on what I think ought to happen. If you place two foundationless frames together, side by side, you may end up with the migration of the drawn comb across the two frames.

Foundationless frames often illicit a discussion regarding small cell foundation. The small cell, usually running 4.9mm as opposed to the 5.4mm in conventional foundation, has perceived benefits, typically surrounding varroa mite control. Theories abound, but a study at the University of Georgia concluded small cell did not have a benefit for the bees or the beekeeper. Still, some people will swear that this smaller cell is their secret to sustainable beekeeping.

One of the on-going theories is that small cells have no room for the varroa mite to develop. It's easy to see how one might draw this conclusion, especially when we're told drone cells, which are larger, are more attractive to the mature female varroa mite which is looking for a cell to start her family.

It's not the size of the cell that matters, it's the length of the pupation that attracts the female varroa mite to the drone cell. Worker bees take twenty-one days from egg to emergence. Drones take twenty-four days. Those three extra days allow the female varroa mite to lay one or two more eggs, which then accounts for more mites when the drone emerges from his pupa stage.

Somehow, those maternal mites are attracted to the drone larvae as somehow they know there is a longer pupation, giving them a greater opportunity to raise more mites. How the mites know this biological schedule simply boggles my puny little mind. Nature holds a million mysteries.

Part of the lure of small cell is the nostalgic urge to return to the days in which honey bees were smaller before human meddling started breeding larger bees, typically thought to create larger honey crops. I don't necessarily buy this line of reasoning, just like I don't buy the presumed opinion that heirloom crops are superior in taste to today's disease-resistant hybrids.

But that's my opinion, and it's another argument for another manuscript. I also don't think that anything from the "good old days" is necessarily better than what we can create today, nor do I think keeping bees like our previous generations did prior to varroa mites is going to work, either. Varroa changed everything. Chemicals in our environment has also messed everything up. If I really want to raise bees like my great-grandfather, I'm going to have to build a time-machine.

Further, if you want to go the route of small cell honey bees, the hives have to be "regressed" from 5.4mm to 5.1mm to 4.9mm, which then means you need extra equipment and micro-manage the process. I may be talking about sour grapes, but as I tried small cell foundation, the bees reworked the sheets of foundation into the size they wanted including a lot of drone comb. I gave up forcing my bees to regress and adapt to small cell foundation. I let them be bees and draw out what they deem best.

Foundationless frames give the bees the option to draw out the size they prefer. And if you measure the cell sizes on a foundationless comb, you'll find the bees draw out several different sizes of cells on the same frame, both "large" cells and "small" cells, which leaves me wondering if forcing the bees into "large" cells is about as bad as forcing them into "small" cells. I'd like more answers concerning small cells.

In the spirit of sustainable beekeeping practices, I like foundationless frames in the brood nest. I highly prefer plastic foundation with added wax in the honey supers, and more and more, I am incorporating a queen excluder to make managing my brood nest and honey harvest easier.

Foundationless frames don't extract worth a hoot, unless you are going to the "crush and strain" method, which in my opinion is not sustainable. Foundationless frames give me the advantage in the brood nest. Plastic foundation in the honey supers, having little to do with the choice of cell size in the brood nest, withstand my extractor's centrifugal force. I have the best of both worlds.

One last topic: frame rotation. It has become a standard practice among many beekeepers to pull out 20% to 30% of their brood frames in an attempt to reduce diseases and the effects of residual accumulations of chemicals. Even foundationless frames become contaminated, even in a treatment-free regime.

The bees are flying brooms and sweep our polluted environment. Our plants are sprayed and even the pollen they bring home contains a lot of chemical residues. These residues accumulate in the wax comb, the wax acting like a sponge. To pull out two or three frames from every brood box every year is becoming a standard practice.

While I'm not enthusiastic about pulling out some of those frames of older, though fully functional, dark comb, I do recognize the beauty of allowing the bees to work with a new frame. I don't like buying more foundation, especially if the foundation I buy from the supplier has a habit of harboring residues of miticides and other chemicals.

I allow the bees the opportunity to draw out a couple of foundationless frames at no out of pocket cost to me as I recycle my refurbished wooden frames. While I sense this rejuvenates the colony, I still count the metabolic investment the bees make in this new wax.

My game plan for sustainable beekeeping, as it pertains to frames and foundation, is to, first, utilize foundationless frames for my brood nest and rotate two or three frames out of each hive body every year.

Actually, when I rotate these old, black frames out, I use them as "bait" in my swarm traps, marking them so I can cut out the comb and reuse the frame at a later date. Foundationless frames give the bees the opportunity to draw out the cell sizes of their own choosing, and I've promised myself not to freak out when I seem to notice what I think is a disproportional amount of drone comb.

Second, I want to use plastic foundation for my honey supers for their resiliency in my extractor. I don't like frames blowing out wasting all the bees' hard work, which then creates more work for me. Plastic frames can be scraped and reused, if necessary. More and more, I'm using queen excluders later in the season so my honey supers do not have quite so much brood raised in them. I know several beekeepers who want 100% broodless honey supers. This is not a priority for me.

Third, I will take great pains to protect the drawn comb and the metabolic investment it represents, regardless of how many pounds of honey it takes to make one pound of wax. Given the size of my operation, I lean toward the Xenteri, but the labor to apply this product tries my patience. It's very labor intensive, but I like the biological control over the chemical treatment.

Sustainable practices are about profitability. Profitability is not just about money, but about time and energy, for me and my bees. When I allow wax moths and mice to destroy the bees' work, I've lost time and energy to clean them up. I've wasted the honey the bees need to consume to draw out the wax. If I'm replacing bad comb with wax foundation, I've got the cost of the foundation and the labor to install it...and the suspected residues.

My advice for sustainable beekeeping is to value that drawn comb, protect it and replace it when it gets old and nasty. Move more and more foundationless frames into your brood nest.

Chapter 7

Knowledge

"Knowledge is power."

That helpful advice was given to me when I was trying to make an important decision. The more information and knowledge I had at my disposal, the better (supposedly) the outcome of my choice.

Another key to sustainable beekeeping, that is, figuring out how to stay in the game and keep on keeping bees, is knowledge. There is no margin for anyone's lack of knowledge in beekeeping. With the Internet, free long distance on our cell phones, the instant communication that comes with e-mail, there is no excuse for failing to find answers to your questions. Knowledge is power.

I love that old expression that says, "If you think an education is expensive, try ignorance." Beekeeping is no exception.

Knowledge informs management, and management is the key to successful, even creative, sustainable beekeeping.

My definition of management when it comes to keeping bees is this: Management is the decisions I make, based on my goals, working with the limits and availability of the resources at hand with the circumstances I find myself in, in order to reach a desired outcome or result.

To break it down more simply, "management" is

decisions....

based on goals...

working with resources and circumstances...

to reach a desired result or outcome

Management is my responsibility and it depends upon my intentions and actions, my intuitions and best guess-timates, whether by commission or omission, on purpose or by mistake.

But good management is informed management. Ignorance is no excuse. This means I'm reading, researching, attending seminars, talking to other beekeepers, listening to them complain about their problems, calculating how to avoid the same problems, giving thanks I don't have their problems.

Sustainable beekeeping cultivates an awareness of the environment and how the bees are responding. It's walking circumspectly, with a respect for the lessons of the past and a vision for the future, while keeping the events of the present in front of our perception.

It's like that poem by Elizabeth Baring Browning,

> *"Earth's crammed with heaven,*
> *And every common bush afire with God:*
> *But only he who sees, takes off his shoes,*
> *The rest sit round it, and pluck blackberries...*

There are so many opportunities around us, but either we fail to notice or we don't know what to notice, and so we sit around plucking apicultural blackberries believing everything is just fine and dandy. But sustainable beekeeping necessitates knowledge.

Knowledge commands an awareness of what's going on, both inside and outside the hive. Anybody can raise bees by being told what to do and when to do it. But great beekeepers develop an attentiveness to what the bees are doing, what is happening and why, how the hive functions, what to expect as the weeks roll from one season to the next and how they adapt their management practices.

It's like cooking. Anybody can bake a cake, but prize-winning chefs understand the complementary nature, albeit the "chemistry" of food, how it harmonizes with corresponding dishes, how certain foods are paired with others, balancing the layers of flavor with the artisanal aspects of this culinary art. In cooking, presentation is everything.

Beekeeping and the culinary arts require knowledge, the understanding and awareness of what's happening and why. It's so much more than peeling the cover from the foil pan I pull from the freezer and baking at 350 degrees for forty minutes. It's so much more than having some bees in a box and letting them "do their thing."

I took a phone call from a woman who just purchased two bee hives. She was so excited and said, "I always wanted to have some bees."

The seller, a beekeeper who was moving closer to his grown children, delivered the hives to the woman that morning. She called me, first identifying herself as one of my honey customers, and, picking my phone number off my jar of honey she bought, she asked me for some advice. "What do I need to know about keeping bees?"

I almost laughed out loud. Where do I start? And what can I tell her over the phone that she would understand? I gave her the standard answer to read everything she can find, search the Internet, join a local association, make some friends, then find a mentor. If she was closer, I offered to be her mentor, but she was about fifty miles away. I told her she was welcome to call, better to e-mail me, at any time.

Her response was unexpected, "I have so much to learn. Maybe I'll just leave them alone and they can figure things out on their own. I'm just not ready for this."

Okay. You're not ready. But this doesn't explain why you decided to buy the hives, but, oh well. The bees will definitely figure things out, but I think this woman is in store for a crash-course education.

Without a doubt, bees can survive very well on their own, to a certain degree. They've survived without human intervention and interruption for millions of years without the aid of white, rectangular boxes with screen bottom boards. Ever see a screen bottom in a bee tree? And bees have been dying for millions of years without our intervention.

There is a notion that natural beekeeping is letting the bees do what they do best without our interference. The idea is based on the irony of bees dying in commercial beehives due to the chemical regime most commercial beekeepers depend on to keep their hives alive. The counter argument is based on the idea, that if not treated, the bees would die. But commercial beekeepers continue to lose hives despite using chemical treatments.

Some people believe the answer is a more natural approach of raising bees without chemicals and without our interference, hoping the bees will figure things out, and they will.

In a nutshell, this kind of management is a benign neglect. We toss our management (decisions based on goals, etc.) and knowledge (an awareness of what's happening) out the window and proclaim how intervention is not necessary, and likely an impediment to the bees and their ability to work out their own problems.

But the "let-alone" method is not without hive mortality, either. This "natural" approach to treatment-free, "let them swarm as nature intended," and "don't rob so much honey you have to feed them" approach to beekeeping is not without problems. Bees die under this management as well.

At the risk of sounding like I'm trying to promote a "natural" versus "chemical," and "us" versus "them," I don't think either side has the silver bullet solution to our present state of affairs. The answer is somewhere in the middle with a sensible intervention and a common sense approach to meeting the needs of the bees, when those needs arise (i.e. IPM). Underlying this answer is knowledge.

We can't live in the extremes of prophylactic applications of synthetic chemicals at one end, nor the ignorant neglect at the other end. I continue to gravitate to the notion of "balance." Can I have my cake and eat it too, or in this case, can I have my honey and healthy bees? Can I intervene, provide sound and informed management and keep my bees happy and productive?

If I were to speak on the two most important aspects of management and how a beekeeper might intervene to benefit the colony, I'd have to address the issues of mite infestation and sufficient winter stores. These are my two areas of concern and when I mess up or procrastinate, the mites or starvation usually are the reasons for my hives dying.

And quite frankly, sometimes I'm so stinking busy with other areas of my life I just cannot find enough time in the day to take care of <u>what</u> needs to be done <u>when</u> it needs to be done. Sometimes the demands of "life" just get in my way of keeping bees. There is no doubt in my mind that I want to become a better beekeeper, and I need to be a better, more organized, more efficient and informed beekeeper. But life happens, so I muddle along to the best of my abilities.

At one of the many conferences I attend in the course of a year, I was deeply touched by one speaker who advocated intervention, almost a scheduled maintenance which I understood as knowledgeable, informed management.

The speaker challenged us by saying, "If you want to keep bees alive and you have to resort to chemical intervention to keep them alive, then go ahead and resort to chemical intervention. In most cases, if you don't do something to combat the mites, they will take down your hive. If you don't want to do what it takes to keep bees alive, then don't keep bees if all you are going to do is kill them or let them die."

Ouch!

Those are harsh words. Yet underlying the speaker's presumptions is the solid understanding that management makes a difference. Actually, *knowledgeable* management is what makes the real difference.

And this is not to say this speaker was advocating the indiscriminate or prophylactic dumping of synthetic chemicals or kitchen sink concoctions into the hive. Knowledgeable management bases decisions on a principle called, "Integrated Pest Management," or IPM for short. It means a knowledgeable beekeeper utilizes the tools available and uses resources in an intelligent manner. There is no room for ignorance.

Despite the benefits and advantages of informed and knowledgeable management, many new beekeepers continue to believe the "let alone" method is superior and more "natural."

The leading question becomes, "Is it then unnatural to intervene and save my bees?" That is, if there was something I could do to increase the likelihood that my bees will survive rather than perish, would I not intervene?

The analogy I draw compares intervention in my hives with our human health. If my children got sick, would I not take them to a doctor? If I came down with an infection, would I not take the prescribed antibiotics? If my dogs were infested with worms or fleas, would I not do something to alleviate their discomfort?

While I'm normally and personally averse to taking unnecessary medications, I want to intervene and address the cause of the problem and not just medicate the symptoms. Why would I see any benefit to simply "toughing it out" if beneficial medication could alleviate my health issues?

Also, I prefer healthy, proactive activities such as good nutrition, adequate exercise and rest rather than finding my comfort in a bottle of pills. In terms of human health, and hive health, prevention is easier than the cure. But you have to know how to prevent those problems (knowledge, again).

Some days the information required to keep bees almost pushes me over the edge. There's a lot to learn and even more to remember. And knowledge alone isn't worth anything unless you are prepared to act upon the knowledge.

I was conversing with a beekeeper and we were talking about getting an early start on the season to prevent swarming. We both wanted honey crops and recognized how swarming diminished that potential. The weather was still a little cool and both of us were hesitant to work our bees and run the risk of chilling our brood.

I went to the long range forecast for the weather which showed a warming trend with nicer temperatures predicted for the next week to ten days. I decided I would go ahead and manipulate my hives and exercise my management objectives to prevent the potential for swarming.

The other beekeeper was more reluctant, irrespective of what the weather service predicted. "I'm more afraid I'm going to make a mistake if I work my bees at this point," was his lament. He chose to do nothing. That was his choice, and management begins with our decisions.

From my perspective, he decision just sounded like excessive caution, at best, and at worst, it appeared to be sheer laziness on his part. A few weeks later, still having done nothing despite a favorable turn in the weather, he complained how his bees "suddenly swarmed," and how he would have, if only he could have, done something about it, but he was now "too busy."

Okay. Sure.

Sometimes in beekeeping, as in life, we have to make some educated guesses, take some calculated risks, take a step of faith, create some new opportunities...but nothing says we have to do so blindly, ignorantly or without some research. Beekeeping is changing every year and sustainable beekeeping warrants our diligence to stay on top of new developments. This is what I call, "knowledge."

In the last couple of years, formic acid treatments have been reformulated from the Mite-Away II pads to the Mite Away Quick Strips or MAQS. The chemical, amitraz, has been released and approved as it is marketed as ApiVar strips. Hardly anyone uses, or should be using, Apistan or CheckMite+ with the resistance and residue issues...except those who have not been reading about the resistance and residue issues.

I see a lot of well-intentioned beginners focusing on treatment-free beekeeping and eschewing any chemical or artificial intervention, even opting for the "more natural" hive designs...and I presume you remember how you can achieve these same "natural" qualities with foundationless frames.

When the natural beekeepers proclaim the advantages of these new-found applications, I often wonder where they acquired their information. It sounds to me as if they went to a seminar, listened to a speaker evangelize about how this new method is the wave of the future to save the bees. Given the problems with chemical applications, I can see how this alternative becomes attractive.

These new beginners become zealous converts and enthusiastically share their wonderment as to why I continue to poison my bees and imprison them in those white boxes.

The irony is they have no idea what kind of protocols I utilize to combat mites. Keeping bees in white boxes does not require synthetic miticides, but they feel compelled, if not obligated, to let me know where I have strayed from the path of enlightened beekeeping. Where do they get this information?

At the other end of the spectrum is a host of old time beekeepers who continue to dump into their hives all kinds of kitchen sink recipes and odd ball concoctions from eucalyptus cough drops to diesel fuel. I personally know of several older beekeepers who continue to use non-registered, illegal and unapproved chemicals because "this is the way we learned to do it and we're still keeping bees."

Ignorance is powerful, and those who only know enough information to be dangerous are, well, dangerous. Another case in point is when I took a person out to look at some of my bees. He expressed an interest in starting up in beekeeping and wanted to get a first-hand look at what I did.

When we drove into the first bee yard, he was critical of my hive placement. I had the hives in full sun. It was a hot and humid, summer day. He thought it would be better if I put the hives back into the trees and under the shade.

I explained how hives in full sun had fewer varroa mites and fewer small hive beetles. He had no idea what either of those pests were and kept suggesting to me it was too hot for those bees to be in full sun. I pointed to a cattle pond about a hundred yards away and told him how the bees collect water and bring it back to the hive for evaporative cooling. He just shook his head and muttered how he couldn't understand why I'd leave the hives in the full sun.

Personally, I would like to put the hives in the shade, but shade only benefits the beekeeper. Some late afternoon shade might be helpful, but with a screen bottom board, there is nothing wrong with bee hives set in full sun...unless you have no clue. Knowledge is not only powerful, it's essential and valuable.

I met some vendors at the farmers market who wanted bees on their organic produce farm. I thought since this farm was managed organically, the bees would be spared from unnecessary sprays and pesticides. The farmers were fairly informed and knew all about the pollination benefits of bees. It sounded like a good deal for both of us.

I brought four hives out to their farm, and before I unloaded the hives, we had to set up a hive stand. I suggested we move about a hundred yards down the fence line, beyond the garden to a strip of shrubby trees. No, the farmer protested, he wanted the hives right next to the garden. I winced and said that would not be a good idea as the bees will be protective, and wary of anyone picking vegetables. Additionally, any tractors or tillers would only aggravate the bees.

No, the farmer insisted, the spot he had picked out was right by the main gate, right next to the middle of the garden. Bear in mind, this was probably a three acre garden with plenty of locations away from the main gate.

I finally gave in and we put the hives right where he wanted them. About a month to six weeks later, he called and said we had to move the hives. The bees were stinging his pickers. I thought how his pickers were probably hot and sweaty in our lovely, sweltering, Missouri summer weather. They probably smelled pretty funky to the bees, and if these pickers were working anywhere close to the hives, they made easy targets.

In addition, knowledgeable beekeepers know that as a hive become larger and more populous, the bees become more aggressive and defensive. What starts out as a nuc as gentle as a puppy often grows into a raging junkyard dog.

What really irritated me was how the farmer made the situation out to be _my_ fault as _my_ bees were the problem, not his insistence upon where we placed the hives. I also tried to explain how I can't simply move the bees to the spot I originally intended as the bees will fly back to the location of his choosing by the main gate.

If I moved the hives, those bees have nowhere to return and rather ironically, cannot just fly around until they find the relocated hives. This is the old axiom of, "Move a hive two feet or two miles." I had to bring new hives out and put them in the new location and then take the old hives back to a different apiary. Eventually, we found ourselves on the same page.

This same situation happens with a lot of beginners who insist on putting their hives in their backyard, not too far from the swing set where the children play and where the grass is mowed every week. Or they put them back by the fence close to where the neighbor has to mow his grass every week.

Bees will fly up to two miles to forage (not sure who decided this or measured it, but it's one of those things we believe...probably because we told ourselves over and over and now it's the gospel truth). If you were to draw a circle with a radius of two miles you are going to cover slightly over 8,000 acres.

You can set hives up anywhere, trusting the bees to find what's in bloom. That's what they do best. You do not have to set them up right on top of the garden or right next to the apple tree you hope to pollinate during that two-week window in the spring.

Knowledge is power. Things are changing every year, but there are many things that don't change. Sustainable beekeeping stays on top of the new developments and does not ignorantly throw out the things that have worked for generations of beekeeping. Every beekeeper, whether conventional or natural, owes it to themselves and to their bees, to be a knowledgeable, informed beekeeper.

There is no room for fools, especially in these challenging times.

Knowledge impacts my planning. Planning promotes success, which is measured by the honey I produce. Planning prevents problems, like the hive that swarms and lands on the neighbor's mail box. Planning produces results, which for me is raising my own queens and getting my hives through another winter.

Thankfully, bees are very responsive to sound management. The bees will be your ultimate report card, the measure of your knowledge. If they prosper, you did well. If not, even if you claim, "I did everything the book told me to do," the bees are the final arbitrator of your claim. There is no curve and the bees will give you the grade you deserve.

Remember, as well, two beekeepers can use two widely and wildly different management practices and both may experience success. There are many ways to manage honey bees and both of these beekeepers can be "right." The bees will let you know where you stand despite your claims of enlightenment.

When I fail to keep my knowledge current and fail to maintain a well-informed management, I will fail to identify problems which could easily be remedied. I'll likely draw false assumptions about needing a queen when it might be the beleaguered support staff ready to crash from a burgeoning mite load.

As an uninformed beekeeper, I might fall into the false assumption that if I can't see any problems (because I don't know what to look for or how to discern them) then I have every right to believe I don't have those problems.

And what do they say about "Denial is not just a river in Egypt?" The misapplication and abuse of miticides and the potential for residues comes from plain ignorance, as do the problems of failing to provide for good nutrition and adequate feed during the winter.

Worst of all, without knowledge, I will probably slip into the "blame game," blaming southern queen producers, the weather, pesticides, nearby beekeepers, sun spots, cell phones, global warming, CCD, giant agricultural corporations, pesticides (again), Chinese imports, GMOs, wax moths, skunks, mites, pesticides (obviously a favorite)...anyone but me and my ignorant management.

We have a quirky way of addressing hive mortality when we suspect a person is not as diligent as they should be managing their bees. When we conclude it's not Colony Collapse Disorder, or CCD that took down their hive, we often suspect "PPB" which stands for "Pretty Poor Beekeeping," or something close to it.

PPB is about a lack of motivation to do what needs to be done when it needs to be done, but it also can mean a lack of knowledge. There's just no room in these challenging times for ignorance.

Knowledge is power, and I need all the power I can find just to keep on keeping bees. Anything less fails to serve me, and my bees. I owe it to myself and my bees to stay informed.

Chapter 8

Swarm Prevention, Control and Management

It was said of President Calvin Coolidge, also known as "Silent Cal," that he was a man of few words and little elaboration.

One Sunday morning he went to church by himself, and upon his return to the White House, his wife inquired, "What was the preacher's sermon about today?"

Calvin's succinct response was, "Sin."

"Oh, really?" his wife responded. "What did he have to say about sin?"

"He was against it."

When it comes to swarming, I am against it. I am the Calvin Coolidge of beekeeping, a man of few words and little elaboration when it comes to swarming. I am against it.

I spent a good deal of time on swarming in Chapter 5, but I want to devote more detail to this nemesis of mine. If you didn't get the memo back in chapter 5, I do not want my hives to swarm and I will work to keep my hives from swarming.

Technically, I don't want to work against the bees, but rather work with them and redirect their energies. They are programmed to build up rapidly in the spring, making more bees, then swarm, making more colonies.

I want to help them make more bees, and keep on making more bees until the nectar flow starts. Once the nectar starts flowing, the swarming urge subsides and they make honey. If they swarm, the honey crop is greatly reduced.

Why Not Let Them Swarm?

The natural beekeeping camp likes to encourage and allow swarming, which is the natural instinct of the honey bee colony, kind of like an insurance policy, to reproduce the species in a given area.

Basically, there is nothing wrong with letting the colony swarm, if that fits your purpose for keeping bees, but I have neighbors, and I'm looking to harvest honey.

Most conventional beekeepers, even those who maintain honey bees as a hobby in their back yard, do not want their bees to swarm. My neighbors across the fence in the back yard to not like to see my colonies swarm. My wife does not want the neighbors complaining to other neighbors about my bees swarming and how the neighbor felt threatened and chose to keep their children out of their own back yard until I removed those bees. This is not good apicultural diplomacy.

In New York city, urban beekeepers are on the rise, but the increased prevalence of swarms disrupting normal city life have city officials wondering if urban beekeeping is such a good idea. Swarming is but one problem which usually leads to municipalities banning beekeeping within city limits. It's a problem we're bringing on ourselves, a problem which can be prevented with knowledgeable management.

Swarming and Potential Honey Crops

Most conventional beekeepers are looking to harvest honey. As I am one of these conventional beekeepers, when I see a swarm fly away, I envision a super of honey taking wing and heading off to the trees. In my opinion, with my purpose for keeping bees, I will work to prevent a colony from exercising that swarming impulse.

Oddly, some of the "prime" swarms I have trapped or retrieved have been monstrously aggressive in their pursuit to draw out comb and make honey. When I've caught swarms from my own hives (after watching them rest in a tree while I get the forty-foot ladder) I notice these bees will outperform the hive from which they came, and this should not be surprising. The remnant colony from which the swarm came from, has to regroup, suffer the injury of successive "after" swarms, regroup, again, and settle a virgin queen to start rebuilding the population.

Once a colony swarms and the prime swarm leaves, before the after swarms start issuing, my advice is to either divide up the remnant colony into nucs, with one frame containing at least one queen cell, or cut out all but one queen cell and let the colony carry on.

By leaving only one queen cell, you won't have the attrition of multiple after swarms wearing down the hive. You may still produce a modest honey crop if enough time remains. In southeast Missouri, our nectar flow is early, then done by the 4th of July. Remnant colonies, even if you cut all but one swarm cell, just don't have the work force to make any honey.

It's always a dilemma when I find a swarmed colony. Swarm cells are considered to be good queens, so if a colony has swarmed, and I concede I've lost the honey potential, the colony is still valuable and it has given me three or four frames with queen cells on them. I consider them a gift and make nucs. In the long run, the nucs may be more valuable than trying to coax a honey crop from the remnant hive.

If you are not familiar with the jargon, when a colony initially swarms with the old, established queen, we call this the "prime" swarm. Just prior to her departure, the colony will start making multiple queen cells for her successors. Sometimes we call them swarm cells, but they contain the queen.

Once these successor queen cells are capped, the established queen leaves with this prime swarm. A prime swarm takes a good portion of the population from the colony, hence, the population of foragers, the work force, is depleted resulting in a diminished honey harvest.

A few days later, the first virgin queen to hatch will take a portion of the remaining bees with her and we call this event an "after" swarm. An after swarm will typically be smaller than the prime swarm, but in heavily populated colonies, it may still be quite sizable.

Since multiple queen cells have been produced, it is not uncommon for a colony to send out multiple after swarms, each taking a portion of the portion of the bees that remain from the previous after swarm. Resulting after swarms can be quite small, even too small to establish themselves and survive.

It is possible that the colony continues to cast off several after swarms, diminishing and weakening the hive. Somehow, the last virgin to emerge knows she's the last queen. She does not swarm off into the trees, but rather stays and eventually goes out on her mating flight. Hopefully she returns, settles down and resumes the egg laying duties and the cycle of life moves on.

Then this colony begins the rebuilding process of getting ready for the winter months. Bear in mind, not all virgins find their way back to the colony from their mating flight, and the colony is basically done for.

It is thought, though with unmarked queens it's really hard to determine such, that a prime swarm with an experienced queen will settle down and establish their new home, then before too much time passes, they will begin plans to supersede the queen with a new replacement.

But in my opinion, this would have to take into consideration how old that queen was and if she was past her prime. Some colonies, like the ones I've observed in known feral locations, cast off a prime swarm every year, thus that swarm queen is but a year old.

Annual swarming, does, however, give rise to the idea of annual requeening and keeping a young, vibrant queen in the colony as a "natural" management practice. Young queens will inhibit the swarming impulse, but let's not kid anyone. If your colony is congested, it's going to swarm.

I make a habit of marking my queens, and any queen that originates in a swarm has their own special color, different than the colors I use to mark the queens I raise. I let the swarm settle in the hive I provide for them, then after a week to ten days I go in and mark the queen.

There's quite a bit of debate as whether beekeepers are able to discern a virgin from an old queen, but I don't waste much time worrying about it. If the queen is old, the bees know to replace her. If I open the hive after a couple of months, I may find the supersedure cells or I may find an unmarked queen. Somewhere I have to trust the bees to gauge the quality of that queen and take the next steps to replace her.

There is also some debate among beekeepers on allowing these "mutts" to remain in the hive. Some beekeepers love to hive the swarm, then make immediate plans to purchase a mail-order queen of known pedigree to requeen the colony.

I'm not sure such actions are warranted. I've hived a lot of swarms. I like feral stock and feral colonies in southeast Missouri exhibit a wide variety of genetic diversity. Somewhere along the way, I have to relinquish my desire to micro-manage every part of the hive and let the bees work things out. They are, after all, a bit smarter than me, and they've been working on perfecting their system longer than I've been keeping bees.

Swarming is written into the DNA of the honey bee. It's a reproductive act of the original colony to send out little honey bee families to start new colonies in the vicinity. Survival of these after swarms is not known, though Tom Seeley has done a tremendous amount of work in the northeast portion of the country.

Quite frankly, all colonies, whether in a hollow tree or a stack of white boxes, whether established or a new swarm, are subject to detrimental forces that challenge its survival. As I stated earlier, bees die, whether in white boxes or in nature. It's a challenging time to keep bees.

Any Benefits to Swarming?

Is there any good that can be claimed from this act of swarming? Well, being purely altruistic, you might contend allowing your hive to swarm repopulates the area and establishes feral (unmanaged) colonies. And there are some beekeepers who simply enjoy keeping bees and letting them follow their bliss. Still, there is no guarantee of survival of either the swarm of the remnant colony, but it seems bees are willing to play the odds.

If my colonies swarm, I do get a brand new queen for free! Well, if you measure a lost super of honey, a quantity I'll guess is about ten quarts, you have an opportunity cost. Getting a "free" queen costs me about $120 in lost production when I sell my quarts for $12 each. That's not exactly a free queen, but I do end up with a queen...provided she can make it back successfully from her mating flight.

Swarming also creates a brood break, a disruption in the reproductive cycle of the colony in which a period of time with no eggs translates into a period of time with no pupated larvae which then culminates in an interruption in the reproductive cycle of the varroa mite.

This is one powerful benefit of swarming. But the brood break also diminishes the foragers down the road which diminishes the nectar collection which diminishes the harvestable honey. This reality dims my enthusiasm for swarming.

There is another benefit in allowing your bees to swarm, provided you can catch that prime swarm. Prime swarms, as I mentioned earlier, are geared up to get down to business. I've caught prime swarms and they produced a super or two of honey. But the key is catching them. This is why I am very enthusiastic about setting out swarm traps around my apiaries, and why I'll set out traps in areas likely to attract swarms, including the locations where I received swarm calls in previous seasons.

I've got a great resource for retrieving swarms, **"Free Bees"** (www.createspace.com/4107714), and the follow up resource to trapping the swarms I can't reach called, **"Keeping Honey Bees and Swarm Trapping"** (www.createspace.com/4106626).

Swarms do not usually fly more than a mile from the originating hive, so I'll set out swarm traps in the areas where swarms are likely to look for potential housing options.

Putting up a swarm trap in my apiaries won't work, but in that 3/4 to 1 mile radius around my apiaries works if I can't prevent the colonies from swarming. Obviously, preventing swarming is the better option.

Be Prepared for Swarming

Retrieving swarms when someone knows to call you is exciting and a very enjoyable aspect of keeping bees. But the real productivity of catching swarms happens when you set out the pheromone-baited swarm traps. There are many swarms that no one sees and the second resource I offer takes the variables out of catching swarms.

But I will also charge you with this caveat: do you have the extra equipment necessary to catch those swarms? It bugs the fire out of me when someone calls, desperate for some bee boxes (and frames with wired foundation, including a top and a bottom...screen bottom preferred, and not too junky and not painted any other color but white) to catch a swarm that just lit out from one of their colonies.

If this is such a big deal to you, first, work to prevent swarming. Do not let your colony swarm, and second, if you really want to catch that swarm, be prepared with the requisite equipment, and have it ready to go.

Suppose your colony swarms and the swarm cluster is fairly close by. Let's pretend you do not have the extra boxes ready to go. You don't want to lose the swarm, but you're stuck...or are you?

At worst, I'll tell you to open up the colony that swarmed and destroy all but one queen cell. Then, take the swarm cluster that just left and shake the swarm back into the colony using a queen excluder to catch the old queen. You can move her to a nuc with some bees or squish her.

You'll end up with a fully populated colony, a new queen on the way, a future brood break and a full potential for a honey crop...and an extra nuc if you keep the old queen.

Now we're pumping up the sustainable model! With the brood break, more nurse bees graduate to foraging duties and this will benefit your honey crop.

When I suggest this last option to unprepared beekeepers who have no extra boxes, they shrug and say, "Well, maybe I don't really want that swarm. I'll just let nature take her course," which usually also includes failing to cut out the pending swarm cells because they heard one time that queenless colonies tend to be a little more aggressive and defensive and they don't think this is a good time to open the hive.

Oh, well. We all have different reasons for keeping bees.

A local beekeeper with two hives called me, all in a lather about this really nice swarm that came out of one of his hives. He wanted to catch it but didn't have any extra equipment. He found my name on the Internet, so he called me wondering if I could bring a box out and help him settle the swarm.

He gave me some directions and I typed his address into my cell phone. My phone said I was twenty-three minutes away. There wasn't much time to lose.

I'm a nice guy, so I dropped what I was doing and assembled a brood box with ten frames of plastic foundation, adding a top and a bottom. This arrangement was sufficient to easily hive the swarm and get it established. The swarm can always be transferred to other equipment later, which is the irony of this story.

Now bear in mind, I have a shed full of used boxes, many of them of painted with different colors of mis-tint or "oops" paint, some with rotting corners big enough to let mice through, some with holes drilled in the front for an upper entrance.

I'm not real picky when it comes to keeping bees in worn out boxes. I'm not known as the "Martha Stewart" of apiculture. On that particular day, I didn't really think much about my box selection. I was more concerned about grabbing the quickest box as catching swarms is a time-sensitive event. You never know when a swarm is going to take off.

As an aside, having spent a good portion of my life, "a day late and a dollar short," I NEVER turn down the opportunity to acquire used equipment at a fair price. Some of my equipment, well, okay, the *majority* of my equipment is really just high-grade kindling, but it works for me and it works for my bees. I'm also a hoarder when it comes to finding sources of used or scrap lumber I can make into boxes and hive bodies. My motto is, "Never despise the day of used lumber!"

I set my hive to catch the swarm in the back of my pick up truck and took off to help this beekeeper hive his swarm. When I arrived at his farm, the swarm was about ten feet high on the branch of a maple tree. He had already found his step ladder and it was in place. I brought the hive body over to the ladder and set it on the ground.

Out of the corner of my eye, I caught him looking at my box with a disapproving glare. He pulled a frame out, noticed the plastic foundation which I lovingly applied extra melted beeswax to make it easier on the bees. He asked, "Don't you have any of that Duragilt?"

Duragilt is a unique kind of foundation produced and sold by Dadant of Hamilton, Illinois. It has several labor-saving features. It's not one of my choices as I prefer plastic or even natural-sized comb drawn on foundationless frames. Still, some of the more traditional beekeepers prefer Duragilt.

"And don't you have a better box than that?" he added.

The irony was I was going to give him the box. If nothing else, he could use it temporarily until he ordered some new equipment, then transferred the frames to his new box. I already gave him a slice of my time that day to come out to his farm and now he's looking this gift horse in the mouth.

Though I was starting to get a little steamed on the inside, I smiled and said, "You don't want this box?"

"Well, I'd like something better, I mean, even a white box would be nice. And I'm not crazy about those screen bottom boards."

I politely nodded and said, "Well, I can go back and see if I have a better box. It will take me a little time. You're sure you don't want this one."

"No, not really, I mean, it's, it's, well, it's nice and all, but I was thinking you'd bring out something that wasn't quite so, so, you know, so rough. No offense, but, I mean..."

I smiled and said, "Okay, so you want me to go back home and see what I can find?"

"If you don't mind, and all," he shrugged.

I nodded my agreement and set the box back into my pick up truck and drove back home. Now I consider myself to be a nice guy, and I'm willing to help just about anyone, but I really like helping those who want to help themselves, especially those who appreciate my generosity of time and effort helping them to help themselves. But this is the kind of beekeeper that tries my patience and breeds my reluctance to remain a nice guy.

I was not yet home when my cell phone rang. It was the call I was expecting, but maybe not quite so soon. "Looks like you don't need to come back out," he said with disappointment in his voice. "The swarm just left. I mean, it just took off. Boy, I sure wish I had kept that box you brought out."

I sighed for affect and said, "Yeah, me too. Maybe next time." After I disconnected the call, I muttered, "That's karma, buddy."

Options With Swarming

You have two options with respect to swarms. You can prevent swarming or you can be prepared to catch the swarms with extra boxes ready to go. If you're not prepared, then you are at someone else's mercy.

You can always take the third option, the altruistic route and claim you're letting your bees swarm to repopulate the natural colonies in the woods. You can pat yourself on the back and tell everyone you're letting the bees be the bees. Try telling that to your neighbor who has to keep her kids in the house until the swarm leaves.

As a honey producer, I want to keep the colony intact, harvest my honey down the road, then make splits. It's fine for feral colonies in the wild to swarm. I want to catch those swarms for many reasons. But once I place bees in my managed hives with Langstroth dimensions, once I successfully bring them through a Missouri winter, I want to redirect the colony's energies from colony reproduction to honey production.

I also want to make my own replacement nucs, which in essence, can be perceived as "artificial" swarms. But before I can make splits and nucs, which I will share in my next chapters, I have to manage the swarm impulse in my colonies. I cannot split a colony that has swarmed. A swarm is the split that flew away into the trees. It's the split I let get away because my management was sloppy.

Some beekeepers like to argue that honey bees were meant to swarm. It's in their DNA. You can't prevent a colony from swarming, no matter what. Bees were meant to swarm and you are wasting your time trying to dissuade them from fulfilling their purpose.

Some beekeepers will even tell you they really tried to keep the bees from swarming and the bees still swarmed. "Preventing swarms is a lost cause," many conclude.

Okay, if that's the way you feel. I'll smile and quietly disagree.

Do Bees Always Swarm?

There were two times I witnessed a dramatic reduction in swarming in my hives and in the calls I received for retrieving and trapping feral swarms. I did nothing to alter the bees from their natural instincts. Nature changed their course of direction. Both of these incidents shed light on dispelling the notion that swarming is the absolute direction every colony takes every year.

The first swarmless incident was in 2005, one of the years I went to Jamaica to do some missionary work. While I was away, the week after Easter, Missouri received a hard freeze late into the growing season. This was not merely a killing frost, but a hard freeze in the first part of April. Every plant in bloom or preparing to bloom froze back. I'm not talking about a little frost bite or a little damage. This was a solid freeze. The plants sustained tissue damage on new growth and many of them lost all their leaves, to say nothing about flowers and developing fruit.

It took two or three weeks for the plants to recover and generate new foliage, but the flower buds were gone, and so was the seasonal harvest from the fruit trees. Gardeners replanted, but it would be weeks before any plant would bloom. Basically, there was no nectar for some time as the plants recovered. Many perennial plants would not bloom at all that summer.

One of the key components of swarming is an influx of nectar. In the absence of nectar, colonies will not swarm. In 2005, my swarm traps went wanting and my phone remained silent as I was hoping for swarms to fill my winter dead outs and vacancies. We eventually had a nectar flow and a honey crop from late season blooms, but it was a weird year.

The second time I witnessed a dramatic reduction in the incidents of swarming was the spring of 2012 when we experienced an unusually early spring that followed an exceptionally mild winter. We were several weeks ahead of schedule and suddenly everything burst into bloom and the bees moved right into the nectar flow. It's like they gave up any idea of swarming.

Again, my swarm traps remained vacant and the phone didn't bother to ring as the swarming impulse was redirected naturally by the bees. Rather than swarm, they moved right into collecting nectar and making honey.

What I observed that spring reinforced the idea that if a beekeeper can entertain his colonies to redirect their energies until the main nectar flow commences, once that flow starts, the swarming impulse will abate and fade away.

Some of my beekeeping colleagues note how they can successfully forestall the inevitable swarming impulse and keep their colony going and growing to produce a nice crop of honey. Since they mark their queens and note a different color for a different year, they can tell me they how they have kept some queens for three or four years. I prefer young queens.

A young queen, with a vibrant queen substance, is like social glue that holds the colony intact and moderates the swarm impulse. I favor a young queen in my hives and I work to keep swarming at a minimum.

Meanwhile, back in the natural beekeeping camp, I am criticized for arresting a natural impulse, as if it frustrates the bees (maybe it does, but I'm the one who is frustrated when they do swarm). The natural camp believes a colony wants to swarm, and beekeepers ought to allow their colonies to swarm. The rationale is the swarming event "freshens" the hive, arguing the point that colonies need swarming to maintain colony health and survive.

I can't argue that logic. I've already cited two benefits of a new queen and the subsequent brood break, but you also let a bunch of bees fly away with a potential honey crop.

When it comes to allowing a colony to swarm, as a management choice, I will, however, choose to disagree. I am against swarming. I have a different purpose in my beekeeping enterprise. I manage a colony to make honey as I seek to work with the honey bee's ability and inclination to fill up the supers with incoming nectar. If swarming is antithetical to a honey harvest, then I am going to manage my hives to resist the urge to swarm.

In managing a colony to resist the swarming urge, I am going for swarm prevention, and if that doesn't work, then I shift to swarm control. I redirect the colony's energies to make more bees not more colonies.

What Causes Swarming?

A brief understanding of what kicks off swarming. First, swarming doesn't just happen. I have heard from many of my beekeeping buddies that the bees were looking good and suddenly, without any kind of warning, the colony swarmed. These buddies claim they never saw it coming.

Really? When my colonies swarm it's because I am not managing them properly to account for the rapid spring build up that precedes the nectar flow. If I don't give my bees extra room, even just an additional super before they need it, I will have problems with swarming.

Promoting early spring build up is kind of a paradox. When we do a good job of managing our colonies in the spring, the punishment for our good management is a swarm. Colonies expect to build up. It's what they want to do. Then we come along and try and prevent swarming, which is something they do not want to do. The key is to work with the bees and redirect their energies, not work against them and frustrate their natural urges.

Swarm prevention is proactive. It anticipates the colony's needs even before they know they need it. The simplest way to prevent swarming is to super your hives before you think it is necessary, and super your hives with drawn comb.

And we've had that discussion about preserving drawn comb, so don't complain to me how you don't have any left from last year.

Swarming is a result of a "state of congestion." Congestion is not the same as crowding. A crowded hive is just a bunch of bees occupying the same space. It's an issue of density, and in the early spring when the bees are trying to keep the brood area covered up and warm, a crowded brood area is a good thing.

But imagine a bee hive, either in a hollow tree or in a couple of deep brood boxes. The weather warms up and the nectar flows. The bees joyfully start bringing in load after load of nectar. The cell space starts filling up with this dilute liquid.

At the same time, the presence of nectar and pollen encourages the queen to lay even more eggs. Remember the gestation period for a developing larva/pupa is three weeks. So the queen starts filling up the cells with eggs and those developing larvae will tie up that cell for twenty-one days. The foragers bring in more nectar, while the queen lays more eggs.

Somewhere there comes a time when all the comb is filled with developing bees and with dilute nectar. A worker bee and the queen bee find themselves staring at each other across the last open cell. Everything around them is full, waiting for the brood to hatch out and free up another cell. But instead, the finite and limited cell spaces are all full, all but the last cell.

Imagine how a worker bee and the queen approach this last vacant cell in the colony. "Back off, your majesty," the worker respectfully intones. "We need this cell for nectar."

"Not on your short little life," growls the queen. "I'm going to lay another egg in that cell. We need more foragers for the honey crop."

The worker responds, "So why don't you just quit laying so many eggs and let us put nectar in that cell?"

"Me?" responds the queen, "why don't you quit bringing in so much nectar and leave this cell to me?"

It looks like the old, Mexican stand-off. Then the worker drops the ultimatum through steely, squinted eyes, "Looks like this hive just ain't big enough for the two of us."

So the queen looks right back at the worker and say, "Fine. If that's the way you see it, I'm out of here. And I'm going to take a good portion of all my friends with me, and we'll go find some other place to make our home."

The worker defensively adds, "Well, they'd better stop filling your mandibles with all that bee bread. You can't possibly fly in the shape you're in. You'll need to go on a diet or you won't be able to fly past the hive stand. But go. We'll raise a new queen more to our liking. Don't let the entrance guard hit you on the abdomen on the way out."

Well, it goes something like that. I can't say, with any degree of certainty, that I've witnessed such a confrontation, but somewhere there will be a shortage of cells for more incoming nectar and the queen's increasing rate of laying eggs. This is a state of congestion.

Congestion is when the struggle for open cell space becomes so aggressive and so competitive that both the workers and the queen are frustrated. Something has to give and it's usually the queen. She'll leave with a prime swarm.

But if you, the beekeeper, intervenes and gives the colony more room, such as adding a super of drawn comb before the congestion reaches a crisis level, you can thwart this swarming impulse. The queen will keep on laying and the foragers will keep on foraging. But be prepared, because on a good day, they may fill up that super with incoming nectar. Be prepared to add additional supers.

There is a common belief among the old beekeepers that feeding syrup in the spring (which acts like a stimulant to get the colony going before the actual nectar starts to flow) will cause swarming.

Feeding, alone, doesn't cause swarming, but feeding is like a sudden nectar flow and the bees will take the syrup and store it away in the cells. Now you have reduced the available cell space, and yes, this will lead to congestion. You stimulate the queen to lay more eggs and you provide syrup that fills up more cells. This is going to cause a problem, and the way the colony alleviates the problem is to swarm.

George Imirie, who I mentioned in the previous chapter on frames and foundation, speaks very highly and stridently about doing three things to alleviate congestion, and hence, retard the swarming impulse.

First, he says, in the spring time, remove all the frames of solid, capped honey. Second, replace these frames with frames of drawn comb. Then third, start feeding a little light syrup in the ratio of 1:1, that is, one part sugar to one part water, the consistency of natural nectar.

"WHAT?" you incredulously exclaim, all in capital letters. "Why should I take away the honey? Isn't that what the bees need to eat? And why would I take it away and feed syrup? That's not natural."

Okay, take a deep breath. Relax. Here's his logic. Honey is a winter food for survival. Nectar is a spring food for raising larvae. Feeding 1:1 stimulates the queen. If the queen increases her production she needs lots of open cells. Frames of solid honey are as useful as a brick wall.

If the weather is fickle, the colony will benefit from 1:1 light syrup, even a 1:2 thin syrup which is one part sugar to two parts water. Both of these syrups are very close in consistency and chemistry to natural nectar. Both of these syrups stimulate brood rearing. The colony will not have much use for honey, though if pressed, they will find water and dilute the stored honey and feed it to larvae, if they have to.

If you prefer not to pull those frames of honey, be sure and add another brood box, providing more frames of open cells, or reverse the brood boxes, and if it's not too cold, slide an empty frame or two into the middle of the brood nest. Add another brood box with drawn comb, and again, if it's not too cold for fear of chilling the brood, pull a frame or two from the brood nest and add it to the new box, replacing those frames with drawn comb. This little exercise expands the brood nest, sometimes modifying the ideals of checkerboarding.

The ideal is to keep providing more frames of open cells. So how does this happen in my apiaries?

Here's how it works for me. First, I like to overwinter my hives in two brood boxes, or a brood box and a medium super. Some beekeepers call this second configuration, "a story and a half."

Second, I hate swarming and I hate what swarming does to my honey production. Having experimented with a modified checkerboarding system of swarm control, ala Walt Wright, I expand the brood nest by adding an additional brood box of drawn comb, typically on top of the existing brood box or medium super. This will make my hives three boxes tall, either a brood-medium-brood configuration or three brood boxes.

By adding another brood box of drawn comb, I am, in essence, providing what the bees will perceive as an action of reversing the hive bodies. I like to do this in mid to late April, about three weeks prior to the main nectar flow. But use common sense. Every year is different and you can't go by the calendar like a recipe or a prescription. Hold off it's too cold or a cold snap is coming. You don't want to risk chilling the brood.

If I find a band of honey along the tops of the frames in that upper second box, I want to pull a few of those frames and replace them with open comb. Otherwise, that band of honey constrains the queen. It acts like a road block and keeps her in the second box which limits the effectiveness of expanding the brood nest with the additional box. I want the queen to move up and lay eggs in that top box, but she just doesn't like moving past the band of honey.

As I work with deep brood boxes and mediums, I am not averse, at this point in my swarm prevention, to using multiple medium supers. Still, at some point along the way, usually when I try and get everything supered up, I'm going to rearrange the boxes so I have two brood boxes on the bottom under a queen excluder, and my supers above the excluder. I may pull a neglected brood box off the bottom of the stack and move it up.

There's a little bit of art to these manipulations. It's not necessarily an exact science. It's one of those things you learn to do "by feel." Later on, as I discuss in subsequent chapters, I'm going to want to make a split or two, and I much prefer to make my splits with brood frames.

So somewhere along the way, I'm going to want to insert a queen excluder to age any brood in the medium supers above and keep the queen laying eggs in the deep hive bodies below.

So when I'm adding boxes and supers to expand my brood nest and while I'm checkerboarding, I'm always thinking ahead to the honey flow. I really, really prefer to extract medium and shallow supers and not brood boxes (brood boxes, or deeps weigh around ninety pounds when filled with honey...and I'm not getting any younger).

The purpose of the queen laying eggs in the top box works me toward two purposes. First, I am alleviating the swarming impulse by avoiding congestion and competition for cell space between the incoming nectar and the queen's desire to lay more eggs.

Second, I am setting up the hive to make a potential split. My main priority is to get my hives into the nectar flow intact, without swarming. I want fully populated colonies. If I can prevent the swarming impulse from kicking in, I'm in very, very good shape. Then after the nectar flow gets under way, I can think about making some splits.

About the first of June, any eggs laid will not contribute to my nectar flow and it's a good time to make a split. If that egg takes three weeks to hatch, and a worker serves in the capacity as a nurse bee for three weeks, by the time it graduates to a field bee, we're now at six weeks our about mid-July. The flow is over.

So I shoot for June 1st to make a split, which, as you might guess, is not the way the majority of traditional beekeepers work, but I continue to modify my schedule to become more sustainable, not conventional.

One thing I think I've been saying along the way, without directing saying it, is this: Sustainable beekeeping is not about doing what most beekeepers do or have done. The common ways of doing things are not working like they used to. I'm looking for that new path of unconventional methods that lead to sustainability rather than conformity.

So in that second week of May, right as the blackberries bloom, we experience a normal cool spell the locals call, "blackberry winter." The temperatures drop and we fuss about the remote possibilities of frost in low lying areas. It's like spring has one last gasp before the hot and humid temperatures hit our area and we experience the full fury of a Missouri summer.

It is in this cool spell I set up my hives with additional supers for employing my concentrated, intensive management practices for honey production, usually just adding the supers on top, at this point. Once the weather warms, this is when I search for the queen, insert a queen excluder, and set my hive for the honey flow and a potential split.

I have to remember my purpose for keeping bees is honey production. I also want to make some splits and raise some queens. Which is what I'll attend to after the nectar flow starts in and my hives are secure and unswarmed.

Sustainable beekeeping is about priorities. My main priority is honey production, and it starts with preventing swarms. My ideals of swarm prevention are not to frustrate the colony or weaken the colony through splitting, but rather to redirect their natural impulses and energies to raise more bees, not establish more colonies.

I have experienced a wonderful success with these methods, and I'm heartened by a quote attributed to C. C. Miller. He said,

> *"If I were to meet a man perfect in the entire science and art of beekeeping, and were allowed from him answers to just one question, I would ask for the best and easiest way to prevent swarming."*

Preventing swarming is a high priority. Space does not allow me the luxury of moving into swarm control, which is the next step when you procrastinate and allow the swarming impulse to move out of the realm of prevention and you are forced now into the mode of controlling the swarm.

Some day I'm going to write a lengthier book dedicated to swarming reduction through prevention and control. It's quite a topic all by itself.

Sustainable beekeeping is also about being profitable. My operation focuses on honey production as its centerpiece. If I allow swarming to occur, I'm giving away my profits and a large portion of my income.

There are several other methods of swarm prevention. What I've presented works for me. You're more than welcome to do what works for you, but the principle we share is the desire to redirect the colony' energies to making more bees, not swarming and making more colonies.

To sum up what I've accomplished in this chapter, I've taken a colony and expanded it, giving the foragers more space to store nectar, and giving the queen more space to lay eggs. I'm setting the colony up to raise lots of bees, priming the pump to produce a sizeable honey crop, and setting the stage to make a nuc or two down the road.

Chapter 9

Mite Suppression

"Perfection is not attainable. But if we chase perfection, we catch excellence." -- Vince Lombardi

I was given some some advice on public speaking by one of those, "old school"-type speakers. She said, "You always want to tell a joke to gain their interest and grab their attention."

However, I found, when I stand up to speak, I have their interest. I don't need to gain it. I have their attention. Most of them are waiting for me to share my thoughts.

So I'm not here to tell a joke; I'm here to pick a fight. I'm going to pick a fight with one of the most insidious pests all beekeepers face, the varroa mite. And I'm not going to talk about wiping out or annihilating varroa. The measures to do so are too extreme and create too much collateral damage in the hive. Killing hordes of varroa is possible, but it comes with a cost, and thanks to the research of Randy Oliver, we don't have to kill all those stupid mites, but just have to suppress them to livable levels. We need to trust the bees to do what they can and should do, without inflicting sub-lethal damage upon them.

So my fight isn't to wipe them out, rather, I'm going to give them a good poke in the eye with a sharp stick. I'm going to whack them across the nose with a rolled up newspaper. I'm going to make them put a bar of soap in their mouth until tears roll down their eyes, then I'm going to put them in a time-out.

The good news is, sharp sticks, newspaper, bars of soap and a time-out are, "all natural."

Still Public Enemy #1

When it comes to the number one problem with keeping bees alive (and keeping beekeepers keeping bees) I would have to say, in one word, "mites."

Tracheal mites used to be a problem, but it seems much of our varroa protocols have worked successfully on the tracheal mites. Tracheal mites have not built up the resistance like the varroa mites. If you are a treatment-free beekeeper, chances are you may be looking at a tracheal mite infestation, but unless you have a 14x microscope and the precision of a surgeon, they are difficult to detect. You just don't read much any more about tracheal mites killing bees.

But not so with varroa mites. Now days, anytime you generally or generically mention the word, "mites," it is presumed you are specifically talking about varroa mites. In the United States, varroa mites are a problem because they suck the bee's hemolymph (body fluid in the bee, not exactly "blood" but a close equivalent). Further, these mites vector viruses and pathogens, causing diseases that inflict a lot of damage to our bees.

Imagine, just for fun, if you had an external parasite the size of a grapefruit, acting like a giant wood tick, hanging on the outside of your body. How could you function? What if it was in an embarrassing location?

What if, if there was some medication to rid yourself of this tick, that once it killed the parasite, you were left with a hole in your skin the size of a half-dollar? What if this wound never healed up, but acted as an entrance for viruses and bacteria? What if it continued to hemorrhage so you could never apply a bandage?

This, "what if," exercise gives you a good idea of what a varroa mite means to a honey bee. In comparison to our bodies, the varroa mite to a honey bee is like a grapefruit-sized wood tick to us.

What if I told you that we have uniquely patented medications to kill most of these parasites that cling to your body, but because 15% of these parasites have developed resistance to that medication, we have to find something better, something stronger, something that may produce more irritation in you (read, side effects) as we try and rid your body of these parasites? What if this medication got rid of the tick but gave you a permanent upset stomach? Or itchy ear lobs? Or it made the soles of your feet so sore you couldn't walk but a few feet before resting? Sounds like the cure might be worse than the problem!

Just for fun, not that it would be fun, suppose our treatment for these parasites was to douse your body in undiluted bleach. Yuck. While it does not pose any direct health problem, not that all that bleach is good for us, we would survive. It would not be pleasant, but we'd survive.

But bleach only wipes out 85% of those parasites. The 15% that survive, now multiply, impervious to household bleach, even though we start bathing in bleach. Someone now discovers that a bottle of liquid drain opener, like Drano®, does a pretty good job on these resistant mites, but holy cow! That stuff is corrosive. It will burn your skin!

Yes, but it really takes care of those mites, right? So we issue protocols suggesting that after dousing your body in Drano®, killing most of the mites, you immediately douse your body in vinegar to offset the corrosive properties of the Drano®. But if you have any open wounds, like from the dead parasites, the vinegar is going to sting. We then have to dust you in baking soda to offset the acidity of the vinegar.

And what if 15% of those mites resistant to household bleach also develop resistant to the liquid drain opener? What's next?

This, "what if," exercise gives you a good idea of what we are accomplishing in our chemical mite treatments. With synthetic miticides we are basically killing 85% of the mites with each treatment, but leaving 15% to multiply.

These 15% of the original population have developed a resistance to this treatment. So we dose our hives until this first chemical doesn't work any more, then we work to strengthen the dosage or find the next, best chemical treatment.

But then we've got those pesky side effects, the sub-lethal consequences that make the honey bee a little queasy, but not deathly sick, and thankfully, not dead. You can bet with stronger chemicals, the sublethal consequences will be even more severe. I wonder how the bees feel when we put this poison in the hive, if they experience a little bit of a setback until they become accustomed to the ill effects of this foreign substance.

I also wonder, though these legal poisons are "safe" and "approved," how they affect a honey bee. Suppose a bee is battling a virus. Will the stress of the added miticide push the bee over the edge? What are the unintended side effects? In my opinion, I just don't see synthetic chemicals as the sustainable option if they promote stronger and stronger mites.

So the mite populations build up and we dose the hive with the next chemical, killing 85% of those mites...leaving 15% which are resistant to our second chemical in our thin arsenal of chemical applications. We run with the killing of 85% until we find it doesn't work any more, than we search, hoping to find the next "best" treatment, which I will almost guarantee is the next "worst" treatment.

Remember, we're trying to kill a bug on a bug without killing both bugs! But are we not breeding a mite with better resistance to whatever we throw at it? Are we not on a "chemical treadmill" ratcheting up the speed and angle, faster and steeper as we try and dominate this mite? Is it not to our advantage to get off the treadmill and find a better way to defeat the mites?

I think the answer to all these questions is, without question, "yes."

As I may have mentioned in an earlier chapter, many of the registered, synthetic chemical treatments are lipophilic, that is they are attracted to fats, such as beeswax, where they take up residence. Residues are a concern of mine. How does the longer-term build up of these residues affect the bees and brood raised in these combs?

Then I wonder how much of this chemical residue migrates into my honey, something I don't really want to know. What are the side effects when a consumer eats this honey? What is my legal and moral obligation to the consumer who buys my honey if I'm treating my hives with synthetic chemicals?

I find myself at this crux of the matter: I need to keep my bees alive and I need to do something to keep the mites at bay. I also acknowledge the fact that even "safe" or legally registered chemicals take their toll, albeit sub-lethal, on my bees and I would prefer to find something which is really safe, and if I dare use the words, "more natural." Perhaps the better description is "less chemical."

I also don't like the idea of having to purchase my treatments or spend inordinate amounts of money finding treatments. So how do I go about keeping my mites under control?

First Principle

The first principle I picked up from Randy Oliver, an exceptional beekeeper in California. Randy generously shares his insights at on a web site at www.scientificbeekeeping.com.

Randy advocates periodical treatments to suppress the mites. He is more than adamant that beekeepers should never allow their mite populations to exceed 2% of the bee population. His idea is to keep mite populations low with several treatments.

He does not believe one should allow the mite populations to reach excessive levels before treating, which is what happens when a beekeeper only treats once per year. He believes in multiple treatments at pre-planned intervals. He does not appear to hold any desire to rid the hives of every single mite, but rather suggests we find a way to knock the populations back to manageable levels, that is, to "suppress" the population.

The concept here is to knock the mite population down, periodically, rather than letting them build up to dangerous levels which require some pretty powerful pesticides.

An Example of Suppression

Think of things this way. Suppose the mites have the potential to reproduce at a rate of 100% every week. Week one, the population of mites sits at 100, at the end of week two the population is 200 mites (a 100% increase). After week three it is at 400 mites (a 100% increase). After week four it is at 800 mites (a 100% increase). After two more months, at the end of the third month, the population would explode to 204,800 mites. Bear in mind, these figures are just to illustrate my point.

Suppose, for example, a powdered sugar dusting has the potential to knock the population back by 50%. So after one month, when the population of mites reaches 800 mites, a dusting drops the population back to 400 mites.

The progression picks up at the rate of 100% and after two more months, the population reaches 102,400 mites by the end of the third month. By suppressing the mites early in the season, the dusting interrupts the reproductive rate and drops the three-month total by 50%.

If a second dusting is applied at the end of the second month, dropping the population back 50%, the population of mites, at the end of the third month sits at 51,200 mites.

Given the only variable is two dustings, one after the first month, the follow-up after the second month, we can conceivably reduce our mite population by 75%

What this crude example shows is that interrupting the reproduction rate, or suppressing the population at intervals in the early part of the growth curve, reduces the mite population later.

Now, here's a problem with this example. I used a linear formula. The mite population does not grow in a straight line, at a constant rate of reproduction. While the example is imperfect, the principle remains the same: disrupt the growth curve in the early stages and the population is smaller down the line.

Conceivably, in theory, we could disrupt the population growth to the point where population at the end of our third month is manageable, and if it fell within Mr. Oliver's 2% threshold, we might not even have to treat for mites. But this means you need to measure your mite load. More on that in a few pages.

An easier way of thinking about curtailing the mite growth is how the population grows by three steps forward and the sugar dusting suppresses it by two steps back. One month later, it's three steps forward, but two steps back with a dusting. Again, not a perfect example, but it illustrates the principle.

With this idea, instead of nine steps forward at the end of three months, we reduce the population to 3 steps (3 -2 = 1) then (1 + 3 - 2 = 2) then (2 + 3 - 2 = 3) a reduction of about 66%.

The figures I used, 100% growth per week and 50% reduction, and three steps forward and two steps back with a dusting were purely arbitrary for the purposes of illustration. The principle shows a partial reduction that disrupts the growth rate. One other fault with my example is sugar dusting only hits the phoretic, or exposed mites. It does nothing to hit the mites safely sealed with the pupae. For this reason, the dustings have to be done early and often.

If there is one thing you gather from all my imperfect illustrations and incorrect, linear reproductive rates, here is what I want you to remember: *do not wait until the end of the season to treat for mites and only treat them with a single application.*

By the end of the season, the mite load is so high, you need strong chemicals and the damage to the bees from virus and pathogens may have already started. Then we have to start thinking about what collateral damage the strong chemicals inflict upon our bees.

Second Principle

The second principle is choosing treatment options which are not harmful to the bees, yet strong enough to suppress the mites. Most of our chemical options inflict some measure of discomfort, and then there are issues of residues in the wax comb.

Many of the so-called "soft" and "natural" treatments vary in their effectiveness, and are generally regarded as safe, or GRAS. But if they are some kind of a fumigant, such as a thymol product or formic acid or any of the essential oil-based applications, they affect the hive's communication process. Do not be surprised when the colony starts to supersede your queen.

The dilemma becomes finding the treatment that fills that gap of being effective yet easy on the bees. This has been a problem finding the magic formula which will be the best of both worlds, effective and safe. Since this magic formula doesn't exist, we have to trade off some effectiveness for safety, or give up some safety for greater effectiveness.

Third Principle

The third principle is my concern about harming my honey crop. What can I apply to the hive that won't migrate and end up in my honey? How can I defeat the mites and protect the integrity of my honey? One simple solution is to read the instructions and only use the treatments in the given time frames or the windows of opportunity/application. But who has time to read the instructions? Apparently only a handful of beekeepers!

One over arching principle is to refrain from making treatments during the time the honey supers are on the hive. Easy enough, unless your nectar flow runs so long that the hives are well into the peak of the mite populations.

For instance, the nectar flow in my northern regions quits about mid-July. This is perfect timing to take off the supers, harvest my honey and treat for mites. Normally, I hit my hives with some kind of treatment in the first part of August, then maybe again in September, depending upon the temperature requirements/restrictions of my treatments.

However, my southern hives, with the longer and later honey flow, won't be harvested until late August, even early September when the mite populations are reaching their peak. Remember how Randy Oliver strives to hit the mites before they reach such damaging levels? This is another challenge to battling these varroa mites.

Use Multiple Agents Against Varroa

One of the keys of sustainable practices is the integration and collaboration of multiple agents. We attack the problems from several angles. The beauty of suppressing the mites is how we do not have to limit ourselves to one weapon. We have multiple options, both natural and soft, and synthetic and chemical.

So what do I do? My first method of sustainable mite suppression is to use the available genetics that are resistant to mites. I like local, feral stock. This stock comes from the feral swarms I catch in my pheromone-baited, swarm traps.

Some people believe in the misperception that "wild" bees are aggressive and defensive, but that's not necessarily the case. In reality, all bees are wild. We have yet to domesticate the bees. Some colonies are managed and some are not, but all bees are technically "wild." Drawing from this feral stock to raise my own queens, I believe that open-mated, locally-adapted queens from these unmanaged feral colonies produces rugged, resistant bees. Much of my analysis is, however, anecdotal.

If I buy mail-order queens, which I do from time to time to interject fresh genetics into my gene pool, I will order queens with hygienic behavior or VSH (varroa sensitive hygiene) traits. While I may lose some of this effectiveness when I raise queens from this stock (hygienic behavior is recessive), I still want to interject a measure of genetic diversity into my breeding stock.

We also live in an age when many queen producers are shifting to treatment-free regimes to produce their queen stock. This does not always mean what works in California, Texas or Georgia is going to work in southeast Missouri, or Minnesota, or Montana, but we've got commercial queen producers thinking the same way we want to keep our bees.

Two other, very simple measures to work against the mite population are screen bottom boards and setting hives in full sun. The screens allow mites to fall from the bees down to the ground, rather than rest on the bottom board where they can reattach themselves to another honey bee. Hives set in full sun do better for a variety of reasons and will have fewer varroa mites and fewer hive beetles. The screen bottom boards allow for better ventilation all year round.

Bear in mind, several university studies have disputed the advantages of screen bottom boards as the sole approach to battling the varroa mites. Additionally, beekeepers are nervous about leaving the bottoms open during the winter months. If nothing else, install a screen bottom board and slide in a "sticky board," usually corrugated plastic "political signs" and smear the surface with petroleum jelly or a deep layer of Crisco®. Mites fall, and when they hit the sticky board they become trapped.

The sticky board will close off the hive from winter drafts, perhaps only in part, and you'll find some solace with this arrangement. I still think screen bottom boards are a good idea, though their effectiveness may be marginal. Still, every little bit helps and it all adds up.

These three things, a) genetically resistant bees, b) screen bottom boards and c) setting hives in full sun, will give you a jump on reducing mite populations, but you'll need more than this.

Powdered Sugar Dusting

My fourth, easy to use, non-chemical approach to mite suppression is powdered sugar dusting. You can run an Internet search for the "Dowda method" for the full details and some variations on this method. You'll want a screen bottom board on your hive so the powdered sugar and mites fall out the bottom of the hive. If you have a solid bottom in your hive, you'll have to add a sticky board or slide a piece of wax paper smeared in Crisco® to catch falling mites and collect the powdered sugar.

Powdered sugar dusting only works on the phoretic mites (that is, the mites exposed in the hive as opposed to the mites hiding in the pupae cells). This process works best in June and will not interfere with the honey crop if your supers are in place, which they are in my apiaries.

Hitting the mites in June, while the populations are low, is an excellent way to keep the mite populations from exploding later. It is, however, somewhat labor intensive and it needs to be repeated. Its effectiveness is also somewhat marginal, but it is one more tool.

I remove the supers to get down to the brood nest. More and more, I'm using queen excluders once I add my supers, and this powdered sugar method works when you dust the brood nest. There is no need to dust the supers. If I want to dust the most bees, I can dust later in the day toward sunset, but be warned: bees get cranky at the end of the day.

I made a 16-1/4" by 20" frame by ripping a 1" rim from an old super. I nailed on first, a 16-1/4" by 20" piece of fine, window screen. To strengthen the window screen, I nailed on a same-sized piece of 8-mesh wire screen. In this order, the frame is upside down.

Flipping it over and setting the rim on the open brood nest (after smoking the bees downward and scraping off any burr comb), I have the screen wire looking up at me, supported by the 8-mesh wire underneath it. I dump one cup of powdered sugar on the screen wire and with a standard bee brush, work the sugar through the wire onto the tops of the frames. This breaks up the clumps of powdered sugar.

Removing the screen wire rim, I brush the powdered sugar from the tops of the frames into the spaces between the frames. Your bees will look like little snow men, uh, snow ladies.

You could, as an alternative, use a flour sifter but many beekeepers report the grinding noise of metal on metal makes the bees hostile. I wouldn't know, and have only used the screen.

The action of the fine sugar granules irritates the bees as they groom and brush themselves off, dislodging the mites in the process. The mites fall downward through the screen bottom board to the dirt below.

Because new bees emerge every day laden with new mites ready to attack your bees, repeat this process in seven days. Repeat it a third time after seven more days. Repeat it again, now for a fourth time after another seven days, which is twenty-one days from the first dusting. Twenty-one days is the total life cycle from egg to adult for the honey bee, and with four dustings covering twenty-one days, you'll catch most of the possible phoretic mites.

Again, hitting on Randy Oliver's notion of not necessarily killing all the mites but rather setting them back at intervals, especially early in the season, you have gone a long ways toward reducing the potential mite population down the road. Your mite load later in the summer is manageable and you do not allow the mite population to grow to damaging levels where your only real option is a strong, synthetic chemical explosion, but in truth, if you let your mite population grow to those higher levels, there is significant, irreversible damage already done to the bees. Your treatment may be too little, too late. Then you'll complain how these chemicals don't work, but the real reason must be laid at the feet of beekeeper management.

Three caveats. First, many people will clamor that powdered sugar contains corn starch, an additive to prevent caking and clumping. The corn starch, when consumed by the bee, binds up the bee's gut, basically constipating the bee. Don't worry. The bees eat very little of this powdered sugar.

If this method was done in the winter and there were no other food options such that the bees were eating the powdered sugar, then this would be a problem. But this is summer, so don't worry about the corn starch.

Second, powdered sugar does not remove all the mites. But the first dusting gets a bunch of the exposed mites. The second dusting catches that first set of mites a second time and hits the second set of mites that emerged from the pupae cells after the first dusting. The third dusting catches the first mites for the third time, the second set of mites the second time...well, you catch my drift. Several beekeepers tell me how they dusted once in September and their hive still died. One dusting won't work, especially in September.

This process takes several attempts, to which many people will say, "Holy Cow! I have to remove the supers and dust, and do it four times?" The answer is, "Yes," as each dusting is not 100% effective and it requires multiple applications.

However, it carries a high degree of total effectiveness when used with something else, and the downside is practically and virtually insignificant...except for the extra labor. A two-pound bag of powdered sugar will do four or five hives at the cost of, maybe, fifty cents a dusting. With four dustings you've invested a couple of bucks with no detrimental consequences.

The most difficult task for me with all my hives is facing that cute little girl at the cash register with my shopping cart loaded with bags of powdered sugar. She usually smiles, then notices the bags and inquiries what I'm going to do with all that sugar.

I usually smile back and lie, "It's grandma's birthday at the nursing home and I've got to make frosting for a million cup cakes."

The little girl smiles back, and giggles, "Tell your grandma, 'happy birthday,' from me." And I get out before someone else wants to know what I'm up to.

No one said sustainable practices were easy. I never said they were lacking an investment in labor. If I ever did say these practices were easy, let me know and I'll apologize. I told you a lie.

But here's the thing to remember: I want to keep on keeping bees. I want to combat these stupid varroa mites. I want intervene with the least amount of poison and I don't want to be bothered with worries of residues and resistance. Sugar dusting in June is a great opportunity to fulfill these three desires.

Third, and this is really persnickety. If I tell you to "feed" your bees powdered sugar by working it through a wire screen, I'm fine. You're fine. The world is fine. But if I tell you to work powdered sugar through a screen to dust for varroa mites, I have turned powdered sugar from a "food" to a "pesticide."

Believe it or not, in a very technical and legalistic sense, powdered sugar is not a legal pesticide, and all pesticides have to be registered and approved by our government.

Seriously.

While it does no harm, while it has no known detriment to our honey bees, I cannot legally tell you to use powdered sugar as an anti-mite treatment in a honey bee hive. And many other treatments, so-called "natural" treatments like patties made of vegetable oil and granulated sugar, have to be addressed as "food" and not "mite treatments." It is the law. Technically, as I promote this method of mite removal using powdered sugar as a miticide, I am breaking the law.

And don't think anyone is going to legalize this process. There is no money for any company to patent this procedure.

So..."feed" your honey bees powdered sugar four times, seven days apart, only over the brood nest in the month of June for long-lasting effects in curtailing...I mean, uh, giving their, uh, well, just "feed" your bees.

While this is done in June, you will still need to do something once your supers come off later in July or even August. Now you are open to some of the other treatment options like formic acid or any of the thymol treatments, which fall under the organic and "soft" regimes.

Still, I am not of the ilk to simply treat for the sake of treating. Formic acid and thymol are fumigants and tend to mess up the honey bee's communication. Both of these treatments will cause the queen to stop laying eggs, and in extreme cases, cause the bees to supersede her. So before I start treating prophylactically, I want to see if I need to treat.

Assessing Your Mite Load

There are many methods of assessing mites, the easiest and least accurate is the sticky board beneath a screen bottom board. I have counted mites and I can tell you strong hives drop more mites than weak colonies. Mites will be a ratio of the population of bees, and if you have more bees you'll have more mites.

I can tell you mite drops will be higher on a sunny day than on a cloudy day, but I'm not sure why. Still, a sticky board will tell you if your hives have mites, but it will not tell you if the infestation is tolerable or not.

The alcohol wash is my favorite over the powdered sugar roll. I don't do the ether roll as that method is about as accurate as the sticky board. You can run an Internet search to find the different variations on the alcohol wash, but here is how I do it. I start with a wide-mouth, pint canning jar. In place of the lid, I cut a circle of 8-mesh wire to fit the ring.

I use two, white, plastic dish tubs, one to catch the bees as I shake them from the frame, the second to dump my alcohol following the wash. I open the hive down to the brood nest and pull out a couple of frames. First, and most important, make sure there is no queen on the frame. Remember what I said about marking queens? A marked queen is easier to find.

I like to shake two frames into my first wash tub. About half the bees will fly up and go back to the hive, about half will roll around the bottom of the tub. After shaking my second frame and replacing each frame to the side of the hive, I use a 1/2 cup measuring cup to scoop up a ball of squirming, rolling bees. Don't fool around as they won't stay in the cup for long.

I quickly dump that 1/2 cup of bees (approximately 300 bees) into my pint canning jar and secure the lid. At this point, I pour enough rubbing alcohol to more than cover all the bees and give the jar a nice swirl. I buy the cheap, 70% isopropyl alcohol from the discount drug store. It works just fine. I set the jar aside and put the hive back together.

Turning back to the jar of bees, don't be surprised if you suddenly see the bees in the alcohol are dead. And don't get all righteous about killing 300 bees. In a small hive of 30,000 bees, this is a small price to sacrifice to assess the mite load that may save the remaining 29,700 bees.

You'll notice in the dish pan where you shook the frames a lot of hive debris and bee poop. This is why I like to use the second dish tub for the alcohol. I dump the alcohol into my clean dish tub, using the 8-mesh wire as a strainer keeping the dead bees in the jar and releasing the mites into the tub.

Pour another cup of alcohol over the dead bees, adding enough alcohol to cover all the bees. I swirl this vigorously and dump that second load in the tub. A second wash isn't always necessary, but it gives me a little more confidence to insure no mite was left behind.

In the white tub, the mites will look like little specks of reddish-brown pepper. My magic number is six. Six mites in 300 bees represents a 2% threshold. Six or fewer mites and I'm comfortable not treating, though I may treat just to be sure. Six to ten mites deems another avenue of control. If you have more than ten mites, you have a problem and it may require more drastic measures of mite control.

I usually pick out the mites and reuse this alcohol. Coffee filters work really good for this filtering. The dead bees are ceremoniously dumped in the grass and I move on to my next hive.

If I were to ask you, "How are your mite levels?" and you can't answer that question, you are shooting in the dark and counting on your lucky rabbit's foot that your bees will live. I always remember how the lucky rabbit's foot didn't do the rabbit much good.

If you don't know what your mite levels are, I'm going to guess you're not, at best, bothering to treat, and at worst, you're treating prophylactically, a potential waste of time and money.

Count your mites and you'll sleep at night. Count your mites and you'll save the money, time and labor on needless treatments, not to mention polluting the hive with smelly fumigants that mess up your queen. Yes, thymol and formic are natural and organic, but they still mess up the hive. I'd rather not use them, if I can get away without using them, but you never know for sure unless you count your mites.

Brood Breaks via Splits

Lastly, one of the best, least offensive ways to set back the mite population is to split your hives. When you requeen, or more specifically, when you allow the colony to raise a queen cell, allowing the cell to mature and hatch, the hive will soon experience a time when there is no capped brood, a time we call a "brood break." This time span is about two weeks.

The mites experience a disruption in their growth. There is a setback, and we have achieved our goal of periodic interruption which knocks down the mite population. Ideally, if I can create a broodless period at a time when I won't put a dent in my population of foragers, I won't penalize myself and my honey production.

For example, I like to make "walk away" splits on June the first in some of my northern colonies in the most remote apiaries. These are the bee yards which have the early nectar flow. I will pull out the queen and a couple of frames of brood on June 1st. Why

June 1st? Well, it's easy to remember, for one thing. For another, it won't harm my honey production.

Here's how that works. On June 1st, the queen lays her last egg and the colony becomes queenless. They will start working on some larvae to become queen cells, but that last egg laid will spend the next three weeks as a larva and a pupa.

Now it's June 22nd as this last egg laid emerges as an adult. It will spend the next three weeks as a nurse bee performing house duties. On July 12th or so, it graduates to a field bee. But guess what? The nectar flow is over by July 12th. No bee that originates from an egg laid after June 1st will have an impact or contribute to the honey production.

Now, there will be some dynamics that hasten the move of that nurse bee to a forager sooner than three weeks, given the lack of young larvae to care for so there will, in actuality, be some contribution. But I won't be penalized.

Key Factor to Splits

Most people like to think of "walk away" splits as pulling out some frames of brood, some frames of pollen and nectar, and the bees attached to these frames and setting them aside in a nuc. Then, you walk away and let the bees do their thing. Yes, given this queenless state, the nuc raises a couple of queen cells and you'll get a free queen, plus a brood break that sets back the mites. The queens fight it out and the victor takes over the nuc. For the limited amount of work involved, you'll get your queen.

However, consider doing the opposite. Instead of leaving the queen in the original hive, think about pulling the queen out and putting her in the nuc, making the original hive queenless. Why?

It's about the resources needed to make good queens. When you move a few frames of bees and age-appropriate larvae to a nuc, even with frames of nectar and pollen, you don't have the volume of bees to make good quality queens. Nine times out of ten, you'll get a queen.

However, the queen is the heart of the colony and you want a good one! Instead of a puny nuc raising a new queen, consider the original colony to do this work. The original hive has more bees and more resources, so I prefer to make the original hive queenless, as opposed to the nuc.

No doubt there will be several queen cells made. No doubt many will be sacrificed by the first queen to emerge. No doubt many good queens will not see the light of day. As savage as it may sound, I let those chips fall where they may. These actions result in a brood break, a diminished mite population, a new queen and a honey harvest. This works for most beekeepers.

But, and there is always a "but," while this works, and while it does not take a lot of labor, and while you do get your queen, is this the best, most efficient way to produce a high quality queen?

The answer is no.

Gary Reuter, from the University of Minnesota, likes to refer to these queens as, "I just" queens. Beekeepers tell him, "Well, *I just* moved some frames of bees to a nuc..." or "*I just* took out the queen."

A lot of beekeepers seem to do okay on "I just" queens. But there is a catch.

Think of the colony when you pull out the queen, or even if you set some frames over in a nuc. The queenlessness of the colony moves those bees to take action. Without a queen, they are toast. So we trust the bees to make the best queen possible. But do we get the best queen possible?

I'm going to say, no.

Look at it this way. The colony goes queenless and you have open brood, that is, larvae in various stages of development. If you read my resource on Nicot queen rearing, I go into detail how the best queens come from larvae in that 12- to 24-hour stage. I might press my luck and use larvae in the 36-hour stage of her development, but the younger the better.

But the million-dollar question becomes, "In a queenless state, when you merely pull out the queen for a walk away split, do the bees only raise queens from larvae in that ideal, 12- to 24-hour stage of development?

I'm going to say, no, again.

Consider this: at the moment of queenlessness, or whenever the bees sense the lack of a queen, you have larvae in these stages:

    Five-day old larvae

    Four-day old larvae

    Three-day old larvae

    Two-day old larvae

    12- to 24-hour larvae

If the bees start grabbing larvae and flooding their cells with royal jelly and reconstructing the worker-sized cell into a queen cell, you'll have larvae of all stages, and queens coming out a different times.

However, as you can probably guess, the first queen to come out will likely kill off her competition. The first queen to emerge comes from the oldest larvae, in this case, the five-day old larvae.

The problem with the queen from the five-day old larvae is her lack of royal jelly. She did not receive the optimal number of days feeding on royal jelly. Her ovaries will not be fully developed. She will not develop her full complement of pheromones. She will act more like a worker bee than like a queen bee, and I'll bet she'll soon be superseded.

She will not be the best queen you can raise, given the circumstances and your lack of labor in this walk away split. Some of you will say, "I don't really care." Well, I do. I need good queens, even if I'm going to pull this method of queen rearing that mostly appeals to the laziness in me or acquiesces to my shortage of time and energy.

When I do this walk away split on June 1st, mostly for lack of time, I make my split taking out the old queen and placing her in a nuc. I trust the workers in the original hive to start making queen cells. Then six days later, I open the hive and cut and/or squish every capped queen cell.

And you're saying, "What? Isn't this what you wanted? Why are you eliminating capped queen cells?"

Because six days after I begin this process, the oldest queen cells, made from the oldest, least desirable larvae, will be capped. I don't want these queens, I want the younger queens which at this point will still be uncapped or in the process of being capped.

On June 1st, I pulled a few frames of sealed brood and the queen and placed them in a nuc. Six days after I initiate the colony to build queen cells, June 7th, I'm going to go in and cut out the capped queen cells. These were made from the oldest larvae.

Five-day old larvae - capped by six days

Four-day old larvae - capped by by six days

Three-day old larvae - close to being capped

Two-day old larvae - about half way

12- to 24-hour larvae - immature cell construction

I also want to count and assess how many queen cells the colony constructed. I may even cut out or squish those cells close to being capped to give my colony the best, most optimally-fed larvae. The quality of the queen depends on how much royal jelly she receives, along with the quality of the young nurse bees who feed her.

On this sixth day, I'm looking at leaving two or three queen cells, maybe more if they look young. Then I'll leave the bees to fight it out. Yes, I could split the colony into nucs, each with a frame containing a queen cell, but my purpose is honey production. If I split the colony too far, I'll lose that potential to make honey.

What do I get through this process? I have <u>ONE</u> nuc with a mature, laying queen, and frames of sealed brood ready to build up into a nice single for winter. I also have a colony that will soon find themselves with a new queen, a potential to produce a harvestable honey crop, and a brood break to suppress the mite population.

Life is pretty good.

Drone Trapping to Remove Mites

I might conclude by briefly explaining drone brood trapping in which frames with drone-sized foundation are drawn out with the intention of raising drones. Drone larvae are more attractive to the female mites that will become the mother/egg layer of more mites. Because the drones take 24 days compared to the 21 days for workers, mites favor drone larvae.

Once capped in the pupae stage, the frames of drone comb can be removed and frozen, killing the mites and the drones, then returned to the colony for cleaning and disposal.

But I need drones for my queens. One option is to move the capped drone frames to a nuc and allow the drones to emerge. In the nuc, the mites do their damage but not to my honey producing hive. What I'm finding, after many years of working with my mite management, is many of my drone pupae don't have any mites at all. It's a simple test to use a cappings scratcher to pull some of the drone pupae out for examination. Not finding any mites is good news on several different levels.

The bottom line is we still need to take care of the mites. In an age of CCD, our mite issues have been overshadowed by media headlines and sound bites on the evening news proclaiming the horrors of CCD. I believe varroa mites are the real problem and cannot be ignored as we worry about CCD.

In our knee-jerk response to chemicals killing our bees, we've allowed the pendulum to swing to the other extreme with treatment-free ideals. We still need to mind the mites, even if all we do is opt for more appropriate genetics in resistant, VSH and hygienic stock. Mites still need to be managed.

I am of the growing opinion that if we can manage the mites, a lot of other problems will disappear with the mites.

Chapter 10

Nucs

If the queen is the heart and the comb is the womb of the hive, nucs are the legs and feet of the beekeeping operation.

If you can raise your own home-grown nucs, you will walk and not grow faint; run and not grow weary. You will find the resolve to weather and survive hive losses in your apiaries without worry and uncertainty. Learning how to split your hives to make nucs will move you forward, by leaps and bounds in your quest for sustainability.

Nucs give you the strength to stand in the gap when everyone else is content to sit on their butt and pluck blackberries...right before they freak out and make a dozen calls because every nuc supplier won't have any more nucs until June. Nucs fit into an integrated management system designed for productivity, resilience and longevity.

I continue to harp on the idea of raising my own queens from locally-adapted stock that meets my objectives and thrives under my management skills (or the lack of them). I also continue to remind you that bees die, irrespective if you keep them "naturally" or "chemically." I continue to put forth the obvious idea that it is better and more economical to raise your own replacement nucs or splits rather than finding beekeepers who will always sell bees, per Kent Williams. I also concede you will not be able to do these things on a conventional, traditional time schedule of the dominant paradigm, i.e., early spring splits prior to the nectar flow in your area.

In the previous chapter, I outlined a very simple method of pulling the queen out to make <u>ONE</u> nuc, preserving your honey production and creating a brood break. These are all good things. The disadvantage is you only make <u>ONE</u> nuc which can be kept and grown, used for replacement purposes or it can be sold. This method is performed on June 1st.

But what if you wanted multiple nucs, say two or three, perhaps even four from the same hive? What if you wanted to make two or three additional nucs in another four weeks from that same hive? It can be done when you dedicate a hive to nuc production rather than honey production.

It's easier than raising your own queens as we're going to trust the bees to make new queen cells via the emergency cell method.

Question: So how do we put this together?

Answer: It's really pretty simple and this method fits smaller beekeepers who only want to add a few nucs for expansion and do not want to learn how to raise their own queens. Here's how it works for me.

Round I

I follow my swarm prevention plan as outlined in Chapter 8, basically adding brood boxes in place of more supers. The concept is the same to give the queen ample room to lay eggs and give the bees sufficient space to store in-coming nectar. This brings me to Mother's Day and our last gasp of cool weather.

Normally, when a hive is destined for honey production, it's all supered up and ready to go by this date. When I dedicate a colony for nuc production, I make some adjustments, namely adding brood boxes in place of the extra supers.

Since I'm going to be messing with open brood, I generally wait until I think this cool spell is over. I am grateful for computerized weather projections, though the crazy weather in southeast Missouri will fool the best computer model the weather service has to offer.

Once we get through the cold weather of what the locals call, "Blackberry Winter," once the weather warms up, I open the hive and sort through my frames of brood. In one of the brood boxes, I will place all my frames of open brood, larvae and fresh eggs. You don't have to be real picky. You don't even need exceptional eye sight to see a frame of pearly-white larvae. The eggs will likely be in the next ring out from the larvae in the middle.

This brood box of open brood is going to be placed on the top of the stack of hive bodies. Under this brood box, as I reassemble the stack of hive bodies, I will place a queen excluder. Obviously, I want to locate my queen and place her below the excluder. I leave this hive for 24 hours. During this time, the population of the hive reorients itself with the young nurse bees relocating to this top box to cover the open brood.

Just as a side note, there's usually someone who wants to know if this manipulation can be done with medium frames. Yes, it can. If you operate in an all-medium operation, it just doesn't matter. Sort through the frames in the same manner. My nuc boxes are built for brood frames, but I could just as easily make the plan work with medium frames.

So I have a top box with fresh eggs and open larvae and the queen below the queen excluder. The next day I will come along and slide a piece of solid paneling under the queen excluder. I use a simple sheet of "luan" plywood or cheap paneling cut 16-1/4" by 20" to match the dimensions of the brood box.

Luan plywood is thin, lightweight and reasonably inexpensive from any lumber yard, but there's a lot of used scrap paneling sitting in a lot of garages. Actually, any piece of corrugated cardboard or recycled linoleum works just as well. Sometimes, when I can find them in my storage shed, I've got some of the old fashioned, light-weight inner covers made out of "masonite" wood. I simply tape over the oval hole.

What I'm trying to do is to cut off the open brood and nurse bees from any smell or contact with the queen. In the absence of the queen, these nurse bees will start making queen cells, often four or five, sometimes as many as fifteen. After 48 hours of isolation, I remove the solid barrier, leaving the queen excluder in place.

In the realm of queen rearing, we call this arrangement a "queen-right cell finisher." Which is to say, the colony has a queen (below the excluder) and with the presence of the queen, the nurse bees will do a better job of finishing and capping those queen cells than if there was no queen. This plan is very similar to those which use a "Cloake Board." Search that term on the Internet if you wish for more details and variations.

We are now looking at a top box with early-stage queen cells on various frames. If there was a downside to this system, you cannot regulate where, or how many queen cells the bees will make on each frame. Life is full of trade-offs so we are trading a sense of control for a greater sense of convenience.

One week from the time I reorganized the colony and sorted through the frames, I will sort my frames and cut out any capped queen cells, as outlined in the previous chapter. I am, however, a little more discriminating as I cut out cells. With this system of making two or three nucs, and given the randomness with which nurse bees will disperse the cells on several frames, I need to think how I'm going to break up this brood box into nucs.

So I cut out those cells which I believe to be from old larvae, leaving the nearly capped larvae intact. I split this top box into two, maybe three nucs adding extra frames of drawn comb to complement the vacancies in the nuc box.

By the way, just as an aside, I make my own nuc boxes and they happen to be six-frame nuc boxes, but that's another story for another day.

As a rule, I like to go out on a Monday to sort my frames. Twenty-four hours later, on Tuesday, I slide in my solid divider. Forty-eight hours later, now on Thursday, I pull out the divider. One week later, the following Monday, I'm ready to cut out old cells and split that top box into two or three nucs. If a frame has multiple queen cells on it, and I believe these cells to be of a desirable age, I let the bees sort things out.

I've had some people suggest, that instead of waiting for the colony to make queen cells on several frames randomly, how about pulling the frames and putting them into nuc boxes with the attending bees? The answer is simple: you'll get much, much better queens when you keep the brood box intact, over an excluder, in a queen-right finishing configuration. It's a no-brainer, though some people tend to over think the process. I covered this question in the last chapter.

One of the concessions I've had to accept is giving up the detail-oriented TLC for the volume of nucs I'm hoping to make. There are benefits to only having two hives in the back yard.

I may move all my nuc boxes to a main mating yard where I can manage them together, or I may leave them in that same yard. Remember, you will have a virgin queen emerge which needs to mate and successfully return back to the nuc box to begin laying eggs. These nucs will also benefit from being fed a simple, 1:1 light sugar syrup. You should have a nice population of nurse bees, but very few, if any, field bees so feeding is a good idea.

I will leave the queen excluder on the original colony and add my supers for the subsequent honey harvest. The working population of the hive is not significantly harmed and I will still harvest a decent to modest honey crop.

Round II

Now, before we take notice of the nucs and their management, remember we have two or three nucs for every hive we forced to make emergency queen cells in our queen-right finisher. We are either down to a brood box and a medium super, or two brood boxes on these hives.

What if, instead of merely supering these colonies for honey production, we now removed the queen excluder and added yet another brood box, preferably with drawn comb? Can we then harvest a second crop of queen cells for another round of nucs?

With another brood box, I like to pull half the frames out of the top box and intersperse new frames of drawn comb in between the old frames. The frames I pull out, likely full of brood, I place in the newly added brood box and add new frames of drawn comb. This is the simplistic basis of checkerboarding.

We allow the queen to move up and around, as if we had reversed the brood boxes and we give her four weeks to lay eggs in these boxes. What if, after four weeks, we pulled the same procedure by sorting the frames and moving all the open brood above an excluder, then after 24 hours, came back and slid in the solid board for 48 hours and forced them to start queen cells, then pulled out the solid board to create a queen-right finisher? What if we then split this top box into two or three nucs for another round of nucs?

It's déjà vu, all over again.

So from one colony that did not swarm, we pull four to six nucs and we allowed them to raise the queens. No doubt, this will now begin to diminish our honey production, but the colony we split was dedicated to raising bees and not honey.

Conceivably, if the weather permits in Cape Girardeau County, I may even pull off this second set of frames into nuc boxes, and then add another brood box to make a third set of nucs in another four weeks.

But this is pushing me into the last half of July, and in a normal year, this is when forage starts drying up. This third set of nucs can be accomplished, but it's got to be a good year with ample rainfall. I need to insure I have drones in my colonies. We normally experience a dearth between mid-July, through August, up until Labor Day. Some queens will begin to shut down.

But if it's a good year, then, Wow! Six to nine nucs from one colony dedicated to the purpose of making nucs. And I still have the original colony. Talk about having my cake and eating it, too. All that's missing is the honey to drizzle over the cake.

Compare the value of those nucs against the value of the honey produced. These results, of course, depend on those queens hatching and mating and finding their way back to the mating nuc. Nobody bats 1.000% and mating nucs attract small hive beetles late in the season. Plan on feeding these nucs, which is extra cost for syrup and labor for feeding.

And if this method is your pleasure, you're going to need a good scheduling system and calendar to keep things straight.

Now let's jump to those nucs we created and see how we need to manage them.

Nuc Care

About 14 days after I move the nucs, I will check for the presence of eggs and larvae signaling a successful nuc. If no eggs are present, I need to move to my conventional queen rearing plans with my

Nicot kit and restock the nuc with a sealed queen cell, or I may combine a failed nuc with a successful nuc. I can always get on the phone and order a mated nuc from one of my southern buddies. Hopefully, after reading my book, they'll still take my call.

Based on the productivity, some of these nucs will need more room. Now I have a choice of making a second brood box for my nuc or moving the frames to a single. I like the second, nuc-sized brood box (bees like to move vertically) but tall nucs are susceptible to blowing over with a strong wind. Since I make a lot of my equipment from scrap lumber, a nuc-sized brood box is no big deal.

This method of forcing emergency queen cells is a modified version of the "Snellgrove" method, also known as the "double screen" method. A lot of my methods are not really original. It's my way of taking a concept and bending it to fit my circumstances. And that's my encouragement for you as well. Take what I present and remodel it to fit your style and comfort level.

The result of either way of making an extra nuc, or nucs, now gives me a free insurance policy in the event something happens to my other hives. I have experienced healthy hives absconding in late summer (with no brood and no stores left behind). I have had hives crash mysteriously right after I harvest my honey in mid-July, going from a robust, healthy hive to small cluster of bees with no interest in foraging and a queen that shows no interest in laying eggs. Some of these hives mysteriously go queenless and I discover a laying worker and tons of drone bees. In these cases, I suspect mite pressures and sometimes queens just give out.

In the old days, under the dominant model of beekeeping, you would find me out in my bee yard, stomping, pouting and cursing my bad luck on having lost another hive. And if I bought a mail-order queen and it was superseded or the colony fell into a laying worker mode, you'd find me exhibiting a weeping and gnashing of teeth. When a whole apiary dies out, it's time for sackcloth and ashes.

In my sustainable model, I have no worries as I have replacement hives coming along to replace this dead hive, or heaven forbid, hives. And what did it cost me? Virtually nothing but my time and labor and some 1:1 sugar syrup, and the opportunity cost of the potential honey crop.

One of the benefits of raising replacement nucs is I let my colonies raise their own queens. This method does not take away a lot of my time and energy, but I cannot raise as many nucs as I would like. Life is full of trade-offs. Allowing a colony to raise a queen during a time of abundant nectar and pollen gathering, when the momentum of the hive is on the upswing and everything in nature is begging the colony to expand makes the likelihood of success very possible. Yes, you are still open to raise your own queens with a Nicot kit or some other grafting method of raising queen cells. I sacrifice some ideals in the wake of volume production and economies of scale.

When I measure, rather randomly, the success rate of mated queens returning to the mating nuc, the emergency queen cell process is a better deal. But, again, I will take the blame of making up an inferior cell-builder colony. I love my Nicot queen rearing kit, but this manner of splitting nucs is getting easier and it's less complicated. I still get to evaluate my queens and pick the best of the best.

If you are a small, back yard beekeeper and don't have a lot of beekeeping experience, if you don't have all the hives for donating extra frames for mating nucs and you want to expand, this is an easy method. It's so easy, a caveman could make nucs this way.

Is there a drawback to making extra nucs? The biggest complaint I hear is from people who say, "But I don't have all those extra boxes, nuc boxes and queen excluders to make these extra nucs."

Please. Give me a break. You either invest your resources in the extra boxes, frames and foundation to become sustainable, or you buy replacement nucs every spring, which quite frankly, doesn't qualify for sustainability under my rules.

With the extra boxes, etc., your nucs become dividends on that investment. When you fall into simply buying more bees from southern producers, you just transfer your wealth and experience to someone else and you receive a negative cash flow in return.

Once you see how easy this equipment can be made in your garage with scrap lumber and a table saw, you can begin to save money by making the equipment instead of buying it.

I keep hearing the echoes of what Kent Williams said in an earlier chapter. You can either learn to manage bees and raise bees or you can find a beekeeper who will sell you bees. Thankfully, there will always be beekeepers who have bees to sell, but that's hardly a sustainable practice. I want to practice sustainable methods.

Chapter 11

Wisdom and Education

*"Hard work beats talent...
when talent doesn't work hard."*

Last year I drove up to St. Louis to attend yet another seminar on beekeeping. I confess I'm kind of a seminar junkie. I rather enjoy listening to other beekeeper's opinions in an attempt to hone my own expertise, somewhat in the spirit of how "iron sharpens iron." There's always multiple ways to do things and I welcome new information. I don't think a sustainable beekeeper ever stops learning.

But more than just gleaning new information, I'm also reminded of the old stuff I forgot or took for granted. We tend to gloss over many of the basic techniques that form a foundation for our bigger plans. Then there are those things we've always done, and we've done them so long we've forgotten why we keep doing them. Frequent reviews and periodic check ups are always in order.

I also attend these seminars for the fellowship. Beekeepers are an interesting bunch of people, depending on how you want to define, "interesting." I've learned a lot from the conversations I've had with others, listening to their gripes and complaints. I think there is more education and experience shared in the hallways between the lectures and over lunch than in the main auditorium.

I love the infinite passion and the indisputable omniscience of new beekeepers. I muse myself, how those who <u>think</u> they know everything upset those who <u>do</u> know everything. And don't we all gravitate to our favorite way of doing things, especially those particular practices we've always done? You can learn a lot from just listening and keeping one's mouth shut.

At this particular seminar, I bumped into some beekeepers who attended one of my beginning beekeeping lectures I taught in early February with the same local association sponsoring this seminar. They were surprised to see me sitting in the audience, taking notes on the lecture.

"What are you doing here?" they asked, almost in unison. "We thought you knew all this stuff."

I simply shrugged and said, "No one knows it all and things keep changing. You got to learn how to roll with the changes."

They then proceeded to ask me several questions about what they were experiencing in their first months of keeping bees. Several others joined our little clump and the next thing I knew I was holding court and delivering another lecture, fielding questions and sharing my opinions. Ironically, I came to learn that day and ended up dispensing my ideas. Apparently it was true: they thought I already knew everything.

There is so much to know about keeping honey bees and so much more to remember. I cling to an old quote, "Knowledge is about the past; wisdom is about the future."

Every year I observe how things have changed and my need to roll with the changes. I still hearken back to my early days in beekeeping, the "pre-mite era" when life was simple and all you had to do was throw those bees in a box and get out of their way. A harvest of honey was almost guaranteed.

Life today is so much more complex and the challenges are greater. Questions have become more complicated. Harvesting honey in this day and age is far from guaranteed and I think you're fortunate if your bees DON'T die. You are the exception instead of the rule.

Thankfully, in these challenging times our information resources are greater. When I started keeping bees, the resources at my disposal were books and a couple old men who kept a few hives of bees in the neighborhood. I wanted to be a commercial beekeeper and they were content with a couple of gallons of honey from their hives. When I'd share my ideas, they'd often chuckle and say, "Well, that sure sounds like a lot of work."

Today we have seminars we can attend in person and webinars we listen to over the Internet while sitting in our pajamas and eating a bowl of cereal. Thanks to www.youtube.com, we can share information visually and store it for instant retrieval at a later, more convenient time.

In the old days, the large retail book stores like Barnes and Nobles were only found in the large shopping malls in the larger cities. Today we can purchase books electronically and instantly upload them to our digital reading devices or download them to our computers.

It's gotten to the point where I don't even visit my local book retailer anymore, and at one time I loved to squander an afternoon browsing the shelves and gluttonously consuming a "grande" cup of overpriced coffee with funky syrups and high-fat diary products added for a delightfully exotic ambience.

Today, I can do just about everything I need from my computer at home, at any hour of the day or night. The resources at our disposal are incredible. And if I wish to enter into an on-line discussion, there are hosts of bulletin boards, forums and blog sites where I can weigh in or simply "lurk" and read the comments of others. I can even disguise my identity with some obscure "handle" or anonymous log-in name. What blows my mind is how this exchange of ideas is instantaneous, where back in the old days we used the snail-mail to send letters as we waited weeks for feedback.

My point is this: with all the information technology we have today, are you staying current on the plight of the honey bee and the most recent developments in honey bee health? I know I waste a lot of time on social media and e-mail, but are we using technology to stay abreast of the changes and new information?

Knowledge is of the past; wisdom is of the future. The old ways of doing things cannot fix the problems they created. Nor can we use the same methods which caused our problems to fix our problems.

Knowledge speaks, but wisdom listens. In my quest to be sustainable, I read a lot of information. I post a number of thoughts on several Internet forums and graciously accept the cranky feedback from certain people who, behind an anonymous Internet name, question my family lineage. I've asked a lot of questions and I've listened to a lot of responders write, "Well, if I was you...."

When I read such a flippant response, I almost immediately think to myself, "But you're NOT me..."

It takes a discerning mind to sort the wheat from the chaff, or as my sister used to say, "You have to kiss a lot of frogs before you find the prince." There's a lot of opinions out there, masquerading as supposedly assumed truth. ("Well, I was reading on the Internet...")

Yet with all the availability of the information I also find a lot of people intimidated by the Internet. I still know some families that refuse to allow this technology into their house, due in large part to their perception that there is a lot of easily, accessible, adult content on the Internet.

And I can tell you they are right, that the potential adult content available to us at our fingertips is not just a perception. Just jump on any popular search engine and request information on something innocuous like, "queen honey bee" and you'll encounter a number of questionable sites.

But that's not my point. My point is there is good stuff out there, if only you would take the time to search for it and read it. And you don't have to open every site or click on every link.

It also doesn't help that simplest of searches for broad subjects, like "beekeeping" yield millions of hits. You lose the trees in the forest of information. And if you find a good site with good information, unless you save it in your "Favorites" file, you can never find it again, even with the same search parameters entered into the same search engine.

When people ask me questions, I'm flattered they think I know so much. But I also detect a level of laziness on their part. I don't have all the answers and what I'm doing may not work for them. We all have different ways of approaching a problem, and at times, I'm looking for the most expedient method because I cannot devote the same time to my hives that the backyard beekeeper has with her two hives.

I often take the path of least persistence, if not the path of least resistance. I tend to manage my apiaries as a whole and not collections of individual hives. I just don't have the luxury of micro-managing a few hives each as separate entities.

When people seek me out for advice, I find myself responding to questions with a disclaimer one of my college professors used to use when fielding questions after his lectures. The professor would listen attentively to the student's question, then pause as if pondering several options. He would begin his answer by drawing in a deep breath and slowing stating, "All things being equal, I would say..."

And in truth, all things were never equal. We have to know our options and alternatives in their proper context. In beekeeping, we used to depend on chemical and pharmaceutical intervention, and some beekeepers still do, but we are shifting to more natural or "soft" chemical intercession, often at lower rates to reduce the sub-lethal effects.

But what are the sub-lethal effects and how to you know what's working and what is doing harm to our bees? You have to do a lot of reading and searching on the Internet to find what other beekeepers are doing, then take that knowledge out to your bee yard and evaluate the results.

Back in the old days, I had to find a book on beekeeping and hope that the book had the information I needed. I also hoped the book had an index to make it easier on me. If I didn't have the book with the right information, I'd trundle into the local library to see if they had any books on beekeeping (which they seldom did).

Today, the Internet is an incredible resource with a million books and blogs at my disposal. The major search engines act like a living index of everything that is out there. But it takes time to search, winnow and glean the right information which fits my situation.

And in our attention-deficit age of impatience and laziness, we don't want to spend a lot of time reading. Just give me the answer. Some days I don't even have the patience to search beyond the first couple of pages on a given Internet search. We are a hurried and harried culture. If often find myself in the kitchen, shouting at the microwave, "Hurry up!"

To share Mark Twain's quote again, "The person who can read books and doesn't is no better off than the person who cannot read at all." This works for beekeepers who can read books and don't, as well.

There's a lot of information out there on how to be sustainable and what to avoid, as well as traditional opinions as to what will really only lead you to be unsustainable. I find much of the material that comes out from our universities and distributed through the agricultural extension services gives the most basic, conventional, traditional, chemical advice from a commercial perspective. It tries to be a one-size fits-all program would never, ever mention natural or soft options. The universities pretty much stick to the conventional program, which makes some people wonder who is funding their programs.

The question I throw out to you is, "Are you reading anything at all?" I love the quote where the person said, "The average beekeeper only reads one book a year; that's why they are an average beekeeper."

The biggest part of reading is separating the wheat from the chaff. Just because it's on the Internet or in a book doesn't make it true (present company not excluded). You need a real discerning spirit to sort out the hype from the simplistic universal answers, i.e., "all good beekeepers need to do XYZ."

As I said earlier, "Beekeeping is more art than science; knowledge is more caught than taught." You can read all you want, but until you actually open the hive and see what's going on, then try something different to experiment a little, you never really know what's going to work in your area. Beekeeping is local, yet many things are consistent. Just as many things are changing, many other things remain the same.

As I said at the outset, these are challenging times to raise bees, and "fools rush in where angels fear to tread." (Alexander Pope) The ignorant beekeeper is the one who brings a knife to a gun fight. The soon-to-be-former beekeeper is the one who says, "Well, I guess it really doesn't matter if I do this, or not."

There's a critical comment floating around some of the bee meetings that goes like this: What do call treatment-free beekeepers? The answer is, "Next year's customers for package bees."

And I don't want to sound too critical of treatment-free options (but be sure and read my last chapter as I discuss if treatment-free beekeeping is the gateway to sustainability). But if you choose to move into alternative practices, you have to know what you are doing. For this reason, I have a hard time advocating treatment-free practices for a beginner beekeeper. But do I want them to pick up the negative consequences of a synthetic chemical practice? Not really!

How I wish beekeeping was like the instructions on the bottle of shampoo: Wet hair, apply shampoo, lather, rinse, repeat.

I want to make a HUGE plea for you to join a local beekeeping association. I also want you to consider joining your state beekeeping association. If you don't know of any, ask at your local county extension office or do an Internet search using words like, "[my state] beekeeping association."

Local associations are essential for networking information and exchanging ideas. If beekeeping is local, then you need local ideas and what makes certain plans work in your area, or things that are peculiar to your geographic location.

I have hives in Cape Girardeau (Missouri) County and in Scott (Missouri) County. My bee yards are separated by a geological formation we call Crawley's Ridge. In the north, in Cape Girardeau

County, the soil is clay and the topography is hilly. In the south, in Scott County, the soil is very sandy and the topography is flat. Two areas and two very distinctive honey flows requiring two different management plans.

And these areas are but thirty miles apart.

One-size-fits-all does not always work. Every hive is different, every location is different, every season is different and every beekeeper is different. A local association provides a wealth of what works in your area, but don't be surprised if answers to your questions vary as there are often many ways to do the same things. Two beekeepers can do different things different ways and both still be correct.

I'd also strongly encourage you to find a mentor. You don't have to necessarily establish a formal relationship or put someone on the spot. Start out by approaching someone you admire and trust, someone who you think is a good beekeeper and seems knowledgeable and successful.

Approach this person and simply ask if you can go with them the next time they open their hives. Or invite them to your place to look at your hives. Tell them you don't know what you're looking at, and that's okay. Most of don't know what we're looking at, either.

A good mentor bridges the gap between knowledge and application. Most experienced beekeepers I know welcome the opportunity to show a beginner the ropes, even helping someone with a few years experience under their belt.

Do not pick the loudest, whiniest, most complaining person who always offers excuses why they cannot find the time to work their bees, and in reality, they don't really seem to care if they work their bees, or not. It seems to me if they really cared, they'd find time to do what needs to be done! Also, they say they're just keeping bees for the fun of it, but they never seem to be having any fun!

The idea behind hooking up with a mentor is to tap into their wisdom. They are the ones who never tell you, "Now that's a stupid question and the answer is obvious." A mentor leads, but does not get too far out ahead of you. A mentor is like a coach, and a good coach keeps you in the game, but they cannot play the game for you.

If you don't have a local association and you cannot find a mentor, find another beginner beekeeper and open up each other's hives. Share resources. In my early days, I subscribed to the *American Bee Journal* and my buddy subscribed to *Gleanings in Bee Culture*. After each of us read our respective magazine, we swapped magazines giving each of us the benefit of a free subscription. We visited each other's yards and opened and worked hives together.

I think of two quotes, one used by my father when I left for college. He said, "Don't let books get in the way of your education." The second comes from a newly released book by Lisa Robbin Young called *The Secret Watch*. In this book she says, "Help is a two-way street. Give. Receive."

To paraphrase another line from a recent movie, "With great knowledge and experience comes great responsibility." Let's share our collective wisdom! What a shame to take it to the grave, and what a shame to allow so many hives to die from what could have been prevented with some preemptive knowledge.

I love the solitary nature of keeping bees, but my experience needs an outlet. So I'll teach and preach, visit and talk, write and post. Hopefully, somewhere in the process, I'll learn a few things. Old dogs can learn new tricks...if only I could remember them.

Chapter 12

Diversity of Forage

In real estate, I'm told the three secrets to success are, "Location, location, location." Actually, that sounds like one secret to me, but I'm not in real estate so how can I really know?

I think one of the secrets to sustainable beekeeping, or three secrets if you are so inclined, is, "Location, location, location."

To put this issue in another context, I want to ask myself, "Where can I place my hives to keep my bees the healthiest and most productive? Where can I set up my bee yard so it benefits the bees as well as meets my expectations for convenience?"

This is really a management issue and the choices we make on where and how we establish our apiaries. As I stated in an earlier chapter, good management is informed management, and setting up an apiary is a decision, based on goals, considering resources and circumstances, for a desired result.

For most beekeepers, this means your back yard, and unfortunately, most of us who start in the back yard do not put a lot of thought into alternative sites. But let's be honest, your back yard is likely more for your convenience than for the productivity of the honey bees. The back yard is where I started, and with all my beekeeping equipment in the garage, it was just plain handy. In reality, I had no other site, but in truth, I really didn't look for another site. My back yard was convenient. My garden was right next door so I figured the back yard was ideal.

As I expanded the number of my bee hives, to preserve harmony in my marriage with young children and to maintain tranquility with my neighbors, I began looking for other locations. In the beekeeping business, we refer to such locations as "out yards."

An out yard is a different location than what we call our "home site" or in this case, my house. I wrote a resource on the five key points when searching for an out yard, as well as about a dozen questions to ask when someone says, "Hey! If you need a place to put some bees, you can put them in my garden." While I don't advocate looking a gift horse in the mouth, I will, at least, examine its hooves.

You can find this resource at www.createspace.com/4044187.

To quote from the description: *"The back yard is the most obvious choice, but there are many factors, including municipal ordinances and relations with the neighbors. Urban beekeeping is on the rise and roof top apiaries are becoming popular. Still, there are several factors that limit and define the most successful apiary site selection."*

When I'm looking for a place to keep hives or establish an apiary, I'm really looking for, as my primary criteria, a diversity of forage. I'm looking for some trees that bloom early in the spring. I'm looking for wild flowers that still grow along abandoned fence rows. I'm looking for drainage ditches or ponds, not just for water, but for plants that bloom during the heat of the summer. I'm looking for untended areas populated with weeds (weeds make for tasty honey), and, after all, weeds are actually flowers once you get to know them.

Diversity of floral sources also means a diversity of pollen and nectar, and not all pollen is the same nutritionally. I want flowers that bloom early and flowers that bloom late. The worst thing I can find is a "green desert" of monoculture, where from one horizon to the other, all you see is one kind of plant or crop. Not only is the window of bloom very narrow, the pollen source is limited as well.

There was a day and age where weeds would grow under the main crop and provide some kind of diversity, but today we spray our crops with poisons and herbicides that eliminate nothing but the main crop.

If bees are required to pollinate a crop grown in a monoculture, you can bet the bees have to be moved following bloom (stress on the bees and the beekeeper) or they have to be fed an artificial diet of pollen substitute or sugar syrup when the blooms quit.

When I find a location that produces a variety of blooms and a diversity of forage and natural pollen, I know I have well fed bees. Well fed bees are healthier bees, and healthier bees are more productive. Diversity of forage is a primary criteria when I select a location other than my back yard.

Some of my healthiest hives are set next to hay and cattle farms in Cape Girardeau County in southeast Missouri. Weeds and clover grow together, and most pastures have ponds and groves of trees. Many of these cow pastures back up to

Interstate 55 where acres and acres of unmowed forage grows allowing the vetch to bloom, followed by the yellow sweet clover, followed by the white sweet clover. And the best part is these acres are never sprayed for insects. Several windows of bloom open and close during the nectar flow.

But always remember that bees will fly two miles. As I said earlier, if you were to draw a circle with a two-mile radius from any bee yard, you encompass over 8,000 acres of potential forage. You have no idea what lies over the next ridge or what your neighbor might be spraying two miles down the road. Unless you live in some region where you have nothing but monoculture, you are pretty much guaranteed your bees are catching a diversity of forage.

But how can you tell? You can watch the colors of the pollen as the bees return from the hive. You can pull frames of brood and check the pollen stores, usually a ring just above the brood area on the comb. While most pollen will fall into the color range of yellows and oranges, you'll also see some red and purple, brown and even grey pollen.

Diversity of forage is about honey bee nutrition and raising healthy, strong larvae. But you also have to watch out for pesticide sprays.

I was approached by an older woman who insisted on buying "pesticide-free honey." I said many of my hives were on fields in the Conservation Reserve Program (CRP ground) and there was, to the best of my knowledge, no spraying going on. She said she wanted honey from these hives, which was difficult for me as I couldn't sort that honey out as it was not distinctive enough for my customers and didn't warrant my special attention.

I also clarified for her, as bees fly more than two miles (covering 8,000 acres) I had no knowledge of what the land owners and farmers were doing over the hill or around the bend, nor did I have any control on which direction the bees choose to fly.

She reiterated, as if she didn't hear a word I said, she wanted pesticide-free honey and she suggested I put hives on her farm and give her some of that pesticide-free honey in trade for putting hives on her pesticide-free farm. I shrugged and said that would work.

Her husband drove me around the farm to look for potential locations to put my hives. As I outline in my resource on where to put hives, I strongly express my desire for vehicle access. I want to drive right up to my hives. I've had it with wheel barrows and hand carts, muddy hillsides and cattle gates.

This particular farm was hilly with lots of woods, cattle pasture, ponds, open meadows, and looked really promising as a potential location to set up a bee yard just off the main road. So I set out a couple of hive stands and some hives. The bees on this farm did pretty well their first year and I still have hives at this location.

As the season progressed, the wife was disappointed in her tomatoes and wondered why the honey bees were not pollinating the blooms. She asked if I thought I should I move a hive closer to her garden. I didn't think that was necessary as the bees fly quite a distance and we set up this bee yard about fifty yards from her garden.

She went on to complain about a couple of other topics, including the bugs that were eating her zucchini, and how even the Sevin® dust wasn't making an impact. I almost fell over. So much for her "pesticide-free" farm!

People like her lump the horrible farmers with "all their sprays" and fail to see their own lawn treatments and garden dusting as harmful to the honey bees. I started a conversation about her use of pesticides in her garden, and how tomatoes don't need honey bees (and how the lack of tomatoes blooms being set was likely an issue with our hot summer that year).

She was on a different wave length and I could see she didn't see her problem because of the problems created by the big farmers and all the chemical interests from "big ag." Our conversation was one-sided as it wasn't the speck in the eyes of the local farmers but her failure to note the fist full of dirt in her eyes.

I still have bees on this "pesticide-free" farm and she still gets a cut of the honey. You meet some really interesting people when you keep bees.

I'm often approached by people who have a garden and want a bee hive to pollinate the garden. This is all good. But they tend to think of their garden as the only place the bees will visit, and they think of the two weeks when the lone apple tree blooms as sufficient to warrant a season's worth of honey.

Bees do well on a diversity of forage, which is part of our problem when hives are hauled out to California for the almond bloom. There is nothing blooming prior to the almonds, so if cold weather delays the blooms, the bees have to be fed sugar syrup or High Fructose Corn Syrup and protein patties made of soy flour and brewers yeast. Then the almonds bloom and the bees do fairly well, but it's not a diverse diet. Because water is so scarce, there are no weeds below the almond trees, sprayed so all the water resources benefit the almond trees.

Then these bees are hauled somewhere else where the bees find another crop grown as monoculture, that is, it's the only thing grown for miles and miles. After that, the bees are hauled to another single floral source. Such is the life of a migratory pollinator.

As I have mentioned earlier, this is also how our modern agriculture works in an attempt to feed a hungry planet and the role of a migratory pollinator fits into this highly intensive production model.

Sustainable beekeeping recognizes the dietary needs of the bees. I am not opposed to feeding pollen substitute patties or sucrose syrup, especially if it maintains the bees until natural pollen and nectar are available. But there is no real substitute for real pollen and nectar.

Sustainable beekeeping recognizes, not just the diversity of the floral sources, but the length of the time the plant is in bloom. I like to think of plants that bloom as "windows." Early in the season, a window opens with a particular plant blooming. This particular plant might bloom for a week or two, then the flowers fade and they go to seed or produce fruit. Then another window opens. When these flowers fade, I want another window to open from another plant, and when that plant quits blooming and that window closes, I'm looking for another window to open.

The best bee yards are those which have a multiple succession of blooming flowers, a series of windows that open and shut, one after the other, as the flower sources overlap into a full season of blooms. This is ideal!

There are, however, seasonal times when there are no blooms. In southeast Missouri, in Cape Girardeau County specifically, the flowers quit blooming around the middle of July. We enter a dry season in which the pastures and hay fields dry up, the vegetable gardens are stressed, and the heat just burns everything up.

This is our normal pattern until Labor Day when we start experiencing rains and a rebirth of the flowering landscape with golden rod, asters and wild sunflowers. We call these dry seasons, a "nectar dearth." It is our hope that we left enough honey on the hive to get the bees through this time, otherwise we have to resort to supplemental feeding. We also hope the frames have sufficient pollen stored away, as well. Feeding of artificial pollen patties or pollen substitutes may be warranted.

Healthy, productive hives are built on a diversity of floral sources. As beekeepers, it is our decision where to keep bees and what locations offer a lengthy season of floral diversity, the series of windows that open and shut in succession.

As I'm selling honey at the farmer's markets, I field a lot of inquiries from people who ask, "I'll bet you're looking for a new place to keep bees. I have five acres, two apple trees and a fifty-square foot garden. I need the pollination and you can keep the honey."

I usually smile at such offers and tell them I'll have to look into their place. I always have more offers than suitable locations. Some of these inquiries are literally around the corner from where I discretely keep bees already, so it's not like they NEED the bees. They probably already have my bees visiting their fifty-square foot garden, which may be impressive to the homeowner, but it's small potatoes (pun intended) to a colony of bees.

And even if this small farm is ideal, it doesn't do the bees any good if the next door neighbor is growing a field of a specialty crop that requires weekly spraying.

I had a yard that did pretty good...until the adjacent neighbor put in a vineyard. Mysteriously, my bees either died or produced no honey and then died. I spoke to the vineyard owner about what he was spraying. We got the names of the sprays and fungicides, and researching them on the Internet, we could find no detrimental effects listed for honey bees.

Still, I took the last surviving hive off that farm and found a better place. And it may not have been the vineyard owner. The problem may have been created by someone else over the hill within those 8,000 acres of diversity, which also includes the potential of undetected pesticides. The vineyard may have been a coincidence, or the synergy of his fungicide reacted with another farmer's pesticide.

If I'm going to keep on keeping bees, I have to find a location that has a diversity of forage so my bees can prosper. That's sustainability.

The simplest forage areas for me are CRP ground and the medium/shoulder strips along the highways. But this past year, in 2013, 1.6 million acres came out of the CRP program across our nation and farmers planted them back into row crops. 1.6 million acres is about the size of the state of Delaware. There are a host of environmental issues (soil erosion, water quality and wildlife cover) that don't concern honey bees, but honey bees will be impacted along with a variety of wildlife. Over the past decade, about 1/4th of the CRP ground is back in production.

We can blame this trend on the higher prices offered for grains, and higher prices come from the higher demand for biofuels. It is the world we live in. It is the state of our production agriculture that we have to live with, though much of this production system works against our future as beekeepers.

Part of the sustainability puzzle is location, and location, and location. It matters where we keep our bees and our back yard may not be the best location for the bees, even if it's the most convenient for us. We have a choice where we place our hives and I hope you feel you are not limited to your back yard. I have been pleasantly surprised at the number of offers I've received, even though many of those offers are not ideal.

One of the tools I use when choosing a location is the computerized satellite maps. You get an excellent view of all the surrounding fields and the topography, including potential flood plains. Flood plains, or as we like to call them in southeast Missouri, "bottom ground," often produce good crops due to the retention of moisture. But they also flood, in season.

Aerial maps also give me a good idea of placing my apiaries with enough distance between the yards so the forage areas do not overlap.

Chapter 13

Time Management and Self Management

I think the BEST thing about keeping bees is how I can set them up in a hive and let them go about their business, basically allowing them to operate on "auto-pilot" to do what they need to do.

After all, these are wild creatures which go out to forage without needing any encouragement on our part. They all come home later in the day in order to go back out the next day. They never go on strike for higher wages. They do not need to be taught or trained how to make honey. They defend the colony without our prompting and they take care of their basic needs without asking our permission. Bees have been doing these very tasks for a million years, and doing a pretty good job of it. They don't really need us.

However, I think the WORST thing about keeping bees is how I can set them up in a hive and let them go about their business, basically allowing them to operate on "auto-pilot," to do what they need to do.

So why is the BEST thing also the WORST thing? Because the bees are so adept at taking care of their needs, there is a temptation to leave them alone, to not "meddle" and to allow the bees to do what they need to do without our intrusion or interference. And besides, every time I open the hive to work the bees, I get stung. I would LOVE to leave the bees alone and let them do their thing all by themselves.

There is a group of beekeepers who intentionally subscribe to this style of management that leaves the bees alone. These beekeepers just let the bees go on their merrily little way, on their own schedule, to do their thing.

Strangely enough, we call this model of management, the "let alone" beekeeping model.

And it will work, to a certain extent, provided you have low expectations of what the colony will produce. When left on their own, a colony seems to make just enough honey to take care of its own needs. But most beekeepers want to harvest some honey, as do their spouses who are looking for a little financial return on the investment in hives and bees, and time. And then there are those relatives and Christmas presents.

In my opinion, bees can and do survive quite nicely without us. History demonstrates this indisputable fact that bees don't need us. I have witnessed several colonies of unmanaged bees living in the walls of apartments and other intractable locations. People call me to remove the bees, to "save" them, often with veiled threats on how they don't want to kill them, but if I don't get rid of them, they'll be "forced to do what needs to be done."

Okay, fine.

The downside is so many of these locations are hard to reach or inaccessible. And I've crawled through attics and removed soffits, sticking my arms into walls as narrow as the two-by-four studs allow while balancing on forty-foot ladders. Bees often find those narrow niches in the mortar of brick buildings, and the last thing I need to be doing is tearing out the brick. Even people with historic homes think all I have to do is wave my magic wand and draw them out.

I laugh, to myself, that if I can't get to those bees, the surly homeowner or uptight apartment manager won't be getting close to them either. Their threats to "do what needs to be done" are supposed to motivate me to sprout wings and fly to a second story roof and take care of the situation.

And, of course, these same people won't pay anyone to take care of the problem and so these colonies live year after year, and I get calls year after year from new managers, sometimes to fetch the swarm cast off by these colonies. Amazingly, these colonies have survived without human intervention in some of the most inhabitable locations.

A couple of times when I've done what we call a "cut out," the procedure of rescuing a colony by removing siding or roofing, the homeowner gets all excited about all the free honey they're expecting me to give them. Some people think this honey is superior to my honey because it is "wild" honey. Maybe what makes it taste so good is all the sawdust, sheetrock dust, dirt, rotten wood and tar paper clinging to the comb. And the quantity, depending on the time of year, can be very marginal.

More and more, I'm doing cut outs less and less. No body wants to pay me, and they don't want to pay a professional exterminator. What they don't know is most exterminators don't want to kill honey bees, anyway. The survival rate on these cut outs is kind of low and it just takes too much time.

These unmanaged, feral bees seem to survive year after year, but they never seem to produce surplus honey (or at least, surplus honey I can harvest). These colonies are not managed to make lots of honey. The bees basically strive to meet their own needs for survival in order to make it to the next season so they can do it all over again. They know how to do this without any training from us humans.

Remarkably, without human intervention, they survive. Oddly, bees in managed hives struggle to stay alive, even with the benefit of medication. The unmanaged hives usually swarm, following their natural instincts. This swarming procedure creates a natural brood break which disrupts the reproduction of the mites as mites need the pupal stage to reproduce.

Thus begins the inquisitive pondering if we are doing our bees any favor by giving them medications which are designed to keep them alive. What is the invisible detriment that we seem to be inflicting upon the colony that causes them to struggle so much? Are we reaching sub-lethal levels of medicine that is actually poisoning our bees? Do the unmanaged hives have a magic "mojo" that keeps them alive?

I confess I am intrigued, and so I trap feral swarms, believing in part they have genetics which have been refined by living in a mode of natural selection through survival of the fittest. I place them in normal hives, and at times, as kind of an experiment, I hold back from treating them. Some of these hives live; some of these hives die out. But then I am reminded that even unmedicated, feral bees eventually die and colonies in trees pass away until a new swarm moves in.

I can see a wonderfully seductive allure to keeping bees without any treatments what so ever. If I believe feral bees in the wild can survive in this manner, I want to keep a box of bees in my backyard and not treat them, basically leaving them alone. Yet having tried it, I can tell you my survival rate is no better and no worse than the hives I manage and treat. The key may be in allowing the bees to swarm. But swarming, aside from my artificial swarm techniques in making a late-season split, is antithetical to my purpose of harvesting honey.

At one of the ABF (American Beekeeping Federation) meetings, a national platform of some of the finest, most astute researchers from all over the world, one of the speakers challenged us by saying, "Supposed we found out that all of the medications and miticides were not working, and the only successful way to keep bees is to let them swarm and accept a significantly smaller honey crop. Would you keep bees in this manner if this was what it came to?"

Most of us nodded in agreement, conditional on the possibility that this is what beekeeping might come to. Maybe we are at that point as we begin to accept the possibility that synthetic miticides are leaving sub-lethal residues and the mites are building resistance requiring ever stronger pharmaceuticals as we ratchet up the chemical treadmill. Maybe the secret is found in that queenless brood break, but we'd have to reduce our expectations for a honey harvest if this became our standard protocol.

If you want to keep a top bar hive or even a Langstroth hive and allow the bees to swarm (better warn your neighbors) and basically give the bees a safe place to raise their family, you are to be commended. But the likelihood of harvesting any honey is, well, unlikely. Just because they are untreated, unmanaged colonies is no guarantee they will survive and prosper. This is where management comes in to play.

Management, to my way of thinking, is defined as this: "Decisions, based on goals, working with resources and circumstances, to reach a desired result/outcome." Those four parts lay out our responsibility to make intentional decisions on how we treat (or not treat) our bees. It is based on goals which are part of our vision, that is, where we want to go with our bees.

Management forces us to work with, and deal with the available resources and to take into consideration life's circumstances such as our busy work schedules or the fickle weather. It is also based on what we want to accomplish, our desired outcomes, our hopes and our dreams.

To simply management, I have to ask two questions: a) what is happening in the bee hive, and b) what do I need to do? Yet I am reminded that management is not so much what I need to do, but what I want to make happen.

As my old college professor from Iowa State University used to say, "You are the MAN in management." Of course, he then clarified his definition to include the "WOMAN" in management, but he drove home the fact that management is what we need to be doing to successfully raise cattle, or corn, or bees.

The key to successful management is being proactive and pre-emptive anticipating the needs of the bees and what I hope to accomplish. This is another way of saying, "Timing is everything."

Management is based on timing, and timing means action. We have to follow through and do what we've decided to do. It needs to be done.

I've noticed three objectives successful beekeepers do in the course of their hobby. First, they have a solid understanding of honey bee biology and the seasonality of the colony.

Second, they have defined goals (which is this "vision" thing again) and these goals inform where they keep their bees, when they harvest their honey, how they treat for mites, etc.

Third, they learn how to incorporate and synchronize those objectives, matching the seasonality of the hive with their goals.

And beekeeping has all sorts of management schemes. There is seasonal management, swarm management, nuc management, mite management, increase management, and dare I include our personal management and time management?

Management is often comically portrayed as nothing short of brutal manipulation exploiting the bees like they were slave labor. I disagree with this portrayal as every responsible beekeeper knows that if a hive is to be productive, a beekeeper needs to respect the work ethic of the colony. We know how to keep them healthy. If a beekeeper abuses the bees, then the bees will not respond favorably.

But if bees are dying, now I have to turn the question around and ask why my management practices are doing to the bees? Is there something I need to change? I keep wrestling with questions that no one wants to answer.

I have some remote out yards that are difficult to reach as they lie in out of the way places. I've had bees in these locations for a long time, establishing these yards when I was first expanding and feeling rather desperate to agree with anyone who offered, "Do you need another farm to put some hives?"

I always said, "Yes," with grateful enthusiasm. Unfortunately, these yards were not always ideal, particularly if you read my book, "Where Can I Keep My Bees" (www.createspace.com/4044187) but they were available and I was desperate.

Since those days, I've become more discerning, much to the frustration of people who think I SHOULD be putting bees on their farm (so they can get the free pollination and a few jars of honey). They can't understand how I can turn down their generous offer. People often think they're doing me this huge favor by offering me a location where I can place one hive (whereas I prefer to place four, preferably eight hives).

They'll encourage me with, "Yeah, we have a couple of apple trees and a garden, and we don't use any sprays" as if that was enough to keep a hive healthy and productive for the whole growing season. Or they have a ten-foot row of berries. Or they want the honey for their allergies. Or they have free-range chickens, as if that mattered.

Mostly, they just want to help, and the only thing they can think of is offering me a spot to put a couple of hives. I think people still have a rather parochial view of beekeepers as small-time hobbyists who only do this stuff on the weekends.

However, I never want to look a gift horse in the mouth. Still, these yards are hard to work into my already complicated schedule. I have more offers for apiaries than I have hives to put there so I am inclined to thank them and tell them I'll add them to the list.

These far-flung, remote out yards are not my most productive apiaries as I obviously ignore and neglect them, except the occasional times when I really need to perform the bare minimum management tasks where I work the hive to prevent swarming, add supers, harvest honey, and winterize the hives. I seldom treat for mites and these are strict survivor bees. I've let them requeen themselves (because they do it before I know they need a new queen) and yes, I do notice the uneven production in some of the colonies from year to year.

If they gave blue ribbons for procrastination, I'd be a grand champion winner. These remote hives are on the end of my priority list and my more productive yards receive more attention on a more intentional time schedule.

I used to acquiesce and assuage my guilty conscience with, "It's good enough." And I'd get just enough honey to justify my neglectful ways, but not so little as to push me to really work these apiaries.

In my quest to become more efficient and more productive, I've increased my attention to these yards and my extra attentiveness has been rewarded.

What I've found is this:

*Good enough rarely is;
not enough usually is.*

Simply put, I don't give them the time they deserve, yet when I do, the bees respond with higher production.

Within reason, the more I work my hives, the more productive they become. Here is a bone of contention with the natural beekeeping crowd, and note that I conditioned my position with the phrase, *within reason*. Many of the beekeepers in the natural camp accept a "let alone" model of keeping bees, only to inspect the hive when absolutely necessary. To a certain degree, I agree with the natural camp.

But if you lack the experience to observe the external behavior of the bees which indicates the internal condition of the hive, then you have to open the hive and pull out some frames to learn what's going on.

I don't mean to be opening my hives every week, which is horribly disruptive, but I want to inspect my hives from time to time and give me the necessary education so I can give my bees the management practices that help them give me a good honey harvest and a decent return on my investment.

Over the years, I can pretty much tell by the way the bees fly in and out, carrying pollen or not, on how the hive is progressing. I don't have to be inside my hives every week, but when I intervene, as needed, my productivity goes up.

And remember how my idea of sustainable beekeeping is to keep on keeping bees, keeping them alive, and producing honey for me to sell at the farmer's markets. Again, this is the power of vision. Sustainable beekeeping is not neglecting the hives nor procrastinating because I'm not up for getting stung.

I keep coming back to my sense of vision, namely, what do I want out of my bees? I am a business man and a honey producer. I am also a pastor, as well as a husband and a father. Time and energy are limited. I don't work my hives as intensely, or intensively, to maximize my optimal production (noting that optimal takes into consideration the theory of diminishing returns) as I might ideally wish.

Still, I work with my bees to give them the resources they need to allow me to get what I want. It's a balance of intervention and equipping against neglect and procrastination.

The secret to sound management is the investment of time. I constantly run into beekeepers who tell me things like, "Well, it looked kind of cloudy and I knew the bees would be ornery so I didn't work them on Monday. Tuesday I had to mow the grass so I didn't want them all stirred up. Wednesday it rained and I had to go shopping on Thursday and that pretty much shot my week. I just didn't get into my bees."

Okay. Sure. We're all busy. I'm looking for results. They're offering excuses. You can't have both...or have I already said that? (Yes!).

Or my beekeeping buddies complain how they didn't have the foundation for the frames because the foundation was on back order, and if those wax moths had not wrecked all the drawn comb....

We've covered this already, have we not? (Yes!)

Bees do function just fine without our intervention, but the investment of time, also called "management," helps the bees fulfill their potential, which, in turn, helps me achieve my vision. Which brings me to one of my favorite excuses, "I just can't find the time to work my bees."

Well, brothers and sisters, let me leap to my proverbial soap box and preach a message that's been drilled into me since the pioneers crossed the open prairie: You don't "find" the time; you have to "make" the time to work your bees. Have we not already gone over this? (Yes!)

I also know we often make the time for what we really want to do. Procrastination is the symptom of what we wish to avoid, hoping our neglect will make it go away. I still leave dirty dishes in the sink at night hoping the magic elves come and wash/dry them. Unfortunately, my wife always sees the dirty dishes before the elves arrive.

I see so much potential in beginning beekeepers, but a few stings dampens their enthusiasm and getting them to open their hives is like scheduling an appointment at the dentist. Then I meet some rather defiant beekeepers who tell me, "Yeah, I only work the bees when I feel like it."

Okay. But are you happy with the results?

The late George Imirie was so critical of beekeepers who never took a real interest in their hives. He referred to them as, "Bee-Havers." These people have bees, but because of their neglect or ignorance, they can't seem to KEEP those bees, they only HAVE them for a season.

It takes time, and a commitment to keep honey bees, but how does one make that time in the wake of our busy lives? The background story is too long to go into, but I find the best way I make time is first, in my notes. Every day I go out to work my bees I take along an ordinary, spiral notebook.

I write three things when I visit an apiary. Those three things are, 1) what I found in this particular bee yard, 2) what I did to these hives in this yard, and 3) what needs to be done on my next visit. Since each hive has a number on it, I can make specific notations in my notebook if there are special circumstances or something unusual. But for the most part, I jot down notes and generally treat the apiary as a whole.

I may visit several apiaries that day, making similar notes in my notebook. By the end of the day, this notebook is sticky with honey and propolis. Then when I get back home, I take my notebook into my office and transcribe my scribblings and crude abbreviations into a new set of clean notebooks. Each apiary has its own respective notebook. Here, I take what I jotted down in the apiary and write clear sentences on what I found, what I did, and what needs to happen next time in the notebooks that never leave my office.

Now here's where my system falls into place in a real critical manner. I look at my calendar and I see I have some free time tomorrow. I check the weather forecast. I decide which yards I want to visit, usually linking several to visit as I lay out an economical and efficient route. Then I pull those notebooks and read my third entry: what needs to be done next as I visit those yards tomorrow.

Knowing what needs to be done, I can load my truck in the darkness of the night before with everything I need to meet the bees' needs. So when tomorrow comes around, I'm not searching for items I cannot find. I'm not forgetting some key equipment as I feel the rush of time slipping past me. I have everything I need loaded on my truck. And some days I have to go into the office at church or make some phone calls or visit the hospital. But when I come home to work bees, everything is ready. I'm set. It's "go" time!

That's how I MAKE time to keep bees. There was a day and time when I'd linger at the office taking one more call, meeting one more visitor, heading out but making one more visit at the hospital, or a run through the drive-through grabbing a burger....only to get home later than I had planned. In those days I'd rush around trying to remember what I needed, hoping I could find it, all the while the day was slipping past me like a freight train on a downhill slope.

Normally, I was not in the right mindset to feel like I was in control and I'd forget things. Then I'd either have to make a return trip home (more wasted time and energy) or do without and hope I could get by with what I had (bad idea and more wasted time and energy...should have gone back home to get what I needed...yada, yada, yada).

You remember when I mentioned something about having either excuses or results? Yeah, I do, too.

The more hives you acquire, the more efficient you must become. I've learned that time management is really self management. There's no room for procrastination in beekeeping if you hope to be sustainable. Further, to be sustainable, I need to take this hobby seriously. I need to make time. I never find time.

When people ask me how many hives I keep, they are impressed with the numbers. Anything is possible when you are organized. There is only so much time in the day, and truthfully, I have only so much energy, physical or mental. But when you are organized, you can accomplish more than you think as you make the most of your available time and energy.

My efforts to be sustainable are often strengthened by an old saying, "As thy days, so shall thy strength be." I am reminded that when situations warrant and I'm called to rise above the challenges, I will be empowered to meet, and overcome those challenges. I can get the job done.

But I have to be organized. A long list is better than a short memory and my memory is getting shorter every day. That's the power of the notebook system where everything is written down.

It's easy to blame something else for our failures. The weather is the easiest, and quite frankly, continues to be the most challenging factor for our success as beekeepers. Our busy schedules, interruptions, mites, pesticides, family emergencies, vacations...the list could go on and on.

In reality, our success and the likelihood of achieving sustainability does fall at our feet. It runs around every corner and beckons us to give chase, never allowing us time to catch our breath.

We bear a lot of the responsibility toward the success of our colonies. Sustainability emerges from sound time management and self management.

Chapter 14

OMG! Do I Have CCD?

I've subtitled this manuscript, "Surviving in an Age of CCD," (Colony Collapse Disorder). As I mentioned earlier, I have not seen CCD in my hives. As far as I can tell, I have not lost any hives to CCD.

Judging from the media reports, dumbed down to the least common denominator to fit the 90-second time slot on the local news, replete with mandatory sound-bite and six-month old "b-roll" before the commercial, CCD is everywhere and is the readily apparent cause of the widespread bee deaths, for which we have no answers.

"Back to Bryan with the weather..."

I often take phone calls and respond to e-mails from downhearted beekeepers who lost their bees over the winter, and after we converse for a while, we work through some of the things they did and the confession of the things they failed to do. Then we come to that universal question when they ask, "Do you supposed I had that CCD?"

To answer, "yes," is somewhat comforting. CCD is mysterious, has no known, single cause and we have yet to come up with any single cure. It's like an inevitable, unpreventable, unexpected plague that catches you off-guard and there is nothing you can do, nothing you could have done.

Stuff happens, and this time it happened to you. It's all random and no one can blame you. We all share our sympathies with your loss.

But to answer, "no," is not so comforting. Now we have to find something else as the cause of death, and then weigh the options of what you should have, or could have done. Now you bear the responsibility of failing to do something which resulted in your hive dying, something which would have prevented this loss.

You experience the guilt and the expense of replacing bees that resulted from your assumed negligence. Even if you cannot shoulder the blame, you'll feel like you should. In these cases, I'd almost welcome a good dose of CCD. In the old days, with these kinds of losses, we'd give you the stony silence of derision. After all, you must be stupid, or lazy, or you're stupid <u>and</u> lazy. But this isn't the old days, anymore, and we're all losing bees feeling like we're doing something wrong. Dying bees is the great equalizer.

But was it CCD and how can I tell?

CCD is defined by a handful of narrowly defined symptoms. When you open a hive that was once a thriving, well-populated, productive colony and you witness a rapid disappearance of the bees, CCD is the first thought that comes to mind. The first thing to look for is the sudden, inexplicable loss of most of the adult bees. The research experts like to call this a rapid "depopulation." The bees simply vanish. They're gone.

Now here is part of the problem. Some very productive hives, appearing healthy because they have a huge foraging force and produce several supers of honey will suddenly depopulate due to what we call a "mite crash." It usually appears later in the season, after the honey flow, when the mite population moves ahead of the bee population and when the queen starts slowing down her egg laying production. It looks like CCD, feels like CCD but it's a mite problem. Still, there is a sudden loss of adult bees and this moves us to the next symptom of CCD.

The second symptom of CCD is not finding dead bees on the bottom board. The bees are gone. The presence of dead bees on the bottom board, in my best guess, is another sign of a mite crash. CCD leaves no dead bees on the bottom board.

Sometimes I've been out to check a bee yard and I notice how a hive which was once active with foraging bees is suddenly, and remarkably vacant. I open the hive and I find no bees, no brood, no honey, nothing but the whisper of a ghostly vacancy and the labored breathing of my frustration.

Yes, this hive mysteriously depopulated, but there are no signs of life other than, maybe, a few wax moths which just recently flew in effortlessly and without any resistance. The hive is empty.

This sounds like common absconding, which in my mind is something the colony does when it is under pressure from varroa mites. The queen stops laying eggs so there is no brood. The colony, en masse, flies the coop to regroup somewhere else. Robber bees soon move in and remove any leftover honey, if there was any left. Robbing leaves the comb torn up and rough, and you'll find a lot of the crumbs on the bottom board. Wax moths, even small hive beetles follow suit and move in.

I've opened vacant, abandoned hives and it appears robbing was the cause of the absconding. Comb is roughly torn up and there will be dead bees on the bottom board and in front of the hive. It's usually a weaker hive to start with and robbing takes it down. Often this happens to nucs or any hive you are feeding in a yard with strong hives...a reason why I like to move my nucs to their own segregated yard. Throw in a nectar dearth and you've got the invitation to disaster.

Then there are those times there are no bees but a host of small hive beetles, beetle larvae and slimed up comb and honey stores. This was the case when the beetles moved in, made a stinky mess and the bees left. Small hive beetles seem to smell some kind of pheromone that tells them this is a weak hive and they move in rapidly.

Sometimes the colony goes queenless and instead of settling to allow a laying worker to continue, the bees simply fly away and supposedly join a thriving hive.

Rapid depopulation is also a sign of pesticide kills. When I suspect absconding, I'll notice one or two vacant hives in the bee yard. With a pesticide kill, all the hives will be affected, and in most cases, the foragers are the ones that die leaving a hive of nurse bees along with the brood. In some cases of non-CCD mortality, I'll find the ground at the entrance to the hive covered in dead bees. With CCD, there are no dead bees.

Swarming is also a rapid depopulation, but the colony leaves behind the tell-tale queen cells and there will be an absence of open brood.

The third symptom of CCD is finding brood and the queen present, along with a very small contingent of workers. The hive is not completely vacated. The fourth symptom is a reluctance of robber bees and moths to enter. The colony sits there, with unguarded honey stores begging to be robbed, and for some strange reason, no other bee will touch it. The fifth symptom is these combs seem to be infectious.

These five symptoms will give you a pretty good, and fairly accurate idea if you have CCD or something else. Oddly, it's easier to diagnose CCD than it is to attempt to discern the other problems which are not CCD. And taking descriptions over the phone is tough, first, because I have someone trying to verbally describe something that I have to interpret visually, and second, I have to ask questions which the caller may not understand or know what I am asking for or what he needs to look for and find in the hive.

The cause of CCD is not known, but is suspected to originate from a composite of several factors, including a mysterious synergy, that is, if we looked at these factors individually, we would find they cause no problems. Yet when combined, several of these factors, together prove to be quite lethal. Unfortunately, we never really know what combinations are possible.

Another problem in finding the cause of CCD is the lack of dead bees. We don't have any of the bees that mysteriously vanished. We have no sample to analyze. They are gone. Further, just when we think we've narrowed the cause down to one or two factors, we find these same factors present in healthy hives.

CCD is obviously some combination of factors, that interact and create a malevolent, undetectable wave of destruction that sweeps through our colonies. It's a mystery. Interestingly, however, some of the latest research continues to point to pesticides as the catalyst that sets other forces in motion, perhaps causing a sensitivity or susceptibility to normally benign factors like viruses and other pathogens.

To add more problems to our detective work, new pathogens are showing up on the scene, old pathogens are evolving and, of course, viruses are always evolving. In the length of time it takes to come up with a cure once we've identified a specific pathogen, the pathogen has changed and evolved and we have nothing to address the new form.

Pesticides continue, and will likely always pop up on our radar, as a favorite suspect, both the pesticides the beekeepers intentionally place in the hive (legally approved and otherwise) and the pesticides the bees encounter in the environment.

We're discovering how legally registered pesticides are safe for bees, until they are unknowingly combined with another substance (i.e., fungicides) and the detrimental synergy kills off the bees.

Let's not discount environmental stress that comes from poor nutrition, such as the suspected pollen in GMO crops, monoculture, herbicides, nor let us rule out other environmental irritants such as air and water pollution. And just how do these environmental stresses affect the bees? We're discovering behavioral effects such as memory problems and learning difficulties, which in turn, lead to a bee's inability to find her way back to the hive when foraging. It's like the bees develop Alzheimer's disease and wander until they expire.

There are physiological effects compromising longevity and the immune system of the bee. What normally is a small bump in the road to the health of bee now becomes a vehicle-engulfing pot hole. A simple cough now becomes cancer.

There are so many possibilities and causes of bee deaths that I'm left thinking the situation is hopeless. Why even bother keeping bees when the odds are stacked against them, and us? Perhaps I'm just too stupid, too stubborn, too mean to give up. Even if I lost all my bees, I'd find a beekeeper who sold bees and I'd refill my boxes. And I'll probably continue keeping bees until they pry my hive tool from my cold, dead fingers.

Any Good News?

Still, CCD brings us some benefits. First, the public awareness of the bees dying and the problem of meeting the pollination requirements of some of our favorite foods has elevated the perception and status of the beekeeper to that of a rock star.

The public has an increased appreciation for these little insects and the role they play in our food supply. Somewhere we've estimated that honey bees contribute $15 billion dollars of production, roughly responsible for one out of every three bites of food.

Second, CCD brings an awareness to us beekeepers about the harmful, sub-lethal practices which may weaken the honey bee's defenses, even contributing to the compromise of her immune system.

I remember an American Beekeeping Federation (ABF) meeting, about ten years ago, when the topic of the misapplication of chemicals intentionally placed in the hive, both legally registered and otherwise, might be contributing to the mysterious bee deaths.

We want so badly to blame the big agricultural corporations and their heinous plans, but when the finger came back around and the researcher implied we were part of the problem, the room fell deathly quiet. I thought we might consider stoning her for her suggestive accusations. How dare she insinuate our illegal concoctions of homemade miticides might be part of our problem?

It seemed each of us felt convicted, recalling our carelessness and procrastination, bad habits and short-cuts, including our ignorance at following the directions on the box of miticide strips. Our guilt inspired better management and diligence in the application of chemical miticides, even vows of trying to find softer and more natural approaches to mite control. We became more responsive and attentive to issues of mite resistance and chemical residues. We changed our management to switching out those old, black combs. There was a rebirth of our consciousness to be better beekeepers.

Third, CCD brings us a wonderful bounty of research dollars to our universities and colleges, agricultural stations and extension centers. CCD happened and our institutions of higher learning took notice. With government funding, they have the tools to continue their work.

Fourth, CCD brings a tidal wave of new beekeepers hoping to stem the death march of hive mortality. While I still cringe at well-intentioned people thinking they know more than some of us beekeepers with several decades of experience, while I ponder at how many of these newbees will end up with dead hives themselves, while I shake my head in disbelief at how some of these good-hearted folks will be selling used equipment after their first year at discounted prices, I still have to thank CCD for raising the public awareness of this hobby that was once thought to be a nuisance.

When I was in college at Iowa State University, working on my slate of classes and figuring out some of the possible electives, my advisor came across "Entomology 222: Beekeeping" taught by Richard Trump. I thought it was an excellent option.

My advisor blew off that idea, implying this was one of those courses, "Popular with the granola crowd. You know, the nuts and the flakes."

Well, I was a member of the granola crowd at that stage in my life. Still am, to a certain degree.

When I started keeping bees I was likened to the crazy old lady who kept a million cats in the rickety, old house on the corner that smelled like urine, even when you stood outside in the street. Who in the world would think beekeepers would now reside on a pedestal, promoted to the front page of the local newspaper, not as a nutcase, but as the savior who secures our local food supply?

CCD has been a challenge, and it's hard to reckon the good in the face of such devastation. You can't make a silk purse out of a sow's ear, but they do make great doggy treats.

Not all of our beekeeping problems can be directly tied to CCD, but CCD has become the symbolic symptom of greater problems in our environment, not just in the way we keep, and have kept, honey bees, but also in the way we grow our food. Consumers are asking questions and demanding answers. But we're still looking for the silver lining to this storm cloud, and at the rate bees are dying, it better be soon.

Until we figure things out, we're just going to have to live with CCD and readjust our beekeeping practices to much more sustainable methods. We really have no choice!

And it may be the greatest challenges are still ahead. I can't imagine anything worse than what we're facing today. In the mean time, I plan to keep on keeping bees. I hope that's your commitment as well. We just need to find that way forward.

Chapter 15

Has Beekeeping Become a Game of Attrition?

Can Anything Alleviate the Effects of Hive Mortality?

It seems hive mortality has become the norm. I don't like it. I can't really change it. I've come to accept it, begrudgingly.

In the wake of these inevitable losses, it seems there are two approaches to staying in business. The first approach is addressing the <u>causes</u> of the losses and finding alternative solutions. That's a topic attracting increased attention and ample discussion, currently. It's my hope to find sustainable solutions to this problem and I've spent most of this manuscript describing how I best go about finding a new path.

The second approach is addressing the <u>effects</u> of the losses, namely, how can we stay ahead of the hive mortality? If it is a given that we're going to lose hives and our alternative treatments and protocols are not effective, how do we keep our numbers up? How do I stay sustainable even if my practices can't seem to address the problem? How do I stay ahead of the game?

The past year has me pondering a new approach to beekeeping I'm going to call, "Beekeeping Through Anticipated Attrition."

I come to this approach with the mindset that there's not a lot I can do to reduce the <u>causes</u> of the mortality that I'm not already doing, but is there something I can do to reduce or minimize the <u>effects</u> of staggering losses and override the consequences to my bottom line? If beekeeping has become a game of attrition, how do I play the game? How do I win?

The basis of attrition is the acceptance that things will wear out, wear down, weaken and drop out. The effects of attrition are felt when these losses are not replaced, such as a budget-strapped business that does not replace their employees lost through retirement. In such a case, the same level of work is now divided among fewer employees. Then some of these employees feel stressed and they leave for better work. Attrition continues to deplete the work force, thus productivity and morale suffer.

But what if this company could afford to hire replacements prior to the anticipated attrition through retirement? There would be no loss of productivity, no stress, no further decline. All it would take is hiring more people to counter the expected losses, and what a benefit to have them trained and acclimated to take over when the inevitable need arose.

So take my attrition theory as it might apply to beekeeping. We start with the idea of "acceptable" losses. At this juncture of our industry, an average loss of 30% is now the norm, a level which can be expected for a number of reasons.

I still mistakenly hang on to the antiquated criticism that if you lost 30% of your bees, you are a horribly negligent beekeeper. Instead, in today's world, 30% is a level which makes us shrug our shoulders, grin and bear it, and soldier on.

I may not like it, but if I can't change it, I have to accept it. I have to remind myself I don't live in "the good old days" when I started keeping bees. I don't want to accept a 30% loss, but neither do I want to accept the notion there is no Santa Claus.

Reality stinks. These are the cards we're dealt; now we have to figure how to play the best hand.

How to Play the Game

So in anticipation of this 30% attrition of our beehives, what if we could afford to enter the winter with 30% more hives? This would be our strategy to stay ahead of our losses, kind of like moving three steps forward knowing we're going to be knocked back two steps.

As an example, suppose I want to keep 40 hives. If I bring 40 hives into the winter, given a 30% loss, I come out with 28 hives (30% of 40 hives is a loss of 12 hives, leaving 28 of my original 40 hives).

Instead of following the standard, <u>reactive strategy</u> of purchasing early season, mail-order queens and making splits (fraught with their own levels of attrition), what if I anticipated the losses and made summer splits prior to going into the winter.

These summer splits could be made after the honey harvest (with the idea of raising my own queens from my best, locally adapted stock), so I would enter the winter with 60 hives. This is a <u>proactive strategy</u> to counter the anticipated potential losses.

Then, just to make the math easy, my 30% attrition rate would account for an anticipated loss of 18 hives (30% of 60 hives) and I end up with 42 live hives (60 minus 18 hives). Now I'm at my desired level and I'm not scrambling to find queens and fight the fickle weather to make splits, not to mention the increasing cost of buying and shipping queens.

This model, however, does presuppose you have the requisite equipment and the locations to handle the extra hives anticipating a normal attrition rate. I still lose bee hives, but the loss is not so cataclysmic. I'm at the level I desire to produce honey and fulfill my markets.

Let's further suppose I want to fill my anticipated market of 2400 pounds of honey, and I can usually expect an average of 60 pounds (about two supers) from each hive. But wait, not all of my 40 hives are going to give me 60 pounds of surplus honey. In many cases, one hive will give me three supers and the one next to it yields nothing.

So back to my attrition theory. If I had 40 hives and 8 of them do nothing (poor queens, ineffective mite treatments, swarming, supersedure, etc.), then I won't have all the honey I hope to sell.

This is a 20% attrition rate from the surviving hives, which means I really need to bring 50 hives successfully through the winter (20% loss of production from 50 hives gives me 40 producing hives).

So if I need 50 surviving hives (40 of which will actually produce), and given a 30% loss from the winter, I really need to enter the winter with 70 hives

(30% loss on 70 hives takes out 21 hives, leaving 49 hives. A 20% production loss on 49 hives takes away 10 hives, leaving me with 39 producing hives with an expected honey harvest).

Responses and Reactions

So to successfully harvest honey from 40 hives (my original goal and intent), I need to enter winter with 70 hives.

When I roll these numbers past my beekeeping buddies, their first response is, "What the *[expletive deleted]*! I don't want to manage 70 hives! I don't want the extra equipment taking up space in my garage! I don't want to have to find the additional out yards to place these bees! This is too much work as it is! Are you crazy? Have you lost your mind?"

But in their next breath, they are complaining on the difficulty of keeping bees today--and yes, it is a challenge to keep bees alive and productive. They complain about shopping around trying to find available queens at the last minute when they realize they need a couple of queens.

They grumble how some of their best hives from last year haven't amounted to anything this year, presuming the queen "played out," or blaming that nebulous specter of the mites. They whine about how beekeeping is really "a rich man's hobby" and it just doesn't pay to keep bees.

Then their spouse usually chimes in on how all the money they made from selling honey last year was needed to buy southern nucs or packages to replace the dead hives. They ask how anyone makes any money with these kinds of losses.

Given this scenario, you can't make money with these kinds of losses. But there is a way to anticipate the losses, plan ahead and account for the anticipated attrition.

What I find ironic is how these same beekeepers share their desire to produce bumper crops of honey and sell it to make giant piles of money to recoup their investment. Yet they won't put up the resources to make this dream come true. Frugality may be one of our industry's real problems.

Accepting Reality

You can complain all you want about CCD or pesticides or poorly mated queens, but one of our symptoms of today's problems is this inevitable attrition and staggering losses that translates into frustration and discouragement, not to mention lost honey production. I hate the notion of 30% losses, but it's what we're looking at. And we need to develop more sustainable models to reduce the negative cash flow every spring.

Personally, I think the answer lies in anticipating this inescapable attrition by working ahead of the losses so we are always in a position of preparation, as opposed to reacting from a position of limited resources. I want to be proactive instead of stressed from circumstances that force me to be reactive.

Even with our beginning beekeepers, we continue to preach the message how it is far better to start with two hives, four hives if they can afford it, in the event something should happen to one of their hives. With two hives, a beginner has covered their potential attrition and frames of brood can be transferred to bolster a weak queen or refill a dead out.

At several of the conferences I've attended, many of the speakers are strongly suggesting the notion of making a nuc from a production colony, keeping it on hand just in case something happens to the original hive. They don't use the word, "attrition," but they suggest taking proactive measures to protect against undesired losses.

This was my thought process when I pull the queen out on June 1st and force the colony to raise their own queen. I could just as easily bought a mail-order queen and introduced it to the nuc but I'm trying to become more sustainable.

Concluding Thoughts

Beekeeping through anticipated attrition means taking a practical line of attack, starting out with more hives than you'd really like to manage, or have time to care for, even a level that may make your spouse nervous.

You know, that despite your best efforts and glorified intentions, all your overwintered colonies won't survive in a normal year, but you have the option to take control and make your gains before you are forced to take your losses.

It's a challenge to keep bees alive and productive in today's environment. We have come to accept we're not keeping bees like our predecessors who would cringe in humiliation and failure with, let alone admit, a 30% loss.

Anticipating these losses with additional bee hives keeps us at a production level where we want to be, preempting that annual exercise of playing "catch up," where we sacrifice our best hives to make up for losses we know we now have to accept.

I want to keep my best hives my best hives. Strong hives produce honey and that's my purpose for keeping honey bees. I don't want to split them in the spring to make up for winter losses.

The figures I used (30% survival loss and 20% production loss) are purely arbitrary and may not realistically fit your situation. If you're a good beekeeper, you've got the records to know your expected loss levels and you can make the appropriate calculations.

The idea behind anticipated attrition is to put yourself ahead of the game and reduce your own level of anxiety and frustration. After all, aren't we supposed to be enjoying this endeavor?

And what if you brought 70 hives into the winter and only sustained a 10% mortality rate? Now you have all those extra hives to sell or keep on hand to make honey.

Wouldn't that be a great problem to have?

Chapter 16

Is Treatment-Free Beekeeping the Gateway to Sustainability?

"Our greatest fear should not be of failure but of succeeding at things in life that don't really matter."
– Francis Chan

I've turned some of this ground earlier, but I'd like to take another swipe at it.

Here are the big questions that seem to be dominating some of the discussions, namely,

- ✓ Should all bee keepers be moving toward a treatment-free regime and totally eliminate chemicals from their production hives?

- ✓ Are we not simply perpetuating weak and inferior bees by using treatments to prop up our hives as if treatments were some kind of "crutch?"

- ✓ Should we encourage beekeepers to go "cold turkey" with respect to eliminating any treatments and let the chips fall where they may as the survivor bees emerge from the wreckage?

The treatment-free movement is gaining traction due to increased bee deaths and escalated hive mortality, ubiquitously accounted as CCD, attributed, in part, to all the toxins (i.e. "treatments"), legal or otherwise, which beekeepers (mostly commercial types) deliberately place in their hives to fight mites and diseases.

Treating hives has been our standard practice for the last three decades, ever since varroa invited itself into our lives. It is a fairly common consensus that these treatments are necessary to keep bees healthy and productive. The hitch in this consensus is the growing ineffectiveness of the treatments and the increased hive mortality that plagues the industry despite treating hives.

It sounds like that old axiom, "Can't win for losing."

Given the problems we are facing, given the perception of the rather obvious, unsustainable nature of the industry as it exists or presently persists, is treatment-free beekeeping the wave of the future? Is this our gateway to sustainability?

We find ourselves, again, sliding into another form of that polarizing division, this time over the options of whether or not to treat honey bees, more particularly treating for varroa mites, though the nature of treating hives in any form, with any substance, becomes a point of derision. And it's a valid discussion as we ponder our future and the sustainability of our practices.

The issue boils down to asking, is treatment-free the only way forward? Is it the best way?

On one hand, we have a rather large group of traditional, conventional beekeepers who treat their bees as a standard management practice. The two most common forms of treatment would likely be some kind of miticide to combat the varroa mite, and some kind of supplemental, seasonal feeding. The varroa treatment may be a synthetic chemical, such as Apivar, or a natural treatment, such as powdered sugar or a thymol product. The supplemental feeding is probably a sucrose syrup or HFCS (High Fructose Corn Syrup).

Now some people argue that feeding is feeding, not treating, but syrups are used to transmit helpful products such as essential oils or fumagilin-B and thus you now have a "treatment." There are those beekeepers who insist that anything artificial added to the hive constitutes a treatment, particularly because you, the beekeeper, took too much of something else away (i.e., honey or pollen). We'll discuss what constitutes treating in a minute.

Over and against these treatment beekeepers come a smaller, but growing number of the progressive, treatment-free beekeepers. To be fully treatment-free, that is, free of treatments, you don't treat. Period. The whole definition is so simple and plain, right? There are no treatments allowed and you do not treat. This group contends you don't need any treatments and any treatments you place in the hive only pushes our precarious unsustainability off the apocalyptic cliff of annihilation plummeting into the slough of despond.

Okay, maybe it's not that bad, but the group contends treating hives is not moving the industry in the right direction. Any treatment, according to this philosophy, continues to imprison the beekeeping profession in a past which has no hope. If there is no hope, any application of treatments is a practice which is, by definition, rather unsustainable.

Part of our problem is coming up with agreeable terms. The sticky point is deciding, and agreeing on the definition of treating and what actions or management regimes constitute a treatment.

I went to one of my favorite web sites is www.beesource.com. I borrowed content, with permission, from a "sticky" copied in their "Treatment-free" forum, the list of prohibited treatments or what constitutes a treatment is, but not limited to:

> Apiguard (thymol)
> Mite-away II (formic acid)
> Apistan (fluvalinate)
> Sucrocide (sucrose octanoate esters)
> Mite-A-Thol (menthol)
> Terramycin/Tetra-B (antibiotic)
> Tylan (antibiotic)
> Gardstar (permethrin)
> Fumagilin (antibiotic)
> Paramoth (p-dichlorobenzene)
> Checkmite (coumaphos)
> Oxalic Acid (dicarboxylic acid)
> Formic Acid (carboxylic acid)
> Mineral Oil (food grade mineral oil, FGMO)
> Sugar Dusting (sucrose)
> HBH (essential oils)
> MegaBee (diet formula)
> Honey Bee Healthy (feeding stimulant containing essential oils)
> Bt Aizawai (bacteria)
> Thymol (crystals, feed, or fogging)
> Essential oils (in general)
> Grease patties (Crisco etc.)

The treatment free group will allow some manipulations and equipment which may include, but not limited to:

>Frequent queen replacement
>Systematic splitting
>Frequent replacement of comb/foundation
>Small cell foundation
>Drone comb removal
>Screened Bottom Boards
>Small Hive Beetle Traps
>Honey Harvest
>Pollen Harvest
>Frame Manipulation
>Hive Body Reversal
>The Use of a Smoker
>Sticky Boards
>Any Method of Breeding

In terms of feeding, these are allowed:

>Sugar syrup
>Dry granulated sugar
>High Fructose Corn Syrup (HFCS)
>Pollen substitutes

This directory is just an arbitrary inventory of treatments, used as the criteria for participation in one particular web site. While it is not a formal or universally agreed upon list outside the beesource forum, it presents a convenient base for our discussion in this chapter.

My heartfelt gratitude to Moderator Barry who has taken a lot of time and a great deal of effort to define what constitutes a "treatment." I want to use this list as the basis for some common ground so we don't have to debate what is, or is not a treatment. If you wonder if drilling holes in supers to let in a little sunshine is a treatment, I implore you to consult the list.

Why is this important? What's at issue with treating and/or not treating? Can't we treat as we've always treated or do we really need to move away from the old ways, shift our paradigm to a treatment-free management regime? Is treatment-free beekeeping in the best interest of preserving the future of beekeeping?

The treatment camp believes treating hives is necessary and permissible. Treatment beekeepers will contend they cannot keep their bees alive and productive without some kind of pharmaceutical or food-grade intervention.

Here's a key question to ask: is this wrong or immoral to treat a colony if that's what it takes to keep bees alive and productive? A key word in this question is "productive." The majority of the conventional beekeeping community bases the measure of their success on productivity, i.e., honey production. Is this motivation improper?

We tend to think of these treatment beekeepers as the commercial types, but this is not necessarily so. Commercial types, the larger beekeepers who keep bees to make honey or pollinate crops, need to keep their bees alive. Many backyard beekeepers want to keep their bees alive, as well. I want to keep my bees alive. Is it wrong to treat if this is what it takes to keep my bees alive?

If the commercial types lose their bees, their livelihood is gone. The lack of bees creates pollination issues that translate into production shortages. Backyard beekeepers can always buy more bees, but where do they turn to buy packages and nucs? Most of them turn to the southern commercial types who are likely treating their bees, due, in part, to keeping their bees alive in order to provide package bees to back yard beekeepers.

It's the circle of life, or death, depending upon how you see it. I would recommend, if you can find a treatment-free producer of nucs and packages to take advantage of their work in this direction. You'll just be that much further along in the game.

So the commercial types, conventional beekeepers, a loose category which I tend to fall into myself, are characterized as requiring synthetic chemicals to maintain healthy bees. But is the actual health of the bees compromised by residues in the comb and sub-lethal effects from exposure to the pesticides that may further compromise the bees' immune system? This is an area of current and ongoing research. Remember we're trying to kill a bug on a bug without unintentionally killing the wrong bug. These poisons have to be incredibly selective.

I am reminded of the days when I kept sheep. I was fresh out of college with an industrial, commercialized education in production agriculture. Sheep are notorious for picking up worms and intestinal parasites. At the time, one of the most effective anthelmintics (dewormers) was lead arsenic.

Yep, you read that right. We intentionally gave our sheep an incredibly toxic poison, but just enough poison to expel the intestinal parasites without killing the sheep. And in the days that followed the treatment, many of those sheep limped around like they had a horrible belly ache. No doubt they did have some digestive malfunctions. They went off their feed. And we knew the lead arsenic was raising cane with the ecology of their rumens and the biological flora that broke down all that roughage we were feeding them.

But this is the way it was done back then. After a few days, their appetite returned and they were so much better off without those parasites. Lead arsenic, setting aside the side effects, was quite effective on intestinal parasites.

I've been out of the sheep business for thirty years so I'm not sure what's working in today's economy. Oddly, back then, no one ever mentioned treatment-free shepherding and if you ever witnessed the devastating effects from the easily eliminated parasites on an old ewe, you would advocate immediate treatment without question.

From my ovine perspective, I ponder why would we allow our hives to accommodate the presence of varroa mites? If you've ever witnessed bees just outside the hive with bent wings in the form of a "K" or bees wriggling around in the grass in front of the hive, unable to get back up into the hive, would you not advocate immediate treatment, given the parameters and restrictions of the miticide? I'm thinking in particular of having honey supers on the hive that would have to be removed before any chemical treatment could commence.

Alongside this synthetic chemical treatment group we find the "soft" approaches. You can see from the directory at the beginning of this chapter how many of the "safe," "soft," "natural," "food-grade," "whatever," treatments are still treatments.

Personally, I like these soft approaches. They are not perfect or particularly effective from the standpoint of being a "give it one shot and be done." They take multiple applications and need other mechanisms such as screen bottom boards. Side effects are not usually an issue, and if so, are usually short-lived.

The treatment-free community eschews any treatment that provides some or any kind of assistance that does not allow for the full expression or potential vulnerability of the genetic code. Any treatment, in reality, is a crutch that props up a weakness. I can't disagree. But sometimes the bees need that crutch. We keep bees in environments with a host of potential toxins and pollution beyond the scope of our control. As a production-oriented beekeeper, I need (want?) that extra edge a crutch provides.

When it comes to bees and parasites, and the beekeepers who administer pesticides, we need beekeepers who read the directions. When Apistan (fluvalinate) first came out, it was heralded as an answer to our prayers in the early days of the varroa mite invasion. At that time, there were two choices: treat your hive or watch your hive die. Treatment was administered without question, and to be fair, we had no idea of residues in combs or resistance in the mites.

The time span to put the strips in the hives was 42 days, clearly stated in the directions on the side of the box. That 42-day period covered two complete brood cycles for the honey bees. Beekeepers were prohibited from applying the strips in the colony when the honey supers were present. Timing was everything, and the beekeeper was expected to follow the prescribed directions. This wasn't rocket science and the instructions were printed in plain English. No box ever listed, "For instructions in English, press 1." It was right there for everyone to read.

I witnessed, first hand, beekeepers who kept the strips in the brood nest all year long, which is a definite violation of the directions. Some beekeepers merely struck a compromise by putting the strips in the hive at the last inspection in the fall and removing those strips when the weather moderated enough to open the hive first thing in the spring.

What part about this not being rocket science did they not understand?

In another lifetime in my beekeeping career, I was helping an older beekeeper with his four hives. This fellow could no longer lift the supers and I was an inexperienced but willing helper hoping to glean some of his wisdom. He kept bees successfully for several decades and was highly respected locally for his wonderful honey. We approached a hive and I pulled the honey supers off, down to the queen excluder...and WTF? (**W**hy **T**he **F**luvalinate?)

Clearly visible, propolized to the bottom of the queen excluder, were the brown tabs from four, nicely spaced, Apistan strips still in his brood nest.

When I gently probed as to why the strips were still in the hive, cautiously mentioning that I didn't think this was the proper way to use them, I got the ignorant response of, "Oh, it's okay if you put them below the excluder and don't rob any honey from the brood area."

Good grief. Where's this information coming from? To paraphrase Mark Twain, again, "The beekeeper who can read and doesn't is just as dangerous as the beekeeper who cannot read." Ignorance isn't bliss and the misappropriate application of these chemicals is part of our problem.

Yes, Pogo, we have met the enemy and it is us.

The use and abuse of a plethora of chemicals only pushed the limits of the respective effectiveness of what had been offered to us to combat the mites. The mites began building resistance and we needed better, stronger more toxic chemicals.

Hello, coumophos.

Then that chemical quit working. As I put this manuscript together, I don't know anyone who still supports the use of fluvalinate or coumophos, though the supply catalogs still sell them.

Up until this last year, prior to the registration of Apivar (amitraz), the commercial and conventional beekeepers were running out of legal options. We still held out hope for formic acid, remarketed as "Mite Away Quick Strips" or MAQS. Canadians still used oxalic acid, but it's not approved in the United States, though many beekeepers use it regardless (technically, they are "bleaching" their top bars, wink, wink).

Thankfully, a couple of thymol-based miticides are still available. Beekeepers have been instructed to rotate the respective miticides as insurance against resistant mites.

So we have some problems treating with synthetic chemicals, some collateral damage, some residue issues. Soft approaches tend to be labor intensive and applications are without standardization.

But what is the alternative? If the treatment-free option is fully embraced, wholly engaged, and I mean adhering to the letter of the law according to our prohibited list, we can expect a horrendous loss of bees, perhaps greater than the collateral damage and the losses accounted to CCD.

Some of the treatment-free beekeepers, the most ardent and radical activists, welcome such overwhelming carnage, a genetic "cleansing." The question arises, are we not just breeding tougher and tougher mites with these miticides that continue to lose their potency? Are we raising an army of resistant mites that will prove imperious and impervious to everything, including the illegal, kitchen sink concoctions? It's a hard to argue against this kind of progression which makes a treatment-free management regime all the more logical.

What if this resistance trend continues? How far will it go? How will this play out? Will the treated hives continue to weaken from residues as we resume raising chemically-addicted bees? Will the miticides continue to decline in their effectiveness? Will we continue to breed resistance in the mites to the point where nothing works?

It's possible. In a fallen world where wonder-working, miracle drugs are saving the human race one week, then have to be pulled from the store shelves the next week due to atrocious and unspeakable side effects, anything is possible. Nothing surprises me anymore.

It's possible, given some rather apocalyptic scenarios and perhaps enough time. It may be our present regime of synthetic miticides becomes so useless the treatment-free course of therapy develops into the default option rather than the protocol of choice. It's a long shot, but I can image the possibility.

Thankfully, we are not at this place in this moment in time. But part of my hope for a sustainable beekeeping practice is to leave some bees for my grandchildren, and their grandchildren to raise. There's a bigger picture than me and my honey at the farmer's market answering questions about local honey and allergies.

The treatment-free crowd points to the evolution of the honey bees in Russia, where no miticides were available when the varroa mites came calling. The way the legend is told, massive losses of colonies devastated the country resulting in the survival of only the hardiest, toughest, most resistant stock of honey bee.

From this point of bottoming out, the numbers began to grow as Russian beekeepers bred queen bees from the surviving remnant. The beekeepers had no choice, and though not unscathed, these beekeepers learned to adapt and survive. A new strain of resilient genetics emerged from the dust and told the mites, "Bring it on! It's game time."

I've tried some bees which were sold to me as "Russians." I have no idea what percentage of their pedigree was truly Russian as any queen I purchase on this level is open-mated, that is, mated with whatever drones she can find in the neighborhood. I liked their color, being darker. This obligated me to mark my queen as darker queens are harder to find amid dark workers.

But the bees were "runny," that is, when I opened the hive after giving them a little smoke, rather than sit quietly on the comb, they rushed around frantically. They were more aggressive and temperamental, but I'm used to vigorous bees so it wasn't an issue with me. They produced an embarrassing meager crop of honey and then they died the following winter.

Honey is my bread and butter, so I had productivity issues with these bees described to me as "Russian" honey bees. While some of my colleagues swear by their Russians, I can only swear at mine. I say, "Good riddance." Some of the successful beekeepers with Russian honey bees have encouraged me to give them another try, that what I had were "not likely very Russian."

The Russian stock evolved out what I described earlier as the "Bond" method, unintentionally. It was natural selection at its harshest with the greatest pressure to live or die...and a lot of colonies could not cut the mustard. Nature worked its heartless purposes out with the most grueling course ever dictated.

Is this what we are facing down the road? Will we experience a total failure of all of our chemical options such that we are forced to become treatment-free? Will we be compelled to let nature take its course, irrespective of the economic cost to the beekeeper, not to mention the loss of pollination? Is the United States beekeeping industry the next

Russia? Is it only going to get worse before it gets better?

No, I don't think so. However, I have personally listened to a host of beekeepers profess their love of treatment-free beekeeping as the salvation of the honey bee, the messianic management tool of the truly omniscient apiarists that will save beekeeping for those who are wise enough to read, and heed, the hand writing on the wall. The rest of us ignorant slobs are just providing the bees a crutch and perpetuating inferior bees that will someday cost us dearly, only proving the superiority of treatment-free beekeeping. We have been warned.

Okay, I will civilly and pleasantly respond that we all still have the option to choose which method and management regime works for us. I provide my bees a crutch. I have my own personal crutch and it's called "corrective lenses." Without my contact lenses or my glasses, my vision is about 20/4000, really. My glasses are so thick they raise the esteem of coke bottle bottoms. I'm literally blind without my glasses. Yeah, I need a crutch, and so do my bees.

I practice Integrated Pest Management (IPM) and measure my mite loads. Yes, it's time consuming. One of the benefits of going treatment-free is you never have to worry about counting mites. The problem reconciles itself without the wasteful energies and worries of mite control.

I'm not at this point in my management. I prefer to know what I'm facing and take the necessary proactive and preemptive steps, but this reflects my purpose in keeping bees which is to produce honey. Dead hives are lousy honey producers. Yes, I have tried this and it is no way to make honey. I need live hives.

I like the alcohol wash which will deliberately take the lives of 300 bees from each colony I sample. I've used other methods of counting mites and I think the alcohol wash is the most accurate. Yes, I've taken samples from the same hive by different methods and the greatest number of mites always, "comes out in the wash."

Doesn't everything come out in the wash?

Please don't get all up in my face with any kind of presumed righteousness about murdering 300 bees. I know some treatment-free activists that will allow a weak, little hive of 20,000 bees to perish just to stick to their convictions and principles that they are ridding the world of inferior, drug-addicted genetics that will only weaken the gene pool. They tell me they have to stand by their principles, and those who don't stand will fall for anything.

Okay, I can respect that position. I actually respect a person who has convictions, even if I disagree. Just don't force me to necessarily buy into it.

IPM gives me the option, based on in-the-field, factual knowledge of what to do next. Knowledge is power, if you were paying attention earlier. Knowledge helps us to make informed choices. So in the course of sacrificing 300 bees, some of which would have been dead in six weeks, anyway, I now know where I stand with respect to my mite infestation.

I now know the best option forward, and if the mite population is low, within a threshold of 2%, I am fine to forego any treatment. Armed with the right knowledge, I have the confidence to go treatment-free, but this is no guarantee of survival.

And as I side note, I am becoming increasing convinced that mite loads are the gateway to desolation. I have no other credence to this statement other than my emergent opinion, that if we can control the varroa mites, we will undoubtedly shove most of our evils (viruses and stress) down the drain.

More and more, I am convinced on the importance of dueling with our old nemesis, the varroa mite, which slipped away from our detection, below the radar and behind the shadows of CCD. I'm becoming attuned to the possible connection between mite loads and CCD, but I've not found CCD in my colonies.

This idea of reducing mite populations as a priority gets back to my earlier statements about changing what can be changed and accepting that which cannot be changed, and the wisdom to discern between the two situations so I can take the appropriate steps to make the situation better.

Personally, I don't like to treat. It's expensive, time consuming and takes away from other tasks that need my attention. I would love to be treatment-free. But given the alternative of losing, say 90% of my bees with a management tool I equate to basic neglect, I will treat rather than take those kinds of losses. It's just smart business.

One of my challenges is that I've built a beekeeping sideline on hives given minimal, soft treatments, but treatments none the less. I cannot identify nor characterize my operation as treatment-free given the previously mentioned list as the defining criteria.

I only want to treat to keep my bees alive, healthy, and productive. That's my business model. To jump into the treatment-free regime, cold-turkey, would be devastating, given the nature and history of my management with my bees which require a crutch.

If pressed, I'll confess I'm enabling their dependence, even with the relative innocuous application of soft approaches. I just think the bees need that little extra boost to give them an edge, even if the treatment-free crowd deems it an unfair advantage. If it's a shoe that fits, I'll wear it. But it gets back to my purpose in keeping hives alive and productive. I produce honey.

It may be, in the long run, treatment-free beekeeping is our real, sustainable option. It's the getting there that bothers me. No doubt, providing crutches will make it take longer. I just cannot reconcile the "cold turkey" method. It's just not practical, nor is it feasible. I just don't think the beekeeping industry can afford such radical losses, even though in the greater cosmic scheme of things, treatment-free beekeeping is perceived as the ultimate, sustainable alternative.

Which brings up another point often not covered in these discussions. What is the percentage of loss in conventional hives, with treatments, when compared to the percentage of loss in the treatment-free hives? Treatment-free does not equate to zero mortality.

I also suspect the actual numbers of dead hives will be smaller with the back yard beekeeper of either conventional or treatment-free practices. Beekeepers with smaller apiaries tend to give the hives more attention. It has been my unsubstantiated observation, that when hive numbers increase, hive mortality increases as well.

It is also my ignorantly presumed opinion, that when someone says they manage their hives according to an "XYZ" regime, and they claim to have zero hive mortality, they are usually working with a smaller number of colonies, most typically of single digits, and they care very little about harvesting much honey or controlling their swarms, which is their choice.

God bless them, anyway. I often amuse myself wondering how many back yard beekeepers, treatment-free or otherwise, never make the statistics nor are they asked to participate in the surveys.

I've met a few treatment-free beekeepers who readily confess they lose hives, and with a genuine sincerity they tell me they are willing to accept these losses in the process of winnowing out the susceptible genetics. They raise replacements from the survivors.

I also know a great number of treatment beekeepers who also admit they experience losses, even with perfectly timed treatments, but ironically, they are less accepting of these losses because they tend to think that treatments ought to work, especially given the time and energy they take putting them in and taking them out of the hive.

I met a beekeeper who felt obligate to enlighten the rest of us. He thought the whole chemical approach was merely a hoax concocted by the pharmaceutical companies to take our money. He also believed the varroa mite was intentionally imported to create a market for the chemical strips. He still treated his hives but just could not keep his bees alive through the winter. I don't know what his problem was, but it was not an apparent case of PPB.

Given the probabilities that synthetic chemicals are not particularly effective, given the likelihood that synthetic chemicals are leaving residues, given the possibility these same synthetic chemicals are creating a sub-lethal environment of "queasiness," I continue to ponder the legitimate prospects that the cure may be worst than the disease. But the disease is no picnic, either. I think moving in the direction of eliminating the synthetic chemicals is a good start.

Yes, treating is expensive, but so is buying new packages every spring. I'm in the honey production business and we all know an over-wintered hive is ten times more likely to produce honey than a newly established package or nuc, even on fully drawn frames from the previous year.

With buying replacement bees lost opportunity costs arise, as well. We also have to realize honey only comes from honey bees. I have embraced an obligation to keep my bees alive, and if it takes a treatment of some kind, I'm willing to concede my need of such. My first option, however, is the softer, more natural methods.

I'm wondering, if our trends continue, if we'll have the twelve-step meetings for recovering beekeepers. I imagine standing before a forlorn looking bunch of beekeepers and introduce myself, "Hi, my name is Grant and I am a treater."

"Hi, Grant."

I am convinced the treatment-free option is not feasible for me and my operation, at least not at this time. The list I provided at the beginning of the chapter is an extreme position to one side of the treatment continuum. I do, however, have some extremely remote bee yards at the end of my prioritized list that fit most of the treatment-free criteria because I have a hard time getting to them.

Many of these bee yards are located at a buddy's house. They are likely an apiary with one, maybe two hives brought out to pollinate their garden, as a favor. These remote yards suffer from my neglect as I have larger, more productive yards that seem to monopolize my time and energy.

These hives seem to thrive, despite my benign neglect, and one of these yards is such a pain to inspect because of the landlord. If this fellow is home, he comes out and talks my ear off. He's an old widower and retired farmer who just doesn't venture far off the farm. He's kind of lonely but excessively friendly, and he loves to visit and recall those childhood days when his grandfather raised bees down in Arkansas. Sometimes he tells me the same story, twice in the same visit.

I like to refer to our little visits as "social rent" that has to be paid. In the summer, we usually walk the garden as he searches for harvestable produce he wants to share with me. After all, my bees are doing him a huge favor and he'd like to give me my share. This can take some time as he relates every plant, every variety, every bug that bit the plant and how he used to grow this one tomato years ago and he'd really like to find some seed but he's afraid they don't grow that variety anymore...tick, tock; tick, tock.

He hits me up for a couple of quarts of honey a year which is cheap given the relative cost of the social rent.

To inspect this yard takes me about two or three hours, for one hive, from the time I drive through the gate until the time I hit the highway on the way back home. These bees seem to do okay, though I do notice old swarm cells so I know the swarming is part of their resiliency. The level of production is usually about a super, much less than my expected harvest elsewhere.

When I find capped swarm cells, I cut out all but one hoping I've still got a little potential production left in the hive. I put up swarm traps in the neighboring fence rows in hopes of catching my own swarms.

No, it's not ideal, but it's more of a ministry to this old man than anything I gain from it. Sometimes I just got to trust the mystery of karma. You reap what you sow.

These are the kind of hives in my apiaries that go treatment-free, not by choice as much by default. And then after a couple of years of treatment-free management, they fade away and dwindle to nothing.

At the other extreme on the treatment continuum, we find the traditional arsenal of legally available miticides purchased through the normal suppliers. I don't like the collateral damage and suspected residues of these synthetic chemical miticides so I don't use them. I don't like the suspected resistance building in the mite population which renders the expense and labor of treating rather useless. I often wonder how much peril I present to my own health as I'm exposed to these synthetic chemicals.

As much as I feel I need to give my bees a little protection, a little insurance, a little boost in the battle against the mites, the synthetic chemicals are not my choice either. If you pressed me for a universal mite treatment, should my IPM warrant such, I would go with formic acid or thymol, though these fumigants mess up the communication in the hive and confuse the queen's productivity. There is no perfect chemical treatment and treatment-free practices are not perfect, either. Still, I would really prefer not to treat at all, if I felt I could get away from the treatments and tolerate the anticipated losses.

I have gravitated to a middle-of-the-road approach, what I consider to be a self-described, common-sense, practical method of beekeeping that I believe is the basis for my sustainability. I do not consider a strict, treatment-free regime to be my gateway to sustainability, but nor do I believe the synthetic chemical path we trod is the method to deliver us from these present evils.

Somewhere in the middle is the balanced approach, avoiding treatments if possible, but treating if necessary, and treating only with the most benign, least offensive, yet still effective option.

Can this dream become a reality? Can we accomplish a sustainable model or is it all a bunch of wishful thinking, the theoretical paper plans of keyboard beekeepers who are all veil and no hives (kind of like armchair cattlemen who are all hat and no cattle)?

I have to believe in the possibilities with the most idealistic optimism. Because if I don't believe it is possible, then I'd hate to imagine where the practice of keeping bees will end up. I can conceive of a future that makes CCD look like a Sunday School picnic, and I've been to some of those Sunday School picnics.

Here's how I see this ideal coming into play in my apiaries, under my management, with my purposes in mind. Most of this I've already covered, so I'm going to present this information rather succinctly and this is not all inclusive of everything I do or everything I've previously mentioned in this manuscript.

I prefer to utilize feral genetics that I catch with pheromone-baited swarm traps. Like the original Russian honey bees, these ferals come from colonies which were untreated, unmanaged and procreate with a measure of natural selection. I also accept the likelihood that swarming and the subsequent brood break creates a benefit that is not entirely genetic.

I also accept the possibility that I may be catching a swarm from a totally, chemically-addicted, ignorant back yard beekeeper just over the next hill. I trust IPM practices to sort out which hives are more and less susceptible to mites. It is from the most productive, least susceptible hives in my apiaries that I target as potential colonies for my queen production.

I am a firm believer in raising locally adapted queens from hives that tolerate my idiosyncrasies, work with my management, and survive under my treat-if-you-need, here's-a-crutch mite suppression. I still lose hives and I raise my queens from the survivors.

In the late summer, the potential queen producing hives are brought in to one yard for convenience and these hives are not treated for mites as they come out of the honey production cycle. I over-winter these colonies with the idea of raising queens from them the following season, using winter hardiness as the final criteria. After all, dead hives make poor queens, though I'll never admit I tried it.

I cannot say these hives are honestly treatment-free, according to our agreed upon list at the beginning of the chapter, because as a production colony I use a number of the soft, "natural" treatments such as powdered sugar dusting. I feed syrup and add a knock-off recipe recognized as a lemongrass oil and spearmint oil, "feeding stimulant," you know, the one that makes your honey bees to be, uh, you know, "healthy," not that I want to mistakenly mention any specific product name!

By the way, you can make your own, uh, healthy bee recipe for about a third of the cost and the resource is found at

www.smashwords.com/books/view/377477

or search www.amazon.com for "essential oil recipes," where I have a Kindle version of this book available.

Once these hives move from my production yards to the queen rearing yard, they do become treatment-free. I like to raise my queens in the following year without the interference and side effects of any possible contaminants, natural or synthetic, legal or otherwise.

Once I make up my mating nucs and transfer or split my production hives following the honey harvest, I will monitor mites using IPM practices and treat accordingly, again with the least offensive insult and minimal potential side effects to the hive.

I use my June 1st splitting option on a number of hives with the "walk away" emergency cell process to create a brood break. Since my greatest loss is through the winter, I will attempt to make additional splits to account for an anticipated attrition.

As much as I hate losing hives, you'd think I'd be getting used to it after all these years. I doubt I ever will. My inability to accept normal losses is a definite stumbling block and keeps me from going "cold turkey" with respect to abandoning my treatments and maturing to the treatment-free level.

Any beekeeping operation can use astute management as a basis for sustainability. We all make choices in where we keep our bees, how much honey we want to harvest, how much syrup we feel we need to feed, how often we inspect our colonies, how long we keep our queens, etc.

I won't totally rule out the possibility of a strict, treatment-free management practice down the road. In the ideal, if we can continue to wean ourselves off of all treatments, this scenario is very desirable. It's how we get there that will take time and patience, perseverance, character and hope.

Some people feel we have no time to dilly-dally around.

It's a process that I don't think can be rushed given the need and the requirement of our agricultural production system. We need all the bees we can produce. I don't like the Russian option of being forced to let nature take its course. Nature can be a real nasty and an unreliable partner in this business.

If the notion of sustainable beekeeping is to keep on keeping bees, then we need to cut our neighboring apiarists a little slack as they choose their own path for what works for them, even if it contradicts every moral fiber in our being.

Two beekeepers can manage their respective apiaries with two opposing and incongruous methods, and despite our reluctance to admit it, we might find both methods approved and acceptable. After all, the bees are the best barometer of our achievement. It's always hard to argue with success.

Thankfully, honey bees are extremely responsive to our management, excessively forgiving of our stupidity, and often do what they were meant to do despite all the crap and garbage we dump into the hive. The future may be brighter than we fear and more productive than we can imagine. Bees have proven to be resilient. Perhaps that's the real lesson we need to learn from them.

In the end, I continue to believe sustainability is an issue much larger than ourselves and our puny-minded, self-serving management practices. There are greater forces at work and maybe the best step forward is to trust the bees more and admit we're not in control as much as we think.

Bees have been around for millions of years. I like to think they know more about how to survive and weather the injury and insult of human stupidity in an industrial society that appears to be doing its level best to be unsustainable.

Personally, I have too much at stake to go cold turkey on the treatment-free option. I have little hope that we will come up with a synthetic chemical treatment that won't continue to accommodate more virulent mites. I will continue most of my "soft" approaches though I can envision trusting more hives to move into a treatment-free realm.

Despite all we do, the bees seem to be resilient and rise above our humanity. Some days, all I have is this hope.

###

About the Author:

Grant F. C. Gillard began keeping bees on the family farm in Glenville, Minnesota, after graduating from Iowa State University in Ames, Iowa, with a degree in Agriculture in 1981.

While in his sophomore year, seeking the easiest class possible to elevate his battered grade-point average, Grant ignored his advisor's derision and enrolled in a seemingly innocuous class entitled, "Entomology 222: Beekeeping," taught by a retired high school biology teacher and adjunct professor, Richard Trump.

Without grasping the potential blessings and lifelong implications this providential twist presented to his academic life, Grant was hopelessly inoculated with the desire to keep honey bees, which would later include visions of commercial aspirations.

Grant was active during his high school years at the First Presbyterian Church in Albert Lea, Minnesota, where he was baptized and ordained as a ruling elder. Returning to his home church after his college graduation, Grant's church members, along with the Rev. Elmer Bates, convinced him he'd make a better pastor than a farmer. Their encouragement spun his life in yet another improbable direction.

In 1987, Grant graduated from Fuller Theological Seminary in Pasadena, California, with a Master's of Divinity degree. It was there he met another Presbyterian student, Kansas City native, Nancy Farris. They married in 1986 during their senior year at Fuller. He later obtained a Doctor of Ministry degree from Aquinas Institute of Theology in St. Louis, Missouri, in 2000.

He's only served two congregations thus far in his twenty-six years of ordained ministry. With his newlywed wife, the two served as co-associate pastors at the White Clay Creek Presbyterian Church in Newark, Delaware. With a desire for more opportunities to preach and teach, Grant moved his young family to Jackson, Missouri in 1993 where he answered a call to serve as the pastor of the First Presbyterian Church PC(USA). His active involvement over the past twenty years redefined his ministry as more of a community chaplain.

Grant combines his passion for beekeeping with his pastoral duties at the church. Grant currently operates around 200 hives and produces honey for local retail sales and farmer's markets in southeast Missouri. He also produces nucs, removes swarms and has published several other publications on the topics of beekeeping and personal growth.

Grant has also published several articles in the American Bee Journal regarding colony management techniques. *"A Ton of Honey: Managing Your Hives for Maximum Production"* and *"Beekeeping With Twenty-five Hives: From Passion to Profits,"* are two of his most noted books. A complete list of his books can be found searching www.createspace.com or search for his name on www.amazon.com.

Grant is currently the past-president of the Missouri State Beekeepers Association, serving as President from 2009 until 2011. He speaks at frequent regional and national conferences sharing his insights and philosophies, his personal vision for keeping honey bees, his field-tested ideas and sustainable methods on how to hang tough, to persevere in the face of adversity, to run and not grow weary, to walk and not faint while trying to keep bees and keep them alive. He received the Missouri State Beekeeper of the Year Award in 2012.

Grant is married with three grown children living in Kansas City, Columbia, and Jackson, Missouri. His wife of 27 years, Nancy, has taken an increasing role in selling honey at the farmer's markets, freeing Grant to take a more active role on the production side of the equation.

Since moving to Missouri, both Grant and Nancy are loyal fans of the St. Louis Cardinals. Despite many lackluster seasons, Grant steadfastly remains an unapologetic devotee of the Minnesota Vikings. And no one knows why.

You may contact Grant for your next conference at: **gillard5@charter.net**

Other books of interest may be found at http://www.Smashwords.com or Grant's personal web site: http://grantgillard.weebly.com/my-books.html

****

Special thanks go to my late father, Jack F. C. Gillard, (1928 - 2012), whose inspirations always gave us children permission to be anything we wanted to be, to do anything we wanted to do, that with the right amount of hard work, with a good education and God's help, anything was possible.

I hope to pass along that same inspiration to my children.

Other Popular Beekeeping Resources by Grant F. C. Gillard

Beekeeping with Twenty-five Hives:
From Passion to Profits
www.createspace.com/4152725

A Ton of Honey:
Managing Your Hives for
Maximum Production
www.createspace.com/4111886

Free Bees!
The Joy and the Insanity of Removing and Retrieving Honey Bee Swarms
www.createspace.com/4107714

Keeping Honey Bees and Swarm Trapping:
A Better Way to Collect "Free" Bees
www.createspace.com/4106626

Why I Keep Honeybees
(and why you should, too!):
Keys to Your Success

www.createspace.com/4043781

Beekeeping 101:
Where Can I Keep My Bees?

www.createspace.com/4044187

Honey! It Turned to Sugar!
Dealing with Issues of Granulated Honey

www.createspace.com/4044721

Simplified Queen Rearing:
A Non-Grafting Approach Using
The "Nicot" Queen Rearing Kit

www.createspace.com/ 4542113

Made in the USA
Coppell, TX
17 February 2020